Steer Clear

Driver education manual

Monica Schaefer

IRISH DRIVERS EDUCATION ASSOCIATION LTD

First published by
Irish Drivers Education Association Ltd
IDEA House
Killarney Road Business Park
Bray
Co Wicklow
www.steerclear.ie

© Irish Drivers Education Association Ltd 2006

Editing team
Maire Daly, Julie O'Shea, Karl Shreeves, Sorcha McDonagh,
Mary Kinsella, Mark Loughran

Director of operations
Brian Murphy

Design and production
William Siddall, Mark Loughran (Identikit Design Consultants),
Tani Pratchayaopak, Anneke Calis, (Tanika Design)

Illustrations and photography
William Siddall, Getty Images, Volvo, NRA, RoSPA (UK),
Haynes Publishing, Big Bad Wolf Animation Team

Author and editor-in-chief
Monica Schaefer

Printing
Printed and bound in Barcelona, Spain by Cayfosa-Quebecor

Dedication
This book is dedicated to the memory of Fr David Boylan
and all of the other men, women and children whose lives have
been so tragically cut short or permanently altered
by collisons on Ireland's roads.

Contents

Contents

Contents

Introduction

Welcome to the Steer Clear Driver Education manual. This book is a key component of Ireland's first comprehensive driver education system.

Steer Clear is a dynamic course that comprises three parts: interactive learning in the classroom; taking formal driving lessons to develop your skills with a qualified instructor; and finally the application of those skills through plenty of driving practice with a mentor, whether a family member or friend.

The first thing we want to tell you, though, is that this course doesn't start with how to change gears or how to negotiate a roundabout. Instead, we begin by showing you why good driving is not so much about what you *can* do—your ability to manoeuvre a car—but more about what you *choose* to do—how you behave when you drive.

That's because driver behaviour is the number one contributor to the overall levels of safety and risk on our roads. Learning to drive well is about adopting the right attitude and developing your ability to make good, rational decisions every time you drive. Having good judgement and committing to being a cooperative and patient driver will substantially reduce your exposure to risk when you're on the road. This will allow you to enjoy with confidence the increased independence that driving offers.

Yet this manual still pays ample attention to the important techniques of driving, such as handling a skid, merging safely and coping with a breakdown. We share ways of dealing with tiredness, distractions or the frustration you might sometimes feel when driving. You'll also learn about the many variables that affect a vehicle in motion, such as road design, the tyres and even the laws of physics. You'll get a sound understanding of how all the parts of the road-traffic system function. And there's advice on how to maintain your car, prepare for the National Car Test and on how to prepare yourself for the driving test.

The complete Steer Clear Driver system incorporates illustrated manuals, videos, hands-on practical demonstrations and workshops, with plenty of enjoyable interaction throughout. All Steer Clear classes are delivered by trained facilitators using specially designed materials and teaching methods to show you how to use the road well and with minimal risk.

The Steer Clear Driver Education course shows how you, the roadways, traffic systems, vehicles, the law and other road users can all work together to make driving a safe and enjoyable experience for everyone. Whether you're a beginner or someone who's been driving for many years, studying this manual and taking part in the Steer Clear course is your first step in becoming the best driver that you can possibly be.

We wish you a safe and enjoyable journey.

The Steer Clear Team

How to use this manual

To get the most from the Steer Clear Driver Education Manual, it's best to read and complete it as part of the full Steer Clear Drivers Education programme, by doing so we think you'll find that all the parts run smoothly together a bit like a good modern car! You can of course just buy this book and read it at home, if you do, you'll still find plenty to help you be a better driver.

Here are some signposts to help you on your journey:

The manual is divided into 12 chapters or modules, each module begins with an introduction to help you to put what you are about to learn into context. **Key Points** are highlighted at the top of each page to guide you through the topics that will be discussed.

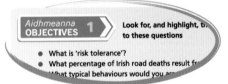

Objectives are poised as questions at the beginning of each topic and we encourage you to look for and highlight the answers to these questions as you read through the module.

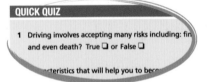

Quick Quizzes are sprinkled throughout the manual. These are a fun way for you to check your understanding of each section. They are in a simple *True* or *False* format so once you have ticked the box, you can see how you did by looking up the answer at the base of the quiz.

Light bulb boxes emphasise information of special interest or importance.

www.steerclear.ie

Weblinks are given throughout the manual. By following these links, you can find tons of additional material on the web.

A **Summary** of all the key points is given at the end of each module. The summary will help you to review and retain information on new concepts and it will be useful for reference when you want to refresh your knowledge in the future.

The **Knowledge Reviews** at the end of each module will help you to test your understanding of the topics covered and will also help you to retain the information in your longterm memory. You should use pen to fill in each answer.

1

'Ability is what you're capable of doing.
Motivation determines what you do.
Attitude determines how well you do it.'

Lou Holtz

Motivation and attitude

Introduction

Why do you want to learn to drive? Most people say they want the independence, freedom, mobility and opportunity that driving brings with it. Having your own car certainly beats standing at the bus stop or always having to ask for lifts.

Perhaps a better question is: What sort of driver do you want to be? Unfortunately, some people see showing off and taking risks as a 'benefit' of driving. At best, this kind of attitude leads to a string of penalty points, fines and escalating insurance costs. At worst and quite commonly, the result is a serious car crash with consequences that will affect you for the rest of your life.

Do you want to be an alert and skilled driver who shares the road and contributes to traffic safety, or a selfish loose cannon who adds to the mounting number of injuries and fatalities on our roads? The answer may seem obvious as you read this, but you can easily lose sight of it amid the potentially angering and frustrating situations you encounter on the road. Decide *now* that you want to be an alert, skilled and considerate driver, and commit to it. Decide *now* that you will

Unless you have the right attitude, it is impossible to drive well

use this course to help you attain this goal. You will learn that being a good driver has a price, just like being a bad driver has.

Decide *now* that you will forego acting in anger when another driver is rude, and that you will inconvenience yourself rather than compromise safety. You will have to be patient and drive defensively instead of offensively. But you will quickly learn that the costs of being a good driver are far lower than the price you pay for being a bad one.

Driver education is not just about learning to drive. It is about developing the right attitudes and the ability to make good judgements that will help to reduce your exposure to risk while driving, allowing you to enjoy the increased independence driving offers. Because driving is an activity with numerous potential risks, drivers carry a lot of responsibility every time they sit behind the wheel. To drive well you must be mature and alert, and avoid unnecessary risks. You must control your emotions while showing care, courtesy and consideration for those with whom you share the road – cyclists, motorcyclists and pedestrians, as well as other motorists.

The right motivation and attitude compensate for poor driving skills far better than good driving skills can compensate for having the wrong motivation or attitude. Think about it: you can know all about safe driving, answer every question correctly and demonstrate your knowledge well in this course but, with the wrong attitude, your skills amount to nothing because you won't apply them when you get on the road. This is why the Steer Clear programme starts with the influences that shape your motivation and attitude as a driver.

Unless you have the right attitude, it is impossible to drive well.

In this module we will discuss...

- Driving risk
- Risk taking behaviours
- Drink and driving

- Drugs and driving
- Emotion
- Resisting negative learning

Driving risk

Aidhmeanna
OBJECTIVES **1** **Look for, and highlight, the answers to these questions**

- What are the risks associated with driving?
- What are the characteristics of a good driver?
- What is the most important factor that influences your risk management on the road?

Risks involved with driving

Every day around the world, millions of motorists drive from place to place without incident. The incidence of injury and death on the roads is exceedingly low. Yet the reality is that travelling on the road as a driver or passenger carries very real risks. These include the financial risks associated with damage to your vehicle or to another person's vehicle. They also include injury risks ranging from minor injuries to those that cause permanent disability and death. Our roads are busy and they present these risks to *all* road users. The likelihood of these risks presenting themselves depends on how much you drive – that is, how much you are exposed to risk – and whether you're a good or bad driver – that is, how well you manage your risk.

Every day around the world, millions of motorists drive from place to place without incident

Characteristics of good drivers

You can think of driving as having a grading system, much as there is a grading system in your other education or work subjects. If you do poorly in maths, business or history, you get a low grade, and you might have some explaining or extra study to do. When you perform poorly in driving, however, the consequences range from financial strain at the least to serious injury, disability, death and bereavement at worst. Driving has a severe bottom-line evaluation: get it wrong and you could pay with your life, someone else's life or both.

Being a good driver minimises your exposure to risk. As you'll learn in this course, there are many facets to being a good driver:

We differ in risk tolerances, so what you consider reasonable risk may be unreasonable to someone else

- **A good driver understands the risks.** You remain motivated to drive well when you remember that the risks include serious injury and death.
- **A good driver accepts personal imperfection and drives accordingly.** You are human, which means you are not perfect. You must therefore drive in a manner that gives you some leeway for error.
- **A good driver maintains good habits.** In this course you will learn many things that you should *always* do, by habit, even when they seem unnecessary.
- **A good driver remains alert to the road.** You probably know that you shouldn't drive when you are very tired, but you should also avoid distractions that range from mobile phones and MP3 players to loud music or an argument with a passenger.
- **A good driver does not act out of anger.** Trying to 'get even' has no place on the road – even when you can argue a good case that the other motorist deserves it.
- **A good driver takes responsibility for their vehicle.** Maintaining your vehicle and ensuring that it's working properly is just as important as your habits on the road. You are just as responsible for a crash caused by brake failure as one caused by failing to use the brakes.

Note that your *behaviour* is the most important factor that affects how you manage risk on the road. You can offset or reduce the majority of risks caused by hazards that you don't control by controlling your own behaviour.

Driving has a bottom-line evaluation: get it wrong and you could pay with your life, someone else's life or both

1 Driving involves accepting many risks including: financial strain, injury, disability and even death? T☑ F☐

2 Characteristics that will help you to become a good driver include: Understanding the risks, accepting personal imperfection and driving accordingly. T☑ F☐

3 Your own behaviour is the most important factor that influences your risk management on the road. T☑ F☐

Answers: 1: T, 2: T, 3: T

Risk-taking behaviours

Aidhmeanna
OBJECTIVES **1** ⟩ **Look for, and highlight, the answers to these questions**

- What is 'risk tolerance'?
- What percentage of Irish road deaths result from human error?
- What typical behaviours would you associate with high-risk drivers?
- How may the forgiving nature of driving lead to a false sense of security?

Risk tolerance

One important factor that will influence your behaviour as a driver is your personal *risk tolerance*. This is the term for how much risk you are willing to accept. People have different tolerances to risk, therefore what you consider a reasonable risk may be unreasonable to someone else. Your personal risk tolerance is based partly on your perception of risk; partly on your belief – whether accurate or not – in your own ability to control or manage that risk; and partly on your understanding of the consequences should the worst happen. If you don't understand the risks involved in driving, if you have misplaced confidence in your driving abilities, and if you don't understand the potential consequences of a collision, then your risk tolerance for driving is going to be too high and it will need to change.

In some activities, you may be relatively invincible and unlikely to make a mistake. You may be an outstanding footballer but, as a new driver, you can't yet make an accurate judgement of the risks. Older drivers tend to be more conservative than younger drivers because they have learned: *that the risks on the road are more immediate than they seem, that you are more likely to make a mistake than you think, and that the consequences of a collision are far worse than you may imagine.* You're taking this course so you can learn to drive safely based on the experiences of others. It is downright stupid to endanger yourself by failing to do what has been shown to prevent crashes, and by repeating what has been shown to cause them.

A lower risk tolerence will increase your safety while driving

Take a moment and think about where you would like to be in 20 years. Where would you like to be living? What kind of career might you have? What leisure activities would you enjoy? Would you like to have a family? Write down three things you see for yourself 20 years from today:

_____

_____

_____

Which of these will not happen if you have a crash that results in serious, life-changing injuries? Which of these will not happen if you live the rest of your life in a wheelchair? Which will not happen if you're blind or seriously disfigured? Which will not happen if you are financially obligated to someone else for the rest of your life? Which would be radically different if someone you love is seriously injured or killed as a passenger while you're driving?

Ask yourself which part of your future is worth exchanging for the convenience of saving five minutes by driving too fast for the conditions. Which part will you exchange for cutting off a rude driver who 'deserves it'? If you don't bother to signal every lane change who, of all the people that will travel with you do you consider expendable?

Despite all the safety equipment in modern vehicles, you can make your life very inconvenient by making poor choices that lead to a crash. Simple everyday things like getting up in the morning, eating, washing or just going to the shops would be a challenge. Even if you don't have a collision, how much money and time are you willing to spend appearing before the courts and paying fines and higher insurance rates? What careers will you have to forego if you lose your driver's licence by accumulating too many penalty points?

Human error and high-risk drivers

Let's look at the hard facts. The media regularly report the ongoing tragedy of Irish road deaths, but you don't often hear about the nearly 10,000 people who are injured every year on our roads. That's 10,000 lives and the lives of 10,000 families seriously altered due *almost entirely* to drivers' mistakes.

Ninety six percent of all Irish road deaths are caused by human error.

The vast majority of crashes are not 'accidents' in the true sense of the word. They are the predictable result of dangerous driving. To be true accidents, they would have to be unpredictable happenings – something completely unavoidable. The behaviours you associate with high-risk drivers – driving too fast, unsafe overtaking, tailgating, driving a poorly maintained vehicle, or crossing the road in a dangerous place – have *predictable* unfavourable outcomes. People who drive poorly by taking unnecessary risks will, sooner or later, end up in trouble. It's almost a statistical certainty.

A forgiving environment

The road is mostly a forgiving environment. If it weren't, the injury rates and death toll would be even more horrific than they are. The truth is, there's some margin for error, which is fortunate because we all make mistakes. A primary difference between a good driver and a bad one is that good drivers constantly strive to maintain their margin for error. Bad drivers erode safety margins in exchange for convenience and by having sloppy habits.

The forgiving nature of driving can lead to a false sense of security because the

The consequences of a collision are far worse than you might imagine

bad driver gets away with bad practices. Repeating the practice without incident reinforces it until it becomes a habit. The bad driver thinks, 'I always take this corner at this speed – I've never had a problem before'. This leads to complacency, so the person pushes the limits a little more each time. Eventually, there's no margin for error – and error is inevitable.

This is why you need to commit to avoiding even those bad habits that seem unimportant, because they gradually lead to more serious slips and a slow, continuous decline in your safety margin. One day, when the conditions aren't as good as you expect or you meet someone else who has similar bad habits – or both – the inevitable crash will occur.

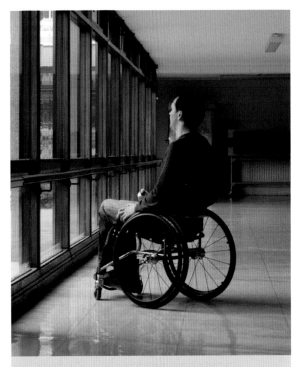

Ask yourself which part of your future is worth exchanging for the convienience of saving five minutes by driving too fast?

The road is a mostly forgiving environment. If it weren't, the injury and death toll would be even more intolerable

QUICK QUIZ

1   Your 'risk tolerance' describes how much risk you regard as reasonable or acceptable.
    T ☑ F ☐

2   The gardai attribute 96% percent of Irish road deaths to human error.
    T ☑ F ☐

3   The forgiving nature of driving can lead to a false sense of security by reinforcing bad habits.   T ☑ F ☐

Answers: 1: T, 2: T, 3: T

Drink and driving

Aidhmeanna
OBJECTIVES **1** **Look for, and highlight, the answers to these questions**

- What percentage of road fatalities involve the use of alcohol?
- Why does even a single drink impair your ability to drive safely?
- Is it safe to drive after drinking if you are within the legal limit?
- How does alcohol affect your capabilities as a driver?
- What kind of driving behaviours indicate that a driver is under the influence of alcohol?
- What plan would you use to avoid driving after drinking?
- What is the bottom-line message regarding drinking, drugs and driving?

The alcohol problem

Even before becoming old enough to drive, you've probably heard about the dangers of drunk driving. The problem affects virtually all countries. According to the Gardaí, 40 percent of Irish road fatalities involve the use of alcohol. Approximately 800 people have been killed here in collisions caused by drunk drivers in the last five years.

When you're sober, it's easy to see that driving after drinking is stupid – but even a single drink can change your mind. You may not feel affected by just one drink, yet that drink can mask good judgement, leading you to believe that you are in perfect control and are fully capable of driving. Human performance tests tell a different story. Even one drink impairs your ability to judge speed and distance. In some people, it causes insensitivity to risks, leading to high-risk driving such as tailgating, unsafe overtaking and speeding.

Although men cause almost nine out of ten serious alcohol-related crashes, women are not immune to the risk. As a young driver, whether male or female, you are in a high-risk category and are very susceptible to the effects of alcohol. Drivers between the ages of 18 and 34 are *three times* more likely to be involved in a crash related to alcohol consumption.

Even if you don't cause a crash, drinking and driving has other negative consequences. According to the National Safety Council, an average of 250 drivers are arrested each week in Ireland for driving while under the influence of alcohol. At the very least, these drivers will have to appear in court and will lose their licences for a minimum of three months.

How your body responds to alcohol

Alcohol goes directly from your stomach into your bloodstream. It doesn't have to go into the intestines to be absorbed, which is why you feel its effects so rapidly. Your gender, weight, usual drinking habits and mood, the alcohol content of your drink and the amount of food you've consumed all contribute to how much and how quickly a drink affects you, but there is *always* an effect.

Once in your system, the speed at which your body eliminates alcohol is relatively constant. Contrary to popular belief, eating food or drinking coffee will not increase the rate at which your body gets rid of it. Time is the only way to clear alcohol from your system.

Many drivers believe it is safe to drive if they are below the legal limit. This is a mistake. The risk of being involved in a crash increases in proportion to the amount of alcohol you consume. Regardless of the amount, alcohol impairs the functions of the brain and even one drink will affect your driving ability. At half the legal limit, you are *twice* as likely to have a collision as if you hadn't been drinking, and at the legal limit you are *six times* more likely. Just because you don't feel affected after a drink doesn't mean you are not impaired – science and collision data show that you are.

'Just one drink will impair your driving. It's your choice, your responsibility and your fault if you decide to drink and drive.'
– Stephen Peover D.O.E. Northern Ireland.

Though it may be legally acceptable to drink a small amount of alcohol and drive, you cannot say that you're just as safe within the legal limits as you would be if you didn't drink at all.

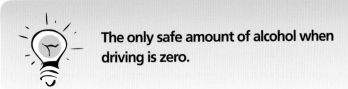

The only safe amount of alcohol when driving is zero.

Alcohol affects your capabilities as a driver in the following ways:

- Alcohol impairs your ability to discern risks, leading you to make bad decisions.
- Alcohol may directly impair your judgement so you overestimate your ability to avoid a collision or underestimate the consequences of a collision. You may therefore drive more aggressively or become aggressive towards other drivers more readily.

- Alcohol impairs your ability to recognise or perceive a hazard, slowing your response to that hazard.
- Alcohol reduces your ability to retain information, leading to poor judgement.
- Alcohol can affect your emotions, causing you to react emotionally instead of rationally.
- Alcohol affects your motor skills, coordination and timing, making it harder for you to control a vehicle – especially in an emergency.

According to the Gardai, 40 percent of Irish road fatalities involve the use of alcohol. Approximately 800 people were killed in collisions caused by drunk drivers in the last five years

Behaviours that may indicate that a driver is under the influence of alcohol include:

- Driving in the centre of the road or over the centre line.
- Driving too fast for conditions (poor judgement).
- Driving at a markedly reduced speed (trying to compensate for slowed reactions).
- Poor judgement of distances.
- Drifting into other lanes or swerving.
- Speeding up and slowing down erratically.
- Braking every time a vehicle approaches.
- Slow response time.
- Stopping suddenly or for no apparent reason.
- Not using indicators or not turning on lights at night.
- Illegal turns or manoeuvres.

It's easy to see that any of these behaviours could result in or contribute to a collision.

The *only* safe plan when going out for a drink is not to drive. Arrange an alternative way of getting home. Never encourage or condone friends who attempt to drink and drive. Never take a lift with someone who has been drinking. With a little forethought and planning, there are always options available to avoid driving after drinking:

- Take turns at being the designated driver.
- Use public transport.
- Take a taxi.
- Stay over if necessary.
- Walk.

If you find that you've been drinking and didn't plan ahead, you still shouldn't drive. If you're tempted to do so because getting a lift and returning for your vehicle later is inconvenient, just remember how inconvenient a collision is. Think about what you do and don't want your life to be like in 20 years. Don't let an inconvenience of a few hours, at most, mess up years of your life, or of someone else's life. You can avoid the entire problem, though, by committing *now* to never drink without *first* – while you are sober – determining a way to do so *without driving*.

The bottom line message

The bottom line message regarding drinking and driving is very simple: **Never, ever drink and drive. It's just not worth it.**

QUICK QUIZ

1 It is safe to drive after drinking if you stay within the legal limit.
   T ☐ F ☑

2 Alcohol affects your capabilities as a driver because it impairs your ability to discern risks, it slows your response to hazards, it affects your emotions, your motor skills and your coordination. T ☑ F ☐

3 The bottom line message regarding drinking and driving is to never, ever drive while under the influence of alcohol. T ☑ F ☐

Answers: 1: F, 2: T, 3: T

Drugs and driving

Aidhmeanna OBJECTIVES **1** > **Look for, and highlight, the answers to these questions**

- What kind of driving behaviours would you expect from a driver who is under the influence of drugs?
- What effect might a small amount of alcohol have when combined with medication or drugs?
- What kind of over-the-counter medications can impair your ability to drive safely?
- How can illegal drugs impair driving?
- What is the bottom-line message regarding drugs and driving?

Drugs

Many prescribed and over-the-counter drugs can affect your ability to drive safely. Do not underestimate the power of medications, which can have the same or similar effects as alcohol, and lead to the same kinds of dangerous driving behaviours.

Always read the labels and heed the warnings. Check with your doctor or pharmacist if a medicine you have been prescribed or intend to take can affect your driving. Drugs with codeine, cough suppressant, antihistamines and salbutamol are particularly problematic.

It may be possible to take an alternative medicine or to take the medication after you have completed your journey. The effects of some drugs, such as cold remedies or cough medicine, are magnified when combined with even a small amount of alcohol. The combination can cause extreme drowsiness, deadly slow responses and other symptoms that are incompatible with safe

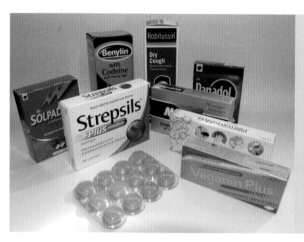

Everyday medications often contain alcohol and other chemicals that can seriously affect your ability to driver safely

driving. Some night-time medications are formulated with a small amount of alcohol specifically to make you sleep.

The following table lists some of the over-the-counter drugs that may cause drowsiness or impair your judgement:

Examples of medicines containing codeine	Examples of medicines containing dextromethorphan (cough suppressant)	Examples of medicines containing anti-histamines	Examples of medicines containing salbutamol (commonly used for bronchitis and asthma)
Benylin with codeine	Nirolex lozenges	Calimal	Salamol
Migraleve	Contact Cough Caps	Piriton	Salbulin
Panadol ultra	Robitussin Dry Cough	Rimarin	Ventodisks
Solpadeine		Semprex	Ventolin
Solpadol		Zirtek	Ventomax
Tylex		Medinex	
Veganin		Nytol	
		Avomine	
		Phenergan	
		Sominex	

Sometimes the drugs that you don't think of as 'drugs' are the ones that cause problems. Even the innocuous Strepsil throat lozenge contains 1.2 mg of alcohol. Always assume that anything you take as a medicine or remedy can impair driving until your doctor or pharmacist confirms otherwise.

Illegal drugs

All illegal drugs impair driving and it is an offence to drive when under their influence. These drugs have numerous effects including confusion, loss of coordination, apathy, euphoria, hallucinations, panic, drowsiness, hyperactivity, inability to concentrate, blurred vision and distortion of the senses. This is not a comprehensive list, but it doesn't need to be, because one thing is certain – there's no way you can drive safely under the influence of an illegal drug.

Drug driving costs lives just like drunk driving does – the lives of users and the lives of the people they meet on the road. Don't do it.

The bottom-line message

The bottom-line message regarding drugs and driving is very simple:
Never, ever drink or take drugs and drive. It's just not worth it.

1   The type of driving you might expect from a driver under the influence of drugs is in no way like that of a driver under the influence of alcohol.
    T ☐   F ☑

2   A small amount of alcohol when combined with medication or drugs has no significant effect on your driving ability.   T ☐   F ☑

3   Over-the-counter medications can impair your ability to drive safely.
    T ☑   F ☐

Answers: 1: F, 2: F, 3: T

Emotions

Aidhmeanna OBJECTIVES   1

Look for, and highlight, the answers to these questions

- In what ways can your emotions influence how you drive?
- How can you regain or maintain control so that emotions don't have a negative effect on your driving?
- Why is it important to detach yourself from emotional situations that arise while driving?
- What should you do if you find yourself in an emotionally charged situation or one that could become emotionally charged when you're driving?
- What effects can feelings of anger, sorrow, frustration, anxiety, fear and hate have on your driving if you do not control them?

States of mind

If you've ever taken a test or played a sport while deeply angered or saddened, you'll know that your emotions affect your performance. Anger, sadness, anxiety, fear and similar emotions distract your thoughts from the task at hand and reduce your concentration. Positive emotions like joy and success can also distract you. Allowing strong emotions to be a distraction while driving can make you less alert to hazards and slow your response to them.

Emotions can also have a direct effect on your behaviour. Almost all of us have, at one time or another, done something inappropriate and irrational out of anger, grief or fear. On the road, anger is a significant problem if it makes your driving behaviour aggressive or retaliatory instead of defensive

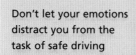

Don't let your emotions distract you from the task of safe driving

and co-operative. A good driver doesn't let emotions affect how he or she makes decisions because in the context of driving, emotional decisions tend to be poor ones.

Regaining and maintaining control

It's useless to say that if you get angry or sad or fall in love, you can't drive. Emotions are a normal part of life and anyway, the emotions themselves are not the problem. The problem is whether you allow emotions to affect how you drive. When strongly affected by emotions, you need to regain and maintain control before getting behind the wheel.

- Don't start a journey if you are emotionally charged. Take time to relax and calm down before driving.
- You may find it helpful to play music that counteracts the emotions you're dealing with – though not at a volume that distracts you, of course!
- Remind yourself that while driving, your attention needs to be on the road and your behaviour needs to be rational, not emotional. Remember that your anger or sadness will be magnified or your elation wiped away by a collision.
- If you find yourself distracted or reacting emotionally while driving and you can't drive rationally, pull over until you can.

Anger on the road

Even when you start a journey in a balanced state of mind, some driving situations can become emotionally charged. You must be able to detach yourself from these situations so that you remain in control of how you drive.

Bad drivers use their vehicles to vent their emotions and have little consideration for other road users. They see their cars as extensions of their

Road rage is a sign
that the driver is not
in control

personal space and take offence when other drivers do things they perceive as rude or as a violation of their rights on the road. Drivers can't communicate directly with each other, making it easy for some people to treat other vehicles as impersonal objects on which to vent their anger. Normally calm people can lose their cool and become critical, unforgiving drivers who use their vehicles as instruments of aggression.

You have a decision to make right now. When you're driving, there will be times when other drivers are not courteous. You will find yourself having to swerve, stop or yield your right of way when other drivers fail to obey traffic laws, fail to indicate turns or pull out in front of you and sometimes drivers may even gesture rudely or blare their horns angrily at you because you made a mistake or because they think *you* did something wrong.

Decide right now that bad driving and rudeness of other drivers will not provoke an emotional response in you. If you find yourself in an emotionally charged situation, or one that could become emotionally charged:

- Stay calm. Think before you act.
- Remind yourself that you must stay in control of your vehicle and your emotions. Emotional driving is dangerous driving.
- Stay focused on your driving first and foremost. Pay attention to other vehicles around you, not just the one(s) involved with the situation.
- Never take anything another driver does personally, no matter how rude, intentional or careless it may seem.
- Treat other drivers as you would want to be treated. Many instances of 'rude' driving are unintentional by otherwise courteous people. You will want others to be forgiving when you accidentally offend them – which you will – so be forgiving yourself. Since you don't know everything that's going on, give other drivers the benefit of the doubt.

- Don't retaliate or mimic the behaviour of intentionally rude or aggressive drivers. Don't use your horn or gesture angrily. All you're doing is rewarding the behaviour and engaging in the fight that the other person is trying to start. The best way to get even is not to get even.
- As appropriate, yield to the other vehicle, slow down, pull off the road or drive away at a reasonable speed to distance yourself from an aggressive driver.
- If a person is being particularly threatening, note the vehicle details if possible, drive to a safe place – such as a Garda station – and report it.

When you can be detached from an emotional situation it is much easier to remain calm and in control. If, for example, a careless driver pulls out from a side road in front of you, forcing you to brake and putting you at risk, it is only natural that you should feel annoyed. – That's fine, but you should put the feelings aside immediately and act only based on what you need to do to drive safely. Acting on or dwelling on your feelings will allow them to grow. If you become distracted and stressed you are more likely to make mistakes or to drive in an aggressive manner yourself. This not only puts you and other drivers at risk, but you may do things that will annoy other drivers. This is why drivers must control their emotions, be patient, forgiving and calm with each other. Stay cool and don't let another driver's mistake become your problem.

Consider the following list of emotions and the effect they can have on your driving if you do not control them.

Emotion	Effect on behaviour
Anger	Shouting, aggressive behaviour, rash decisions, road rage
Sorrow/grief	Crying, unable to focus properly, attitude of not caring what happens, poor decision-making
Frustration	Aggressive behaviour, road rage
Anxiety	Indecisiveness, slowness of response, poor decision-making
Fear	Unable to focus properly, poor decision-making, indecisiveness
Hate	Aggressive behaviour, lack of respect for others

1   Emotions can influence how you drive by reducing your concentration, slowing your response time and causing aggressive or retaliatory responses.
    T ☑   F ☐

2   Don't start a journey if you're emotionally charged, if you are already driving, pull over until you have calmed down and can drive rationally.
    T ☑   F ☐

3   It is important to stay detached from emotional situations so that you can remain in control of your driving.   T ☑   F ☐

Answers: 1: T, 2: T, 3: T

Resisting negative learning

Aidhmeanna OBJECTIVES **1** > **Look for, and highlight, the answers to these questions**

- How can the media cause or encourage reckless driving?
- How can peer pressure affect how you drive?
- How should you handle peer pressure when you are driving?
- In what ways can role modelling cause you to drive badly?
- In what ways can improved safety engineering encourage you to take inappropriate risks?

Given everything you have learned to this point, you may wonder why bad driving is much of a problem at all. It's no secret that drunk driving, failing to follow traffic laws and becoming agitated are unsafe. Few people are so ignorant that they don't know this. So why do people still do these things?

The reason is that we don't always make decisions based on rational thinking; sometimes we make decisions based on emotions. There are times when decisions *should* be based on emotions – for example, you choose to paint your bedroom based on colours you like. There is no rationally correct colour. The problem arises when you make decisions based on emotions in situations where the decisions should be based on rational thinking – and often these situations pertain to driving. If you're not careful, there are plenty of influences that can encourage you to imitate poor driving behaviours because they are often associated with positive emotions.

The media

Media and marketing tend to glamorise different lifestyles. They do this to entertain and to influence the choices we make as consumers. You've probably seen movies or television programmes that depict a favourite actor driving a high-performance vehicle on a daring, risky chase involving improbable stunts that range from driving against traffic on the wrong side of the road to jumping over a chasm. Picture James Bond with one hand on the wheel as he talks to a woman while speeding down a narrow mountain road at 120 km/h. In advertisements, car manufacturers promote the perceived benefits of their car over all others. They try to persuade us that driving their model will make us cooler, more attractive, safer and faster. They sometimes do this by glamorising bad driving, such as demonstrating their latest model manoeuvring at high speed through a tiny, picturesque village.

The subliminal message all these images convey is that it is cool to be reckless and drive fast. They may cause you to associate positive feelings, such as excitement and a sense of prestige and self-esteem, with dangerous driving. But these feelings are as fictional as the media that stir them in you. What you see may be great entertainment, but it doesn't reflect reality. Shows like *Top Gear* are very entertaining as they demonstrate impressive and risky manoeuvres, but remember they *always* use professional drivers in the safe confines of off-road tracks with safety precautions in place.

The truth is that if you try to drive the same way to 'be cool', you will not only be dangerous, but no one will see you as 'cool'. In real life, we see risky, fast drivers as inconsiderate, selfish and uncaring, or just plain stupid and ignorant.

Enjoy the entertainment the media provide, but don't let the emotions you feel when you're watching a show carry over onto the road.

Peer pressure

Young drivers accompanied by other young people are at a greater risk of being involved in a fatal crash. Research, from the *AAA Foundation on Road Safety*, shows that teenage drivers accompanied by one other teenager are twice as likely to be involved in a fatal crash as those driving alone. Teen drivers with two or more teenage passengers are *five times* more likely to be involved in a fatal crash then if they were travelling alone. On the other hand, those accompanied by a parent or other mature adult can *cut their risk considerably* and are the least likely to be involved in a car crash. Teen drivers accompanied by adults have only half the number of crashes then those driving alone and they are involved in ten times less fatal crashes then those driving with a group of their peers as passengers.

Accompanied driving – more than just the law – it's a life saver!

Consider this…The number of young and inexperienced drivers involved in fatal car crashes is lowest when new drivers are accompanied by experienced adult drivers.

Research data on teenage motor vehicle deaths collected from U.S. coroners reports and delivered to the American Automobile Association foundation for road safety symposium on teen driving shows that:

- The number of young drivers killed in fatal crashes doubles when inexperienced drivers drive alone.
- When young drivers are accompanied by a young friend the risk of being involved in a fatal collision is double that of driving alone and four times that of being accompanied by an experienced adult driver.
- And when a young inexperienced driver is accompanied by two or more of their peers the chance of being involved in a fatal car crash is increased by ten fold.

Why is this? At least one reason is that if you are a teenager, peer pressure can be a major influence on how you drive. Other teens in the car may not only distract you, but they may induce you to take risks and do things that you would otherwise avoid. Peer pressure commonly leads to showing off, speeding, not using safety belts or driving after drinking. Peer pressure can masquerade as 'not being afraid of the road' or 'not driving like you're old', but no matter how it's framed, peer pressure still encourages risky driving.

To handle peer pressure, you must know what causes it. Peer pressure is an emotional response caused when you perceive a need to improve or maintain your peers' view of you. It is a type of emotional immaturity associated with measuring your self worth based on what others think.

Teen drivers with two or more young passengers are five times more likely to be involved in a fatal crash

Peer pressure can be so strong that people have *died* rather than lose face. Clearly this is an irrational choice. Peer pressure can be one of the most difficult pressures for you to deal with as a new driver and it is the main reason why, as a learner, you are required by law to be accompanied by a qualified driver while driving on a provisional licence. Whether or not you think you will be stopped by the Gardaí is not as important as your safety. Take full advantage of this beneficial regulation because it cuts your chance of being killed or seriously injured in a car crash tenfold.

You should handle peer pressure by recognising it for what it is – childish thinking. It is putting your self-esteem ahead of rational thinking and safety. Your friends might pressure you to drive at a high speed or to take chances. But even though they are encouraging you, your passengers are usually thinking, 'What an idiot!' or 'I can't believe he/she is doing what we said!' If you get stopped by the Gardaí or if you have a collision, don't expect your friends to explain how they talked you into it – you're more likely to find yourself dealing with the situation alone. If you feel pressured by your friends:

- Recognise that peer pressure results from childish thinking. Be an adult and do what you know is right.
- If they're receptive to discussion, you may try explaining why what they're suggesting is wrong.
- Whether you discuss it or not, continue to drive properly. Everyone in the vehicle, including you, is counting on it.
- If your friends continue to pressure you to drive poorly, don't offer them lifts again.
- Remember your own risk tolerance and don't allow others to compromise it.

Finally, think about this: would you encourage someone you care about to speed, or to drive drunk, or not to wear a safety belt? Of course not. What does that say about someone who encourages you to do these types of things?

Role modelling

Most of us spend many years in cars as passengers before we learn to drive. During that time, you learned much of what you need to know when you become a driver. For example, unless you've recently moved to Ireland from abroad, it's almost certain that you recognise the meaning of most traffic signs and signals. It is also possible, though, that you witnessed plenty of bad driving habits as well. This may mean that you have learned some things that you need to *unlearn* before they become your habits, too. Don't take it for granted that the driving behaviours you witnessed as a passenger are all necessarily appropriate – even if they never resulted in a collision.

Hopefully most of the drivers you've travelled with have been good role models. But in this course you're likely to learn some things that differ from what you've seen some experienced adult drivers do. Take this opportunity to learn about driving and road use for yourself and see what behaviours, attitudes and habits have been proven to reliably minimise risk and maximise safety.

Safety features

Because today's cars and roads are much safer than those used 30 years ago, it may sound odd that safety engineering can actually lead to dangerous driving. Thanks to ABS brakes, today drivers often stop in situations that used to lead to unavoidable collisions. Thanks to airbags, crumple zones and side-impact bars, people walk away with only minor injuries from collisions that used to kill. Today's vehicles handle better and are more 'survivable' than ever.

The down side of this is that safety engineering can lull you into a false sense of security. The more you rely on safety engineering instead of safe driving, the more you erode your safety margin. As you learned before, eventually you have no safety margin. One day when a safety device fails or isn't enough, the inevitable crash comes.

The following list of improvements to roads and vehicles, illustrates the safety and the risk involved in each innovation:

Innovation	Safety benefit	Inappropriate risk
Improved lighting at night	Improved vision	Driving too fast for the distance you can see ahead
Superior road surfaces	Better stopping ability	Tailgating
Better handling at greater speeds	Easier to maintain control	Speeding
ABS braking	Controlled stopping in poor conditions	Driving too fast for conditions
Faster acceleration	Accident avoidance	Aggressive driving
Crumple zones & air bags	Collision survivability	Increased tolerance to collision hazard

Remember that safety engineering exists to increase your safety margin. It isn't intended to replace safe driving. Ultimately, safety features only reduce your exposure to risk when you drive safely.

QUICK QUIZ

1 Peer pressure can affect how you drive by encouraging you to take risks you normally wouldn't. T ☑ F ☐

2 Role modelling can inadvertently teach you bad driving habits.
T ☑ F ☐

3 Safety engineering can encourage you to take inappropriate risks by causing you to rely on safety devices that don't work. T ☑ F ☐

Answers: 1: T, 2: T, 3: T

Summary points ≫≫≫≫≫

In this module on motivation and attitude you learned:

1 Driving involves risks that include financial risks, injury risks and the risk of disability and death.

2 Good drivers understand the risks and accept that they are human and can make mistakes. They keep good habits, remain alert, don't act out of anger and are responsible for their vehicles.

3 A serious crash can completely alter the course of your life or of someone else's life.

4 Ninety-six percent of Irish road deaths are caused by human error, not by unpredictable or unavoidable events.

5 The forgiving nature of driving can lead to a false sense of security. At some point, habitual risk-taking catches up with you, resulting in a crash.

6 Alcohol consumption contributes to as many as 40 percent of road fatalities. Approximately 800 people have been killed in drink-related crashes in the last five years in Ireland.

7 Drivers tend to be more aggressive or more likely to get involved in aggressive situations after consuming alcohol and drugs.

8 Alcohol and drugs have an adverse effect on all aspects of safe driving: judgement, coordination, reasoning, alertness, response time, emotions, information retention and hazard perception.

9 It is not safe to drink and drive just because you are within the legal limit.

10 If you are going to drink then don't drive. The two do not mix. Never drink without first determining a way to do so without driving.

11 Never encourage friends to drink and drive and never take a lift with someone who has been drinking.

12 Read the labels or check with the pharmacist to see whether it is safe to drive while under the influence of prescribed drugs or over-the-counter medicines.

13 Driving a car when emotional reduces your ability to concentrate and stay alert. You should apply strategies to help you cope with overpowering emotions.

14 Do not use your car to express negative emotions. Never take what another driver does personally. Treat other drivers as you would want to be treated.

15 Decide now that you will not allow poor driving, rudeness or aggression by other drivers to prevent you from remaining rational.

16 Don't allow media representations of driving or peer pressure affect your driving behaviour.

17 Be aware that you may have learned bad driving habits from role models, and that you need to unlearn these so that they don't become your habits.

18 Remember that while safety engineering has made roads and cars safer than ever, these innovations do not replace safe, responsible driving.

In this module we will discuss...

- Driver co-operation
- Your limitations as a novice driver
- Physical principles governing driving
- Momentum: braking, slowing, stopping

- Road design
- Vital signs: road signs, signals and markings
- Law enforcement

Driver co-operation

Aidhmeanna
OBJECTIVES 2 ⟩ **Look for, and highlight, the answers to these questions**

- In what two ways can you interact with other road users?
- Why is it important for drivers to cooperate with each other?
- Why should you be willing to give way to other vehicles even when you have right of way?
- Why should you give way to pedestrians and other vulnerable road users?
- Why should you be especially cautious around children?

You can interact with other drivers in two ways. You can treat driving as a *competitive* activity or as a *co-operative* activity. More than likely, you've seen both attitudes in other drivers. Competitive drivers are, for example, those who try to 'win' by overtaking unsafely to get ahead of the car in front of them, or by refusing to allow another driver to merge or change lanes. They approach driving as if their agenda is more important than anyone else's, and as if everyone else is in their way. Competitive drivers are selfish drivers. People who treat driving as a competitive activity put themselves and other road users at risk, reduce traffic flow, inconvenience and aggravate other drivers and have a negative effect on everybody's driving environment.

Driving is actually a *co-operative* activity, by design *and necessity*. Safe, efficient driving requires co-operation because all road users need space and time to execute their manoeuvres without pressure, hindrance or risk. A word of warning here: while it is important to be considerate towards other road users, you should never encourage them to make a manoeuvre that could put them at risk. Don't wave anybody onto or across the road – you may not be able to see all the potential hazards and your actions could lead to a collision.

As a co-operative driver, however, you *should* allow other drivers to merge, diverge, change lanes and so on when you can – it costs nothing and it benefits everyone. A competitive driver sees letting someone in as a delay but as a co-operative driver, you should realise that doing so actually *saves time* because it helps the traffic

Co-operative drivers facilitate other road users allowing traffic to flow smoothly and reducing driver tension

system to flow as designed. It is also important to be ready to give way, even when technically the other driver should yield to you. This is because other drivers make mistakes (just like you) and, as a co-operative driver, you try to accommodate and adjust, just as they should for you.

When you drive co-operatively, you make your actions as predictable as possible to other drivers so they know what to expect from you. It is also important to give other drivers as much notice as possible about your intended actions so they have time to adjust, if necessary. This is particularly important when you make a mistake (which you will). For example, suppose you start to make a lane change without realising there is another vehicle in the way. If you use your indicator before changing lanes, as you should, you'll make the lane change predictable – hopefully predictable enough so that the other vehicle can let you in, use the horn or otherwise avoid the collision.

Co-operative driving extends to motorcyclists, pedestrians, cyclists and other vulnerable road users. A car or lorry can easily kill or severely injure an unprotected person at speeds that would have no effect on you as a driver. Therefore, it is important to give way to pedestrians and other vulnerable road users when circumstances require it. Give unprotected road users a wide safety margin and pass them cautiously and at a reduced speed. If you hit a pedestrian, the chances are high that you will either kill or seriously disable the person.

A car or lorry can easily kill or severely injure an unprotected person at speeds that would have no effect on you as a driver

Children's movements can be unpredictable. Slow down and allow plenty of room for the unexpected

Be especially cautious around children. Lacking adult judgement, children behave far more unpredictably than adults with respect to traffic. Slow down and be attentive as you approach and pass children on the roadway. The younger they are, the more likely they are to do something unexpected.

Ninety percent survival versus 10 percent survival
If you think slowing to 30 km/h (or slower) is a waste of time around pedestrians and children, consider this.

- Pedestrians have a 90-percent survival rate when hit by a vehicle travelling at 30 km/h.

- Pedestrians have only a 10-percent survival rate when hit by a vehicle travelling at 60 km/h.

- Slowing down not only increases your chances of avoiding a pedestrian, it also increases the pedestrian's chances of surviving if an incident occurs.

There's no doubt that competitive drivers increase the risks for all road users and when you see competitive drivers on the road, you may wonder why they don't cause more collisions. The reason is that co-operative drivers adjust for the competitive drivers' selfishness to prevent collisions.

You now understand why co-operative driving is so important to safety, but a word of caution: we all have a competitive driver inside us who tries to get out when we're late for work or in a hurry. Competitive drivers are not only unsafe, but seldom arrive significantly earlier anyway – much later if they crash, hurt somebody, or get pulled over and given penalty points and a fine.

Your limitations as a novice driver

Aidhmeanna
OBJECTIVES **2** Look for, and highlight, the answers to these questions

- What is the most dangerous period for novice drivers?
- What should you do to compensate during this period?
- According to research, how long does it take to reach average driving competence?
- What are the differences between experienced drivers and novice drivers?
- What are some of the possible limitations of other road users?

Here is some bad news: in crash statistics, novice drivers account for the greatest number of incidents. As a novice driver, you need to pay attention to that fact. Statistics show that the first year after passing the driving test is a particularly dangerous time for new drivers.

Why is this? It's because as a new driver, you're limited in your driving judgement: your perception of risk, your ability to respond to hazards and your ability to predict driver behaviour. You're also limited in the basic motor skills of driving, such as vehicle handling, steering, and braking. The problem is that you will acquire the basic motor skills much more quickly than you acquire the experience you need for good driving judgement. Relatively quickly after you pass your driver's test, you will feel confident in your ability to handle a vehicle. Unfortunately, this is a *false* sense of confidence because while you have the motor skills, you still don't have the judgement that comes with experience. *Statistics show that if you let this*

Novice drivers are overrepresented in crash statistics. The first year after the test is a particularly dangerous time for new drivers

confident feeling determine how you drive, you're highly likely to have a crash.

The good news is that you are not a statistic. You can choose to compensate for your inexperience during this dangerous period and come through it without incident. You can do this by recognising your inexperience and driving accordingly. Drive conservatively and co-operatively, giving yourself a bigger safety margin and more room for error than feels necessary. Assume that you will encounter hazards that, due to inexperience, you won't recognise, because *it will happen*. Remember and apply what you learn in this course. The reason you take this course is to learn from the experience of others instead of having to learn the hard way yourself.

Although the first year is the most dangerous, research from the USA suggests that it takes about *five years* to reach average driving competence. The benefit of experience shows in the statistics, clearly marking the differences between novice and experienced drivers.

- Experienced drivers make correct decisions more quickly and easily than novice drivers.
- Experienced drivers generally recognise their own limits and their vehicles' limits better than novice drivers.
- Experienced drivers recognise hazards more quickly than novice drivers.
- Experienced drivers are better at predicting where hazards or problems are likely to occur than novice drivers.

Experience will help you predict and prepare for hazards. For now, leave more room for error than feels necessary

Drivers of large vehicles need more room for stopping and manoeuvring

The only way you can go safely from novice driver to experienced driver is by gaining careful experience. During a few years of driving, you will see diverse situations from which you'll learn to predict what to expect on the road. But no matter how many years you've been driving, you need to stay alert, keep your driving knowledge up to date and never become complacent.

Just as you have limitations, so do other drivers and road users. For example:

- Older drivers who have slower reactions.
- Learner drivers who lack experience, may be nervous and need time to execute manoeuvres.
- Visually impaired or deaf pedestrians and other people with disabilities.
- Cyclists, motorcyclists, horse riders and pedestrians – our most vulnerable road users – need space, time and consideration.
- Drivers of very large vehicles, vehicles towing trailers, farm or construction vehicles need more time to accelerate, more room to stop for a given speed and more room to manoeuvre.
- Large vehicles and those towing trailers may have significant blind spots in which they cannot see you.

Being a co-operative driver means adjusting to accommodate the limitations of other drivers, just as you would have them do for you.

Finally, keep in mind that your limits constantly change. Today you're a novice driver. One day you may drive a slow, big construction vehicle and in time, you will be an older driver. As your limits change, you must change your driving behaviours to stay within your limits, and accept that other drivers must do the same.

QUICK QUIZ

1 The most dangerous period for novice drivers is during the first year of unaccompanied driving.
T ☑ F ☐

2 As a new driver you should compensate for your inexperience by leaving a larger safety margin and more room for error then feels necessary.
T ☑ F ☐

3 According to research, it takes about two years to reach average driving competence.
T ☐ F ☑

Answers: 1: T, 2: T, 3: F

Physical principles governing driving

Aidhmeanna OBJECTIVES **2** Look for, and highlight, the answers to these questions

- What is inertia and why is it important to driving?
- What are friction and traction?
- Why is traction important and what can affect it?
- Why do tyres have tread?
- What driving behaviours affect traction?
- How does gravity affect traction?
- What is centrifugal force and how does it affect a vehicle on a bend in the road?
- How does the tilt of the road affect your vehicle as it goes around a bend?

To understand the forces that affect you and your vehicle on the road, we need to look at some physics. We're not getting into nuclear particles and we're not going to get overly technical, but we'll look at the basic principles that dictate how a stationary or moving object must behave according to natural law.

Inertia

The most important physics concept to understand in driving is *inertia*. Inertia simply says that a stationary object remains stationary and a moving object continues to move in a straight line *unless a force acts upon the object.* If your car is on perfectly level ground, even with the brakes off it will just sit there, due to inertia. For it to move *requires* an applied force, such as pushing it or engaging the engine.

Now suppose you're on perfectly level ground, with perfectly aligned tyres, driving at 60 km/h. You put the car in neutral. Although the motor's disengaged, you don't stop, of course, but continue to coast. This is again due to inertia. To stop, you need to use the brakes. Eventually the car does stop on its own because the road and air act as forces that slow and eventually stop it (more about this shortly), but obviously not fast enough for control in most traffic situations. What you need to remember, then, is that due to inertia, once your car is moving, its tendency is to *continue to move in a straight line*. Steering and stopping *require* influence by other forces.

Friction and traction

In driving, the most important force that counteracts inertia is *friction*. Friction is simply the resistance that occurs when one substance rubs over the surface of another. In the previous example your car slows down after coasting at 60 km/h due to friction – the resistance of the air and the road surface combined with the minimal restriction within the wheel bearings. When you apply the brakes, the brake mechanism uses friction to hinder the turn of the wheels, slowing the vehicle. When you start the car moving, friction between the tyres and the road allows the force of the engine to propel the car into motion. If there were no friction between the tyres and the road, your wheels would just spin and the car wouldn't move.

Friction between your tyres and the road allow the power of the engine to propel your car into motion

Traction is the degree of friction that your tyres have – in other words, how well your tyres grip the road. Whether you're driving a two-wheel or a four-wheel-drive vehicle, it is traction that allows you to accelerate. Rubber tyres have traction because rubber is sticky (relatively speaking) and doesn't glide easily over most surfaces, even smooth, dry surfaces. Compare sliding a pen cap and a pencil eraser over a smooth surface. The eraser resists sliding much more because it has more traction – *i.e.,* friction.

Traction is important because it is necessary for steering, acceleration and stopping your vehicle. With good tyres and in good road conditions, you have maximum traction. This allows you to accelerate without spinning your wheels and to stop without skidding. A car stuck in the mud is stuck because it has no traction – the wheels spin rather than transfer the engine's power into vehicle motion. You can't stop or control a car sliding on a slick surface

Worn tyres cannot effectively eject water, therefore your traction in the wet will be significantly compromised

because the tyres have no traction. The brakes stop the wheels, but the wheels don't grip the road. Turning the steering wheel does nothing because there's no traction to overcome inertia and force your car into a new direction. Instead, inertia slides the car in a straight line from the point where it lost traction to the point where it either collides with something or slides onto a surface with sufficient traction to regain control.

You can only expect the best traction (rated 1.0) on a smooth, dry surface. Water, oil, ice, mud and other conditions reduce friction and thereby reduce traction. Slide a pencil eraser over a table top, then wet the table top and try again. You'll find it slides more easily. If you apply oil, the eraser slides with very little resistance at all. The following table lists how much traction you can expect on various surfaces:

Traction	Road surface
0.90	smooth dry asphalt
0.70	average dry road
0.60	wet asphalt-based road
0.50	wet or dry gravel
0.40	wet concrete or oily gravel
0.35	damp road or melted ice
0.20	muddy or frozen asphalt
0.05	ice

Your vehicle's tyres have *tread* to increase traction when road conditions are less than perfect. In wet weather, tyre tread design improves traction by ejecting water through the grooves to maximise the friction. As the tread wears out, however, the grooves become thin so that they don't effectively eject water. If there's water on the road and you're travelling faster than your tyres can displace it, you can literally drive up onto a water layer. This is known as aquaplaning or hydroplaning. Practically speaking, you have zero traction in this situation because your tyres cannot grip water.

Snow can clog the grooves in your tyres and reduce traction, so snow tyres have a special tread. Off-road tyres have treads designed to provide traction in dirt and mud. However, tread design cannot *guarantee* traction. In general, even with good tyre tread, traction is reduced in direct proportion to how slippery the road surface is. When the road surface is icy, or covered in oil, mud or frozen snow, traction can be reduced to nothing or nearly nothing.

Your driving behaviour also affects traction. For example, although you have less traction on a wet road, you still have *some* traction. If you allow ample space between your vehicle and others, accelerate slowly and brake gradually, you can control your vehicle within the traction limits. Starting or stopping too quickly, may cause your tyres to spin or slide and you will lose all traction. On a dry road, if you 'stand on the brakes', you may lock the wheels and skid. This *lengthens* your stopping distance because during the skid, heat from friction melts the tyre tread into a liquid that acts as a lubricant, further

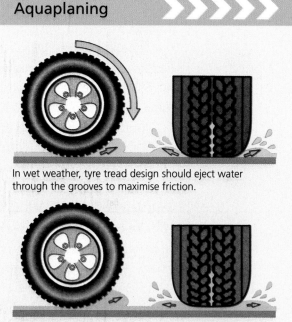

In wet weather, tyre tread design should eject water through the grooves to maximise friction.

When water volume is too great and speed is too fast, you risk driving up onto a water layer leading to zero traction.

reducing traction. This is why antilock brakes improve safety – on a dry road, they allow you apply the maximum braking power without skidding, though you can still skid with antilock brakes on water or ice, or if your tyres are worn, for example.

Another aspect of driver behaviour that affects traction is taking care of your tyres. If you over or under-inflate tyres, you reduce their traction. Under-inflated tyres aquaplane more easily because they don't eject water properly. Over-inflated tyres have less contact with the road, reducing traction in all conditions. Check your tyres regularly for proper inflation,

When driving in wet conditions, allow ample space between your vehicle and others, accelerate and brake slowly. Control your vehicle within the traction limits

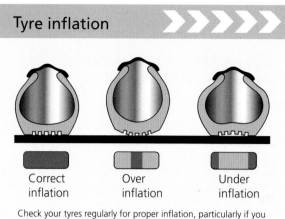

Tyre inflation

Correct inflation | Over inflation | Under inflation

Check your tyres regularly for proper inflation, particularly if you are carrying a heavy load.

particularly if you are carrying a heavy load. Additionally, be sure you have the legally required minimum of 1.6 mm of tread, and use tyres with uniform tread. Mismatched treads cause uneven traction, which contributes to poor handling. You should also use the appropriate tyres for your vehicle's purpose, e.g., everyday tyres for general use, off-road tyres for gripping on unfinished roads, and snow tyres for driving in snow.

Gravity

When discussing inertia, we looked at examples of what happens when your vehicle is motionless or moving over a _perfectly level surface_. This is because if a surface is not level, a second force – gravity – acts upon your vehicle. Gravity also affects traction on all surfaces. We'll look at this first.

Gravity affects traction because it gives your vehicle weight. All else being the same, a heavier vehicle has more traction. Returning to your eraser, drag it over a surface, pushing down lightly and again pushing down heavily. Pushing heavily creates more friction and resistance to movement, just like a heavier vehicle would. But, note that when you drag the eraser over a wet or oiled surface, pushing down heavily doesn't increase the resistance that much. This is why the practice of loading the boot with weight for more traction may help a little in marginal conditions, but it won't help much in the poorest traction conditions.

On a slope, gravity also acts as a force that pulls your vehicle down the slope. This is common sense: you tend to speed up going down a hill and may have to use the brakes, and you tend to slow down and the engine has to work harder going up. If the road tilts to the right or left, it is said to have _cross-fall_. This means gravity tries to pull the car off the road to the side. The reality is that there is no such thing as a perfectly level road. In fact, engineers may intentionally tilt roads for drainage and to improve handling (more about this in the next section). Sometimes roads have a pronounced tilt because there's no practical way to correct it. It is traction that counteracts gravity and keeps your vehicle on the road and in control. When cross-fall is pronounced, traction becomes critical because tyres that don't hold the road allow gravity (and other forces) to carry the vehicle out of control.

Centrifugal force

Another important force that affects driving is *centrifugal force*. To understand how this force affects your vehicle, consider what happens when you whirl a small weight in a circle with a piece of string. Due to inertia, the weight wants to fly away from the centre of the circle (your hand) in a straight line, but it can't because the string holds onto it, forcing the weight to keep moving in a circle. If the string were to snap, the weight would fly away from the circle's centre in a straight line. This tendency to pull away from the centre is called centrifugal force.

Centrifugal force is arguably the most dangerous force at work when you drive. It comes into play when you turn and go around a bend. As the car turns, its inertia tries to carry it along in a straight line, away from the centre of the curve. The 'string' that keeps the car on the road is traction. Losing traction is like cutting the string – the car travels in a straight line away from the centre of the curve. This almost always means losing control and having a collision.

Besides losing traction due to road conditions, you can also lose traction simply due to speed on a turn. Let's go back to whirling a weight on a piece of string. The faster you whirl the weight, the stronger the string must be or it will snap and the weight will fly away. Put another way, the weaker the string, the slower you must whirl the weight to keep the string from breaking. Similarly, you're more likely to lose traction and control, when making a turn at a higher speed, than at a lower speed, because there's more centrifugal force at work on your car. This is why it's especially important to slow down at bends in wet or icy conditions – it often doesn't take much extra speed to lose traction. Think of poor traction as having weaker string holding you on the road.

A tilted bend can work for or against you in dealing with centrifugal force. Centrifugal force tends to make the car want to travel in a straight line away from the centre of the curve. So, if you're curving to the right, the tendency is for the car to go left

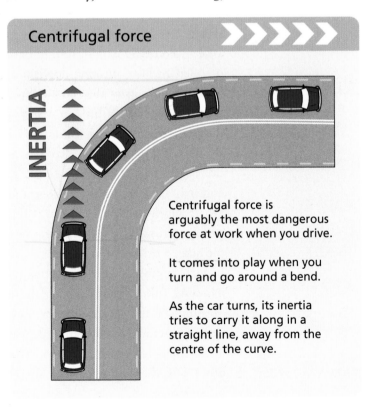

Centrifugal force

INERTIA

Centrifugal force is arguably the most dangerous force at work when you drive.

It comes into play when you turn and go around a bend.

As the car turns, its inertia tries to carry it along in a straight line, away from the centre of the curve.

Tilted curves

Engineers sometimes use camber to counteract centrifugal force by tilting (or banking) a curve, so that the inside of the curve is lower than the outside.

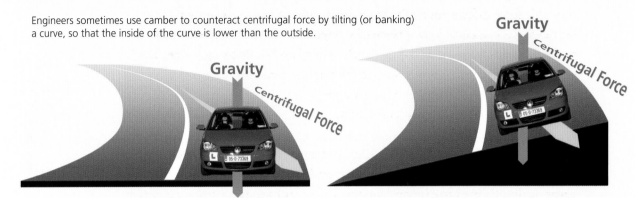

relative to the road, and vice versa. Remember, though, that gravity crossfall tends to pull your car down a slope. Engineers use this to counteract centrifugal force by tilting (or *banking*) a curve, so that the inside of the curve is lower than the outside. As you go around the curve, centrifugal force pushes you to the outside of the curve, but gravity pulls you to the inside of the curve. The forces counterbalance, making it easier for you to maintain traction and negotiate the turn under control. However, this assumes that you don't exceed the curve's design speed, *i.e.*, the speed limit. If you're going too fast, the centrifugal force can be too great for gravity to counterbalance and you will find it difficult to maintain traction, especially in slippery conditions.

QUICK QUIZ

1   Traction is important because it is necessary for acceleration and stopping your vehicle.
T ☑   F ☐

2   Tyres have tread to improve their traction in all conditions.   T ☐   F ☑

3   With respect to centrifugal force, the tilt of the road has little or no effect.   T ☐   F ☑

Answers: 1: T, 2: F, 3: F

On some roads, the tilt works against you. This happens when a road tilts towards the outside of a curve. In these instances, gravity and centrifugal force combine instead of counterbalancing, trying to force you away from the centre of the curve. This situation, combined with a slippery road, poorly inflated tyres or anything else that compromises traction is a frequent cause of collisions. Approach any curve that is 'banked the wrong way' with caution and negotiate it at a reduced speed.

Momentum: braking, slowing, stopping

Aidhmeanna
OBJECTIVES **2** **Look for, and highlight, the answers to these questions**

- What is momentum and why is it important in driving?
- What counteracts the momentum of your vehicle when you brake?
- What transfers the momentum of a driver and passengers to the vehicle when you brake suddenly?
- What governs the amount of damage suffered by a vehicle and its occupants in an impact?
- What are the most dangerous types of collisions, and why?
- How does momentum affect traction on a bend?

Momentum

In the last section, you learned that inertia is the tendency for a resting object to remain at rest and a moving object to remain in motion in a straight line. You also learned that you have to apply another force to make a stationary object move or to make a moving object stop or move in a different direction. Now let's look at some other aspects of inertia.

If your car isn't moving, you have to apply a force to begin moving it. Through experience, you probably realise that to reach a given speed, it takes more force to move a heavy object than a lighter object. This is because the heavier a vehicle is, the greater its inertia. For example, on a level surface it's very easy to push a child on a tricycle to a speed of 1 km/h, but it would take several people working hard to get a heavy lorry rolling that fast.

Momentum

It takes a lot of effort to get the Giant Ball rolling by pushing, but once moving, it's hard to stop!

This principle also applies once an object is moving. Continuing our example, it takes a lot of effort to get a lorry moving by pushing, but once it gets going, it's not hard to keep it moving. This is because the force that goes into moving an object stays with the object. This force is called *momentum*. Once an object has momentum, it keeps that momentum until another force counteracts it. On a level surface, you only have to push the lorry hard enough to replace the momentum that it loses to friction, both from the air hitting the truck and from the resistance of the wheels as they roll along the road.

Now think about *stopping* the child on the tricycle and the lorry, both rolling at 1 km/h. You probably realise that you can stop the tricycle easily with one hand, but it will take just as much work to stop the lorry as it took to get it rolling. This illustrates that the force required to counteract momentum is equal to the force that was required to get the object moving at its present speed. For two objects moving at the same speed, the heavier object has more momentum. For two moving objects that weigh the same, the faster one has more momentum. Based on this principle, it's possible to mathematically calculate an object's momentum if you know its weight and speed. We'll return to this shortly.

Stopping

Let's apply all this to driving. It takes a lot of force, or energy, to get your car moving, but once you reach a given speed, it takes much less force to keep it moving. On an open motorway, you gently control the accelerator applying just enough power to replace the energy lost to friction or lost to gravity as you go up a hill. As you already know, if you were to put your vehicle in neutral, it would coast a long way (assuming level ground) before friction with the air and the road would counteract the momentum enough to stop you.

If you don't have sufficient traction, the brakes can't stop the vehicle, no matter how well they're working

Therefore, you need the vehicle's brakes as a strong counteracting force against momentum. When you want to stop, you ease off the accelerator, that is, you stop applying force that builds momentum and apply the brakes. As you already learned, friction between the brakes and the wheels, along with the traction between the tyres and the road, create the force that counteracts your momentum. You also learned that if you don't have sufficient traction, the brakes can't stop the vehicle, no matter how well they're working.

It's important to recognise that the more momentum you have, the harder your brakes have to work to stop the vehicle. This usually translates into requiring more distance to stop. The less traction you have on a wet road for example, the longer this distance becomes. This is one reason why the faster you're going, the more space you need to allow for stopping. For a given speed, the heavier the vehicle, the further you will travel between first applying the brakes and coming to a stop. You may need more stopping distance with four passengers than if you're travelling alone, for example.

You, your passengers and contents

Anything moving has momentum, and that includes anyone or anything in your vehicle. To stop safely, your momentum and the momentum of your passengers and any contents must transfer to the vehicle to be counteracted by the brakes and tyres. When you stop gradually, this happens naturally. When you stop suddenly, the safety belts capture the momentum of the occupants and transfer it to the vehicle.

The forces involved here are more significant than you may realise. Momentum equals half the weight times the velocity squared. Don't worry about the maths, but realise that speed has a bigger effect on momentum than weight. When you double your weight, you double your momentum, but when you double your speed, you *quadruple* your momentum. A person who weighs 70 kg has about 1,400 kg of momentum when moving at 70 km/h. It therefore takes 1,400 kg of counteracting force to stop that person.

In a sudden stop, like when jamming on the brakes or in a collision, there isn't sufficient time for momentum to transfer naturally from an occupant to the vehicle. This is why a safety belt is so important. If an occupant is not wearing a safety belt, then little momentum transfers to the vehicle and the person continues to travel forward with the force of momentum. In a collision or very abrupt stop from a vehicle moving at 70 km/h, a 70 kg unrestrained occupant hurtles forward with as much as 1,400 kg of force – more than enough to go through the windscreen, even from the back seat if not blocked by the front seats or other occupants. Sudden stops with a safety belt can result in discomfort and injury, but tests and data show that the risk of serious injury or death is substantially higher without one.

Similarly, don't underestimate the effect of momentum on baggage or anything else in your vehicle. A loose object behind you or a passenger can cause serious injury, even death, when it flies forward in the event of a sudden stop. Be sure the contents of your vehicle are restrained or placed so they cannot become projectiles.

Impact

The most abrupt way to stop is by collision with another object. The momentum of the vehicle and passengers must go somewhere – where it goes and what happens to the vehicle and its occupants depends upon the nature of the impact. The amount of damage suffered by the occupants and the vehicle is governed by how quickly the momentum is released. The faster it happens, the more dangerous it is for vehicle occupants. Consider these situations:

- If a vehicle runs off the road onto a grass or gravel verge, resistance from the uneven grass/gravel surface helps to dissipate momentum reasonably slowly. The vehicle may be damaged, but the occupants are likely to be unharmed.
- If a vehicle hits a light object like a bush or a small tree, the object will absorb some of the momentum and help to slow the vehicle, probably resulting in minor injuries.

The amount of damage suffered by the occupants and the vehicle is governed by how quickly momentum is released. The faster it happens, the more dangerous it is for vehicle occupants.

- If a vehicle hits a heavier object, such as a wall or larger tree, the object absorbs a moderate amount of the momentum and may crumble. The vehicle stops quite quickly, causing some harm to the occupants and a lot of damage to the vehicle.
- When a vehicle collides with an immobile object, it stops almost immediately and the object absorbs almost all the momentum abruptly. The force experienced by the occupants will be severe and likely to cause serious injury and even death.
- The most dangerous collision is when two vehicles collide head on, with the worst effects on the vehicle with the least momentum. This is because the vehicles transfer momentum instantly. The vehicle with the lower momentum becomes the agent through which the other vehicle dissipates its momentum. These types of collisions are usually serious and quite often fatal.

Safety innovations such as air bags and crumple zones only help to reduce the risk of serious injury, they do not guarantee survival

Many modern safety innovations are intended to transfer momentum more safely from occupants to reduce injury risk. These include safety belts, head restraints, air bags and side impact bars. Crumple zones sacrifice the vehicle to protect the occupants by designing it to collapse like a giant shock absorber on impact, slowing the loss of momentum. However, all these features have their limits, and while they improve your chances in a collision, they're no guarantee of survival. The best way to survive the effects of momentum is not to have a collision in the first place.

Momentum and traction

In the last section, you learned that the faster you go around a bend, the more traction you need to keep centrifugal force from pulling you off the road. You probably recognise now that centrifugal force results from momentum; the more momentum, the more force. It also means that a heavier vehicle must take a curve more slowly than a lighter vehicle, because a heavier vehicle has more momentum.

Passengers will increase your momentum by adding to the weight of your vehicle. You need to be aware of this particularly when cornering and stopping

1 Momentum is the energy or force within a moving object. T ☑ F ☐

2 When you brake suddenly, the safety belts help to transfer momentum from the occupants to the vehicle. T ☑ F ☐

3 On a bend, momentum affects your traction by increasing the cross-fall. T ☐ F ☑

Answers: 1: T, 2: T, 3: F

Whenever your vehicle is carrying more weight, including passengers, be aware that you have more potential momentum fighting your traction on bends and turns, so slow down to reduce your momentum. The poorer the road conditions and the heavier your vehicle, the more slowly you should negotiate bends and turns.

Road design

Aidhmeanna OBJECTIVES 2

Look for, and highlight, the answers to these questions

- What philosophy do road designers apply when designing and building roads?
- What are some examples of how road designers apply this philosophy?
- What are the possible consequences of violating the design speed of a road?
- What are the four main categories of roads in Ireland and how would you recognise them on Ordnance Survey maps?

There is more to building a road than simply bulldozing a path and laying down asphalt. In designing and building roads, road designers apply the philosophy of making roads as safe as possible by accounting for driver psychology and physical principles, including those you've learned about up to this point.

The National Roads Authority (NRA) and the Department of the Environment, Heritage and Local Government (DOEHLG) designs and builds Irish roads based on years of research, development and assessment. In a relatively small country like Ireland, costs can constrain the best design practice, with other social, environmental or historical factors also affecting road design.

However, as much as possible, road design takes both driving physics and driver psychology into account. This not only includes the slope, direction and width of the road itself – among other things – but also the signs, signals and markings that apply as you negotiate the road. If you ignore these directions, you put yourself and other road users at risk by going beyond what the road was designed for. In general:

- A road is built as straight as possible, but without extremely long straights on single carriageways. This is because such long straights make it difficult to judge the speed and distance of oncoming vehicles.
- Unavoidable bends have as big a curve as possible to allow for full overtaking sight distance, or very tight curves to discourage unsafe overtaking.
- Road surfaces on bends are 'super-elevated' or tilted to counteract centrifugal force. At the intended speed, the imposed tilt (known as 'camber') assists you in controlling the car in the bend. If you exceed this design speed, you risk losing control of your vehicle. This is why speed limits are as much a part of the road design as the road itself.
- Engineers optimise sightlines at junctions, though sometimes they deliberately reduce them to ensure that drivers stop at junctions and don't enter the main road too quickly. Where sightlines are unavoidably restricted, engineers reduce the speed limit on the main road. This is another example of how you can put yourself at risk by exceeding the design speed; you may not see a slower vehicle entering the main road in front of you until you are too close to stop.

Modern Irish roads are designed and built based on years of research, development and assessment.

- Slip lanes and acceleration lanes allow safe and easy merging and diverging.
- Roads arch slightly in the middle to keep the surface as dry as possible in wet weather.
- Road surface materials are designed to give maximum traction and road holding. The surface is also designed to reduce noise, dry quickly and improve stopping ability.

There are four types of Irish roads: National Primary Roads, including Motorways; National Secondary Roads; Regional Roads; and Local Roads.

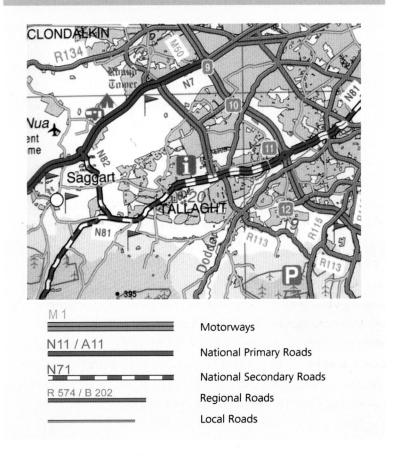

M 1	Motorways
N11 / A11	National Primary Roads
N71	National Secondary Roads
R 574 / B 202	Regional Roads
	Local Roads

National Primary Roads

National Primary Roads are the major long-distance routes linking the cities, towns, ports and airports of the country. They are designated by the letter N, except when the primary route is a Motorway. In that case, the letter M is used. On Ordnance Survey Maps, these roads are represented by green or blue lines.

National Secondary Roads

National Secondary Roads are medium-distance routes serving medium to large geographical areas and are also designated by the letter N (in Northern Ireland A) They're shown as green and white lines on OS Maps.

Regional Roads

Regional Roads are the main feeder routes for the National Primary and Secondary Roads. They're designated by the letter R (in Northern Ireland B), On OS Maps, look for red lines.

Local roads

Local roads include all remaining rural and urban roads. They usually have names rather than numbers, such as 'Trees Road'. They're referred to as third class roads in Northern Ireland and shown as yellow lines on OS Maps.

Vital signs

OBJECTIVES 2 ⟩⟩ **Look for, and highlight, the answers to these questions**

- Why do we need a system of road signs, signals and markings?
- What are the five types of signs, and what is the purpose of each type?
- What must you do when you see a Regulatory Sign?
- Where can you find a full list of all Irish road signs?
- Why do we have traffic signals as well as signs?
- What are the meanings of the different lights and symbols on traffic signals?
- What are the meanings of the different road markings?

In this module, you've learned that driving is a co-operative activity and that physical laws affect your safety as a driver. For these reasons, our road network needs signs, signals and markings for efficient road use by all of its users and to minimise risk. With respect to driving as a co-operative activity; signs, signals and markings help you and other motorists share the road. They tell everyone who has priority, where vehicles should or should not go, when to stop and when to go, so that traffic moves efficiently with the least risk possible.

With respect to physical laws; signs, signals and markings also help you avoid physical hazards. You've already learned that curves may have design speeds, and that engineers may reduce speeds to account for limited sight distance. Similarly, various markings alert you to permanent, temporary and conditional hazards, or give instructions to help drivers avoid a hazard.

Road signs

When you drive down the road, you pass lots of signs. You may not have thought about it before, but there are actually five types of road signs.

Information signs are usually rectangular and sometimes have one pointed end indicating the direction to follow. These signs allow you to navigate from one road to the next and help you find your way.

- Motorway signs have a blue background with white lettering.
- National primary route signs have a green background with white lettering.
- The signs for other routes have a white background with black lettering.
- Tourist information is given in white on a brown background.

Regulatory signs indicate either *mandatory* or *prohibitory* traffic regulations. Mandatory signs tell you what you must do, for example, 'stop', 'keep left' or 'yield'. Prohibitory signs tell you what you must not do, for example, 'no entry' or 'no left turn'. They also show speed restrictions. You must obey regulatory signs. They are for your safety and the safety of other road users and it is an offence not to obey them. Failing to follow a regulatory sign can result in a crash at worst, and penalty points at the least.

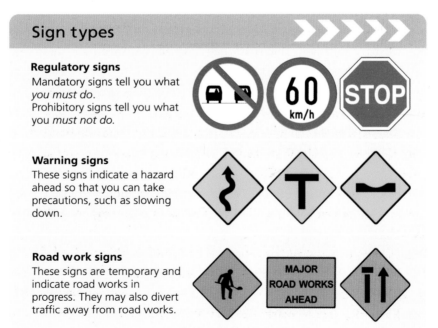

Sign types

Regulatory signs
Mandatory signs tell you what *you must do*.
Prohibitory signs tell you what you *must not do*.

Warning signs
These signs indicate a hazard ahead so that you can take precautions, such as slowing down.

Road work signs
These signs are temporary and indicate road works in progress. They may also divert traffic away from road works.

Warning signs indicate a hazard ahead so that you can take precautions, such as slowing down. These signs have a diamond shape with black symbols on a yellow background. A black outline surrounds the yellow diamond. For example, intersection or junction ahead.

Road work signs are temporary signs and indicate road works in progress. These signs are either rectangular or diamond in shape with an orange background, black borders and symbols or lettering. Road Work Signs alert you to related hazards, related regulations like a reduced speed limit and the presence of workers near the roadway. These signs may also divert traffic away from road-work areas.

Motorway signs are specialised regulatory signs. They have a blue background with white lettering and symbols that indicate motorway rules and regulations. They are generally well placed and larger than regular signs so that you can read them from a distance while travelling at the maximum speed of 120 km/h.

You can find a full list of road signs in the *Rules of the Road*. As a driver, you're required to have a thorough understanding of their meaning, so be sure to review them.

Traffic signals

Signs are useful for telling drivers who must yield right of way, but they always give the same message, no matter what the traffic is like. At junctions between heavily-used roads, one road may back up with traffic if there's no flexibility in who has priority. Therefore, we need traffic signals as well as signs to allow traffic to move efficiently. Traffic signals govern traffic and pedestrian movement, and they are regulatory. That is, like regulatory signs, it is an offence to disobey signals. You're probably familiar with the different lights and symbols on traffic signals, but here's a quick review:

- **Red light**
  You must stop at a red light and not proceed beyond the stop line while the red light is illuminated.
- **Amber light**
  You must not proceed beyond a traffic light or stop line when the amber light is illuminated, except when the amber light comes on after you are too close to the stop line to stop safely. You are expected to safely clear the intersection before the light turns red.

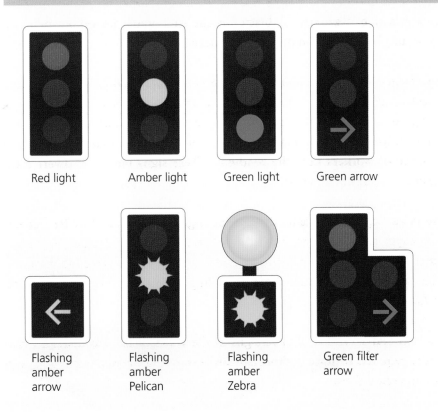

Red light

Amber light

Green light

Green arrow

Flashing amber arrow

Flashing amber Pelican

Flashing amber Zebra

Green filter arrow

- **Green light**

  You may proceed past a green light provided the way is clear.

- **Green arrow**

  You may proceed in the direction of a green arrow, provided the way is clear and it is safe to do so.

- **Red arrow**

  If you are in a turning lane governed by this arrow, you must stop.

- **Flashing amber arrow**

  You must give way to pedestrians and vehicles on the adjoining road and only proceed when the way is clear.

- **Flashing amber lights at zebra crossings**

  When approaching pedestrian crossings, you need to be able to slow and stop for pedestrians wishing to cross. You must yield to pedestrians at zebra crossings and must not encroach on the marked crossing area. Parking and overtaking is prohibited within 15 m of pedestrian crossings or on the zigzag lines at the edges of the road approaching the crossing.

Road markings

Road markings seem to be the least understood element of the road system, yet they can be extremely valuable because they send a continuous message. Road markings provide guidance, hazard warning and regulatory information. A good rule of thumb is that the more paint a road marking has, the more important its message! Here are the different types of markings and what they mean:

Transverse markings run across the road, perpendicular to the centre line. A continuous transverse line on your side of the road shows where you must stop, *e.g.*, at a stop sign. A broken transverse line on your side of the road indicates that you must give right of way to traffic on another road, *e.g.*, at a yield sign or when traffic is already on a roundabout.

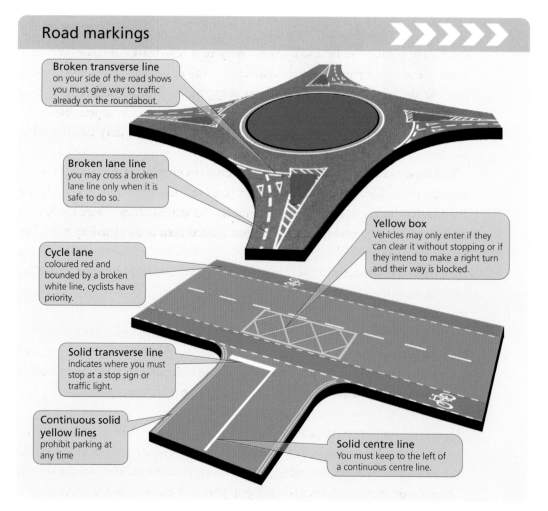

Road markings

Broken transverse line
on your side of the road shows you must give way to traffic already on the roundabout.

Broken lane line
you may cross a broken lane line only when it is safe to do so.

Cycle lane
coloured red and bounded by a broken white line, cyclists have priority.

Yellow box
Vehicles may only enter if they can clear it without stopping or if they intend to make a right turn and their way is blocked.

Solid transverse line
indicates where you must stop at a stop sign or traffic light.

Continuous solid yellow lines
prohibit parking at any time

Solid centre line
You must keep to the left of a continuous centre line.

Longitudinal markings are centre lines, lane lines and edge lines. They set the right and left side limits within which you must drive.

Centre lines may take several forms. You must keep to the left of continuous single or double centre lines. You may cross a broken centre line only if it is safe to do so. A centre line that is broken on one side and continuous on the other allows traffic only on the broken side to cross when it is safe to do so. Double broken centre lines tell you that a continuous white line is a short distance ahead.

Lane lines that are broken white lines separate lanes on dual carriageways and motorways. The marks are closer together where lanes or slip roads merge.

Edge lines that are single broken yellow lines indicate the edge of the road or hard shoulder. The hard shoulder is not an extra lane but on single carriageways it may be used temporarily to allow traffic to pass provided there are no pedestrians or cyclists already using it. Continuous double yellow lines at the edge of the road prohibit stopping or parking at any time, and continuous single yellow lines prohibit parking at posted times. **Bus/tram lanes** may not be crossed when the line is continuous but may be crossed at the tapered ends to allow access to side roads. Be aware that some bus lanes allow buses to travel in the opposite direction to normal traffic flow; these are called contra-flow lanes. Taxis and bicycles can use most bus lanes but not contra-flow lanes. Red shaded areas designate shared lanes where cyclists or pedestrians have priority. When the red shaded area is bounded by a broken white line other vehicles may cross and share the lane but when it is bounded by a continuous white line they may not. An example is a transverse stop line at a junction.

Markings at level crossings, roundabouts and junctions take several forms, depending upon the location's requirements. Level crossings are well signposted: they usually have flashing red light signals, a gate and a thicker stop line drawn across the road. Approach them with caution.

Roundabouts come in a variety of styles but the same general rules and road markings apply. A broken line and a yield triangle painted on the road indicate that approaching traffic must yield to traffic already on the roundabout, but may proceed without a stop if the way is clear. At traffic-signal-controlled roundabouts, traffic must stop behind the line when the light is red.

Broken lane line
you may cross a broken lane line only when it is safe to do so.

Hatched markings
separate traffic approaching a hazard such as a junction. You may only enter a hatched area in an emergency

Hatched markings
separate a merging area, they can only be crossed in an emergency.

Edge lines
indicate the edge of the road or hard shoulder.

Straightforward white line markings govern most junctions, but where traffic flow is affected a **yellow box** is marked on the road. Vehicles may only enter the yellow box if they can clear it without stopping or if they intend to make a right turn and their way is blocked by oncoming traffic. Drivers should not enter the box to turn right if it will obstruct other traffic.

Worded markings are self-explanatory markings that indicate schools, parking bays, bus and cycle lanes, for example. They warn you of special circumstances or hazards.

Pedestrian crossings are marked by 'zebras' – alternating thick black and white stripes laid parallel to the centre line of the road. A broken yield line is positioned just before the black and white stripes to indicate that vehicles must yield to pedestrians using the crossing. Pedestrian crossings with stop signals have a solid white line to indicate where vehicles must stop. Zigzag lines at the side of the road leading up to or away from a pedestrian crossing indicate the approach to the pedestrian crossing. You may not park or overtake in this area, and you should prepare to slow down or stop if pedestrians wish to cross the road. Pedestrians must cross at the designated crossing area and should not cross the road elsewhere within the area.

Hatched markings separate traffic approaching a hazard, bend, junction or slip-road merging area. The usual white boundary line rules apply: you should only enter the hatched area in an emergency as its function is to provide a safe separation area. In general, the closer together the hatched markings, the greater the potential hazard.

Use your *Rules of the Road* book and the *Driver Theory Test Manual* to study Irish road signs, signals and markings. You need to do this to be safe on the road and to answer the questions at the end of this module, in the Steer Clear Final Exam and in The Official Driver Theory Test.

Law enforcement

Aidhmeanna
OBJECTIVES 2 > **Look for, and highlight, the answers to these questions**

● What happens when drivers violate traffic laws?
● Why is law enforcement necessary?
● What is the purpose of the penalty points system?
● How many penalty points result in disqualification from driving?

By now, it's obvious to you that for the safe, effective operation of our road network all drivers need to follow the same rules and regulations. Traffic laws exist to govern motorist behaviour. They assist you in cooperating with other drivers and in avoiding dangerous behaviours.

Motorists who violate traffic laws upset the whole system. They're unpredictable, and they compromise traffic flow, their own safety and the safety of other road users. They place a burden on other drivers to compensate for their bad driving.

Law enforcement is necessary to correct bad driving or driver misconduct. There are actually two ways misconduct occurs: either by mistake, when a motorist is ignorant of the law or by intent, when a motorist disregards the law. Both are subject to correction and penalty, but the latter is a worse offence because the individual knows better but behaves as if the law doesn't apply to them.

The purpose of the points system is to correct driver misconduct helping to improve road safety for all road users

A system of penalty points was introduced in 2002 as part of a major road-safety initiative to address the unacceptable level of death and serious injury on Irish roads and to instil greater responsibility in drivers. The purpose of the points system is to correct driver misconduct and, when necessary, to remove those who don't drive properly from our roads.

Under the penalty points system, drivers who commit road traffic offences accumulate points on their licence. For example, the penalty for speeding is two points and a fine of €80. If the driver contests the matter, the penalty can increase to four points with a fine of up to €800 if the court finds the driver

Under the penalty points system, drivers who commit road traffic offences accumulate points on their licence. Twelve points disqualifies a driver for six months

guilty. Penalty points stay on the licence for three years. The accumulation of twelve penalty points automatically disqualifies a driver for six months.

The system will be rolled out in stages and will ultimately include sixty-nine offences. The advantage of the points system is that it applies both corrective and punitive action. If you break the law through ignorance, receive a fine and penalty points and learn from it, you probably won't repeat the offence. You will have an incentive to learn and stay informed so you don't earn more points and put your licence at risk. Individuals who know the law but refuse to follow it, however, do not suffer from ignorance, but from an inappropriate attitude. They must either change their attitude about following the law, or continue to accumulate points and lose their licence. The points system provides an incentive to learn and to follow our traffic laws, and a method for taking those who refuse to do so off the road.

Summary points ⟩⟩⟩⟩⟩⟩⟩

In this module on understanding the road you learned:

1   Driving is a *co-operative* activity by design and necessity.

2   Good drivers behave in a way that makes their actions predictable to other drivers. They are ready to give way when other drivers make mistakes.

3   Novice drivers account for the greatest number of incidents in crash statistics. This is because they tend to have a false sense of confidence in their driving skills though they lack the judgement that comes with experience.

4   You compensate for your inexperience by driving conservatively and co-operatively and by leaving a bigger safety margin and more room for error than feels necessary. Remember and apply what you learn in this course.

5   Once your vehicle is in motion, it tends to continue to travel in a straight line until acted upon by another force. This tendency is called inertia. The force within your vehicle is known as momentum.

6   The primary force you use to control your vehicle is friction. Friction from the brakes slows the wheels. Friction between the road and the tyres is called traction. Traction allows friction in the brakes to slow the vehicle, and it allows you to steer.

7   Water, ice, oil, snow and tyre condition all affect traction. The less traction you have, the easier it is to lose control of your vehicle.

8   Gravity causes cross-fall, which tries to force your vehicle off a tilted road. Traction is necessary to counteract cross-fall.

9   Centrifugal force tries to force your vehicle away from the centre of a curve. It is arguably the most dangerous force at work when you drive. You must drive within the limits of traction to counteract centrifugal force and keep your vehicle under control.

10   Engineers sometimes tilt a road so that cross-fall helps counteract centrifugal force. Such roads are lower on the inside of the curve. You must remain within the road's design speed to remain within the intended balance between the forces. Roads tilted so the outside of the curve is lower can be hazardous because centrifugal force and cross-fall combine instead of counteract.

11   Momentum increases with weight and speed, but speed has a greater effect on momentum. If you double the weight, you double the momentum, but if you double the speed, you quadruple the momentum. Due to momentum, it takes just as much force to stop an object travelling at a given speed as it takes to get the object moving at that speed.

12   Everything travelling in a vehicle has momentum. When you stop, momentum must transfer from occupants and contents to the vehicle. In a sudden stop, safety belts capture occupant momentum and transfer it to the vehicle. Without safety belts occupants can hurtle forward with tremendous force due to their momentum.

13   In a collision or impact, the more suddenly momentum is released, the worse for the vehicle and occupants. The worst collisions are head-to-head with another moving vehicle. The vehicle with the lesser momentum becomes the agent through which the vehicle with the greater momentum dissipates its energy.

14   Despite modern safety innovations, the best way to survive the effects of momentum is not to have a collision in the first place.

15   The heavier your load and the poorer the road conditions, the more slowly you should negotiate bends and turns.

16   Road design tries to account for driver psychology and physical factors. Ignoring signs, signals and markings creates risk for you and other road users by taking you beyond what the designers intended when they built the road.

17   Regulatory signs indicate things you either must do or must not do. It is an
      offence to disobey a regulatory sign. Traffic signals are used where a sign would
      make traffic flow inefficient. It is an offence to disobey a traffic signal.

18   Road markings provide visual information about where your vehicle should or
      should not be on the road, and they also provide information to help you avoid
      hazards. It is an offence to disobey road markings.

19   When drivers violate traffic laws, they upset the system by reducing traffic
      safety and traffic flow. They compromise their own safety and the safety of
      other road users, inconvenience everyone else and place a burden on other
      drivers to compensate for their bad driving.

20   Law enforcement provides a means for correcting drivers who break traffic laws.
      The points system provides an incentive for learning from mistakes and provides
      a means of removing those who can't or won't learn to drive according to
      the rules.

3

'The best car safety device is a
rear view mirror with a cop in it'

Dudley Moore

Understanding your vehicle

Introduction

Owning and running even the most economical vehicles requires a considerable
investment. Not only will you need to consider the cost of buying a car, but there are
the associated costs of running and maintaining it as well. You have a responsibility to
ensure the vehicle you're driving is in good working order.

Therefore, you need a basic understanding of how a car's systems and parts work.

The car is an amazing machine made up of literally thousands of parts, but a
failure of any one part can seriously compromise its performance. Routine vehicle
checks and maintenance, and your ability to recognise possible problems, will allow
you to avoid costly repairs and assure reliable, safe and efficient performance.

You don't have to be mechanically minded to carry out routine checks
and simple maintenance on your vehicle. This module will give you a better
understanding of how your vehicle works and help you to carry out the simple
routine checks needed.

In this module we will discuss...

- How your car works: parts, systems and functions
- Routine checks
- Basic maintenance

- Vehicle modifications
- Appropriate and inappropriate modifications
- Breakdowns and personal safety
- Managing breakdowns

How your car works: parts, systems and functions

Aidhmeanna OBJECTIVES 3

Look for, and highlight, the answers to these questions

- What are the main parts and systems of your vehicle?
- What functions do they perform?
- Which systems are necessary for safe driving?

Each component of a vehicle has a specific purpose, and must also interact with all the other parts and systems. The loss of any one of them seriously compromises function, so that it may not work or be safe to drive. So let's look at systems and the functions they perform, basic considerations for keeping them in good working order and servicing requirements.

- ■ Mild Steel
- ■ High Strength Steel
- ■ Extra High Strength Steel
- ■ Ultra High Strength Steel

The integrated chassis structure of a modern Volvo uses up to 4 different strengths of steel for maximum safety

Chassis and body

The chassis and body form the skeleton of your car – an integrated structure that holds the vehicle together and creates a light, strong protective frame around the occupants. Car bodies are designed with crumple zones that collapse and give way to dissipate energy in the event of a crash.

The shell gives your car its style and look. It is light and aerodynamic to minimise drag and turbulence. It includes the doors and roof and it holds the windows in place, to protect you from road debris and weather. It contributes to safety, performance and economy.

The chassis and shell are the parts of a vehicle that need the least maintenance from a safety and performance point of view. Aside from periodic chassis lubrication at pivot points, unless you have a crash, there's

The shell gives your car its style and look. It is light and aerodynamic to minimise drag and turbulence

little maintenance beyond washing and waxing the shell. If you have a collision, however, shell damage will require considerable professional repair. Impact damage to the chassis can affect vehicle safety; cars in crashes strong enough to damage the chassis are seldom economically repairable.

Suspension

The **suspension** is a spring-loaded system that supports the chassis over the wheels. **Shock absorbers** dampen the spring action, providing comfort on rough and uneven roads. The suspension system connects to the axles which have bearings on which the wheels turn.

The suspension controls how the vehicle's load transfers to the wheels and tyres. This is especially important on turns and corners and when stopping quickly. If the forces distribute improperly, you lose traction, which affects your ability to control the car. Shock absorbers wear out over time and require replacement. If you notice unusual handling or squeaking over bumps have a mechanic inspect the car's suspension system.

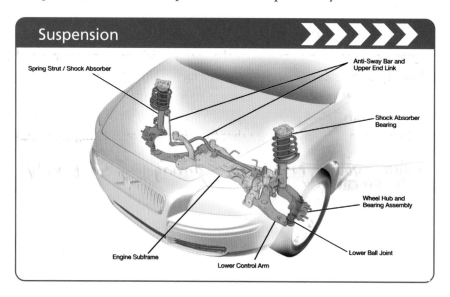

Steering system

The **steering system** gives you control of the front wheels, which give your car direction. A healthy steering system is essential for safe driving.

Most cars use a **rack-and-pinion** steering mechanism that links the front wheels with a cross-bar or '**rack**' that pushes the wheels left or right when you turn the steering wheel. The steering wheel links to the rack via a steering gearbox that converts the rotational movement of the steering wheel to the linear movement of the rack.

Many vehicles have **power steering** which uses hydraulic power provided by the engine to assist you in turning the steering wheel. This gives you more control, though it may make you less sensitive to road-surface conditions. Except for emergency circumstances, don't turn the wheels with the engine off if you have power steering, because doing so causes excessive wear and strain on the system.

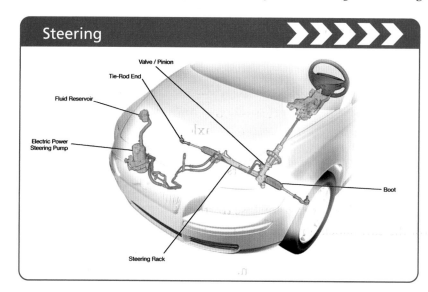

Steering

Valve / Pinion
Tie-Rod End
Fluid Reservoir
Electric Power
Steering Pump
Boot
Steering Rack

Engine and propulsion system

The **engine** and **propulsion system** make your vehicle go. They consist of several sub-systems, all of which must work for your car to run.

The **engine** is where chemical energy and/or electrical energy transform into the mechanical energy that moves your vehicle. Almost all modern vehicles have an **internal combustion engine** that functions by combusting (burning)

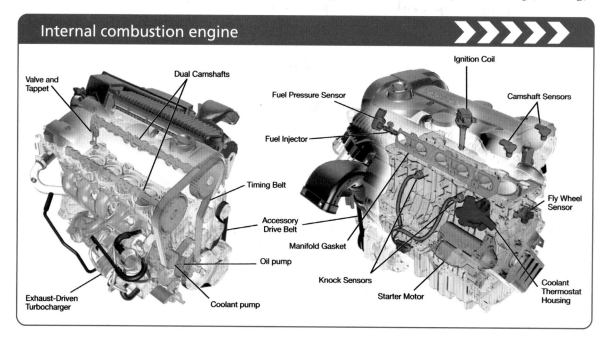

Internal combustion engine

Valve and Tappet
Dual Camshafts
Ignition Coil
Fuel Pressure Sensor
Camshaft Sensors
Fuel Injector
Timing Belt
Fly Wheel Sensor
Accessory Drive Belt
Manifold Gasket
Oil pump
Knock Sensors
Coolant Thermostat Housing
Exhaust-Driven Turbocharger
Coolant pump
Starter Motor

fuel to create motion. Most vehicles use petrol, diesel or petrochemicals (methane or propane) as fuel, though the trend is toward renewable fuels. These include vegetable oils and ethanol. Hybrid designs use electric motors and a smaller internal combustion engine. The electric motor gets its power from batteries and the internal combustion engine drives a generator that recharges the batteries. Some hybrid designs allow both the electric and internal combustion engine to power the vehicle directly.

Internal combustion engines always work the same way, regardless of the fuel they use. The engine receives fuel from the **fuel system,** which stores and filters the fuel and pumps it to the engine as needed via metal piping called the fuel line. When you press on the accelerator pedal, you're allowing the fuel system to deliver fuel. The faster you give the engine fuel, the faster it runs. The fuel system has filters to keep dirt out of the engine.

In the engine, fuel mixes with filtered air to form a highly combustible vapour. Most cars use an electronic **fuel injection system** to mix the fuel and air in the proper proportion. The mixture flows into a **piston-cylinder assembly.** The mixture combusts with explosive force, driving the piston downward in the cylinder to the vehicle.

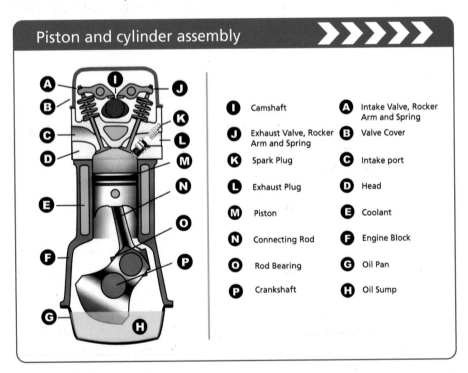

Piston and cylinder assembly

I Camshaft	**A** Intake Valve, Rocker Arm and Spring		
J Exhaust Valve, Rocker Arm and Spring	**B** Valve Cover		
K Spark Plug	**C** Intake port		
L Exhaust Plug	**D** Head		
M Piston	**E** Coolant		
N Connecting Rod	**F** Engine Block		
O Rod Bearing	**G** Oil Pan		
P Crankshaft	**H** Oil Sump		

When the piston is fully inside the cylinder with the fuel/air mixture, combustion starts the process by forcing the piston downward, delivering the power that propels the vehicle. The piston then cycles back up, pushing

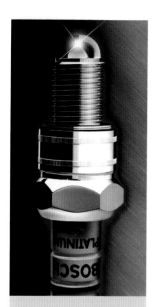

A spark from a spark plug is required in petrol engines but diesel engines rely on the heat of compression to trigger combustion

waste fumes out of the cylinder, then down again, drawing in the fuel/air mixture. It then comes back to the top, compressing the mixture to be ready for the next spark that repeats the cycle. Valves on the cylinders open and close in time with the strokes to control the flow of fuel, air and waste fumes. Combustion requires a spark from a **spark plug** in petrol engines to start the process but diesel engines use the heat of compression to trigger combustion and don't require spark plugs. The plugs receive power from the **electrical system,** to produce the spark as needed. The typical engine has anywhere from two to eight pistons and cylinders working together.

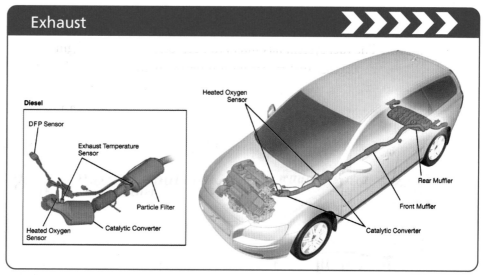

Exhaust

Diesel

DFP Sensor

Exhaust Temperature Sensor

Heated Oxygen Sensor

Particle Filter

Catalytic Converter

Heated Oxygen Sensor

Rear Muffler

Front Muffler

Catalytic Converter

The waste fumes discharge through the **exhaust system,** a series of pipes captures the fumes and channels them to the rear of the vehicle. In petrol vehicles, they pass through a catalytic converter that changes toxic carbon monoxide into relatively harmless carbon dioxide. The fumes flow through a silencer, to make your vehicle quiet and then are expelled through the exhaust pipe.

Internal combustion produces a lot of heat. The **cooling system** carries heat away so that the engine doesn't overheat or seize. Usually the cooling system pumps a liquid coolant in a continuous cycle through the engine block and the radiator. The coolant picks up heat as it travels through the engine block, and loses heat as it passes through the radiator. A fan maintains air flow through the radiator even when the vehicle isn't moving to assist the dissipation of heat from the coolant. Some vehicles, such as motorcycles, have very small engines that can be cooled with air flow alone. 'Cool' is a relative term, an engine at normal working temperature is still hot enough to give you severe burns if you touch it.

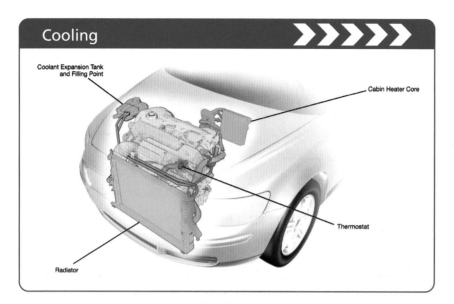

Cooling

Coolant Expansion Tank and Filling Point

Cabin Heater Core

Thermostat

Radiator

Pistons move up and down hundreds of times per minute. Without lubricating oil, the engine would overheat and wear out in a matter of minutes, even with a cooling system. The engine **lubrication system** cycles the oil to keep all parts lubricated, and to keep the oil cool enough to prevent it from thinning out. A filter removes small particles and debris from the oil, which would otherwise contribute to engine wear. Over time, the oil loses viscosity (thickness), so you need to have it changed at regular intervals. Different types of engines need different oils, so you must use the correct type.

The pistons connect to a **crankshaft**, which is below the engine, via a set of rods. The rise and fall of the cycling pistons rotates the crankshaft. As you increase or decrease fuel flow into the engine with the accelerator, the speed at which the crankshaft turns (revolutions or revs), increases or decreases, resulting in the vehicle moving faster or slower.

The **drive shaft** has a large, heavy metal disk called the **flywheel** fixed to one end. The flywheel keeps the power from the crankshaft to the tyres constant by using inertia to smooth out the intervals when pistons are not producing power. The flywheel connects to the electric starter motor. When you start your car, the starter motor spins the flywheel, which turns the crankshaft and pulls the pistons up and down. This begins the internal combustion process.

The crankshaft is not connected directly to the wheels, if it were, the wheels would have to be turning all the time when the engine is running. But as you know, you can stop your car – that is, stop the wheels turning – without stopping the engine.

The engine lubrication system cycles oil to keep all parts lubricated. Without lubricating oil, the engine would overheat and possibly seize in a matter of minutes

When you press the clutch pedal, the clutch plates separate from the crankshaft to allow the engine to run in neutral. When you ease off the pedal, the clutch plates come together and grip

The **clutch** mechanism, allows you to control when the engine power reaches the wheels. In a manual-transmission vehicle, when you press the clutch pedal, disks called the clutch plates separate from the crankshaft to allow the engine to run in neutral without giving power to the wheels. When you ease off the pedal, the clutch plates come together and grip, causing the crankshaft to turn the **gearbox**. The gearbox then passes the power from the engine and crankshaft to the **drive shaft**, and on to power the wheels.

The gearbox provides the engine with a greater range of operating speeds. The gears do the same job on a car as they do on a bicycle. The lowest gears provide more power to the wheels, but they don't allow the drive shaft to go very fast. You use these to get the vehicle moving, or when carrying a heavy load up a hill.

The gears do the same job on a car as they do on a bicycle. The lowest gears provide more power to the wheels. Once you build up speed, you switch to a higher gear

Once you build up speed, and hear the engine revving. You switch to a higher gear to build upon the momentum you've created. You press the clutch to momentarily stop power from going to the wheels, change to the next gear with the gear stick, then release the clutch to send power to the wheels again. The engine now turns at a slower speed and you continue accelerating in the higher gear. You repeat this until you reach cruising speed, at which point you can usually ease up on the accelerator because you need only apply enough power to replace the energy you lose to friction. Cruising is the most fuel-efficient way to drive and causes the least wear to your vehicle. When you need to climb a steep hill or to slow down, you reverse the process, shifting into lower gears to increase power and decrease speed.

Vehicles with an automatic gearbox use only the accelerator and brake to control speed. The system automatically changes gear based on speed and load. Automatic gearboxes are controlled electronically, though you can override them if you want to stay in low gear. You would do this for extra power with a load, or to keep your car from going too fast when driving down a mountain, for example.

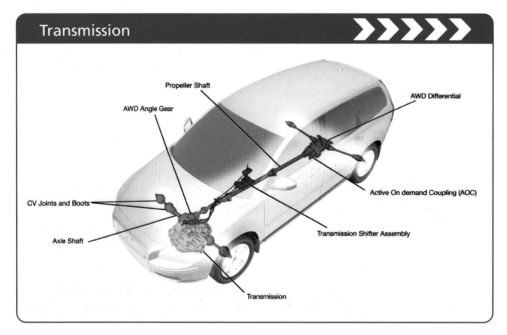

Most modern cars have front-wheel drive (this means, the power turns the front wheels to pull the car), though older cars and some current models have rear-wheel drive (where the power turns the rear wheels to push the car). A few vehicles, especially those designed for off-road use, have four-wheel drive. It's likely that you'll learn to drive in a front-wheel drive vehicle.

When you go around a curve, the wheels on the inside of the turn rotate slightly slower than the wheels on the outside. To overcome this difference, your car has a **differential gear system** that allows the wheels to turn at different speeds and to apportion the torque (turning power of the crankshaft) between them. The differential system channels the power from the drive shaft to two half-shafts, each linked to one wheel by a constant velocity (CV) joint. The CV joint couples with the two shafts so the wheels don't have to be rigidly aligned with each other and can therefore rotate at different speeds and so that you can change the wheel direction for steering.

Your car has a differential gear system that allows the wheels to turn at different speeds and to apportion the torque between them

The electrical system gets power from the alternator, which is an electrical generator driven by a belt that turns when the engine runs. However, you need power to start the engine, so the electrical system also has a battery that turns the starter motor. The electrical system supplies the power for the fuel injection, instruments, lights and for the accessories like electric windows and stereos. On hybrid vehicles, the electrical system and electric motor can provide the primary propulsion. These vehicles have multiple high-capacity batteries and a significantly larger generating system.

Brake system

It's obvious that you need the brake system for safe driving. All brakes work in essentially the same way: by creating friction that slows down the wheels, turning momentum into heat. Hybrid cars are designed to absorb some of this momentum to generate electricity and charge their batteries, reclaiming some of the energy that conventional vehicles lose through braking.

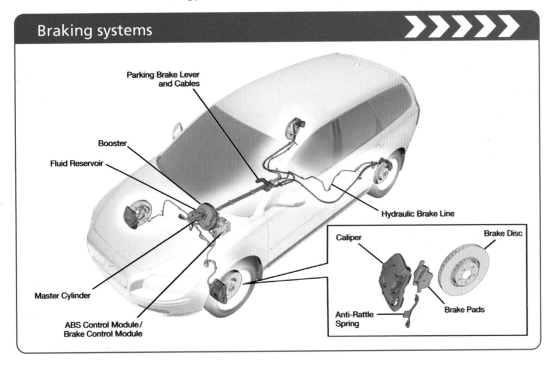

Braking systems

Parking Brake Lever and Cables

Booster

Fluid Reservoir

Master Cylinder

ABS Control Module/
Brake Control Module

Hydraulic Brake Line

Caliper

Brake Disc

Brake Pads

Anti-Rattle Spring

Disc brakes slow or stop a vehicle by clamping brake pads onto a spinning disc that is part of the wheel mechanism.

When you depress the brake pedal, you apply pressure to brake fluid in the braking system. The fluid transmits the pressure through tubes to the brakes at each wheel, causing the brake pads to move and stop the car. The harder you press, the more pressure you apply to the fluid and the harder the pads press against the braking surface.

With power-assisted brake systems, engine power helps provide the braking pressure. If your engine stops, you can still brake, but you have to push *much* harder because you no longer have the engine's assistance. Modern anti-lock brakes (ABS) use electronics to monitor wheel speed. The system redistributes braking power as necessary to maximise braking action in an emergency, without locking the wheels.

Systems and safety

By now you will realise that to drive safely, *all* your car's systems must be functioning properly. You can't drive safely if the steering system doesn't let you steer or the brake system doesn't let you stop. You can't drive safely if the suspension system doesn't properly distribute the load or if your electrical system doesn't operate your indicators or windscreen wipers. You can't drive safely without reliable power when you need it, so any problem that affects the engine and propulsion systems compromises safety.

Are there any parts of your car that can malfunction without affecting safety? Of course there's always one exception and in this case, it's the stereo!

Disc brakes slow or stop a vehicle by clamping brake pads onto a spinning disc that is part of the wheel mechanism

QUICK QUIZ

1 The cooling system performs the function of carrying heat away from the engine.
   T ☑ F ☐

2 The chassis connects the steering wheel to the crank shaft. T ☐ F ☑

3 The only system crucial to safety is the brake system. T ☐ F ☑

Answers: 1: T, 2: F, 3: F

Routine checks

Aidhmeanna
OBJECTIVES **3** Look for, and highlight, the answers to these questions

- What five routine checks does your vehicle require?
- What does each of these checks include?
- Why is each of these checks important?

To keep your vehicle running properly, you need to give it routine checks and maintenance. We'll look at some of the specifics in the next section, but now let's look at the five routine checks you should do most often. These involve lubricants, battery, coolant, lights and tyres.

Lubrication

As you learned in the previous section, your car's lubrication system is necessary to keep the engine running. One thing drivers often do is let the lubrication system get low on oil between manufacturer-recommended oil changes. In a relatively new car, you may not need to add any oil between changes. In older cars, though, the pistons may fit slightly more loosely due to wear, which allows a little bit of oil to seep into the cylinder and burn. This should be minor so that you'll only have to add a small amount of oil after hundreds of kilometres of driving. If you car burns more oil than that, you should have it serviced by a mechanic.

Check the oil level with the engine's dipstick. Be careful not to overfill the oil reservoir, as this can lead to other problems

Check the oil level with the engine's dipstick. You can top the oil up yourself, or have your mechanic take care of it. If you do it yourself, be careful not to overfill the oil reservoir, as this can lead to other problems. Generally, you should have the oil changed every 4500 kilometres or so. When a service mechanic does the oil change for you, he or she will also change or top up the lubricants in the gearbox, differential, suspension and bearings and change the oil filter and the filters associated with other systems, if necessary. Worn filters no longer protect your engine, and may hinder performance by obstructing lubricant flow.

Battery

Sealed batteries are typically maintenance-free for the life of the battery. Some batteries on older vehicles or on motorcycles are not sealed, however, and require checking. The mixture of acid and water may need to be topped up with distilled water if evaporation causes the water level to drop below a critical level. If this happens, not only does it reduce the battery capacity, but it can damage the battery.

If you have a hybrid vehicle, consult your mechanic and the owner's manual about battery maintenance requirements.

You need to maintain your cooling system to avoid overheating and engine damage. If you find that the coolant is low, top it up and have a mechanic check the cooling system for leaks

Coolant

You need to maintain your cooling system to avoid overheating and engine damage. In a well-maintained vehicle, you should not need to top up coolant in your cooling system. However, overheating or an undetected minor leak can make the coolant level drop, so you should check the levels every so often. If you find that the coolant is low, replace it and have a mechanic check the cooling system for leaks. If you see coolant dripping or notice a pool under your vehicle, have it checked immediately.

Although you can use water as a coolant in a pinch, you should use antifreeze as your regular coolant. Antifreeze coolant prevents cracking the engine block during the winter because it doesn't freeze readily like water does. Antifreeze coolant also carries heat more effectively than water, and it has anti-corrosion chemicals to reduce rust damage inside the cooling system.

Every one to two years, get your mechanic to flush the cooling system and replace the coolant. This process removes debris from the system and prolongs its life because fresh coolant has fresh anti-corrosion chemicals.

Indicators and lights

As a good driver, you should make your driving predictable for other drivers. Part of this means making sure your indicators work. Also, you don't want to drive at night or in fog without working head lamps. Bulbs are probably the least reliable items in your car, but they're easily replaced.

Have a friend walk around your car to check that your headlights, rear lights, brake lights and indicators are working

The easiest way to check all the lights is to have a friend walk around your car while you turn on the headlights, press the brakes and turn on the indicators. Also, get in the habit of using reflections to check your lights. For example, when behind another car in stopped traffic, you should be able to see the reflection of both headlights or the blinking of your indicators on the body of the other car.

Tyres

Tyres provide the traction you need to control your vehicle. Over- or under-inflated tyres result in traction loss.

You should routinely check for proper inflation, and tread depth. Not only does proper inflation give you the best traction, but it prevents premature wear so that your tyres last as long as possible.

To maximise tyre life, have them rotated, balanced and aligned annually. Tyre rotation is swapping the front tyres with the rear wheels diagonally to even out the wear – front tyres wear more quickly. Balancing tyres is a process of adding a small weight to the wheel so it spins smoothly. This helps ensure the smooth running of your car. Alignment is the adjusting of your tyres so they're in a straight line with each other. This keeps your car from tending to drift to one side of the road or the other, and reduces tyre wear and wrist/shoulder fatigue of the driver.

Tyres have tread-wear indicators between the grooves to alert you when a tyre has worn down to the point where it needs replacement. Usually you should replace all tyres at the same time with matching treads.

You should routinely check for tread depth and proper inflation. Tyres have tread-wear indicators between the grooves to alert you when a tyre has worn down

QUICK QUIZ

1 You should add oil monthly, whether low or not. T ☐ F ☑

2 The best coolant for your car is antifreeze coolant. T ☑ F ☐

3 A properly maintained cooling system is important for avoiding overheating and engine damage. T ☑ F ☐

Answers: 1: F, 2: T, 3: T

Basic maintenance

Aidhmeanna OBJECTIVES 3 ➤ Look for, and highlight, the answers to these questions

- Why do you need to make sure your car stays roadworthy?
- How do you keep your car roadworthy?
- What problems can a poorly-maintained vehicle cause?
- How and why do you keep a service record?
- How do you; open the bonnet, change light bulbs, replace wiper blades, check or change tyres and add fluids to your vehicle?
- How can you best prepare for the NCT?

Keeping your car roadworthy

Not only is it unsafe to drive a vehicle that's not in proper working order, it is also illegal, bad for the environment and ultimately expensive, since a poorly-maintained vehicle costs more to run than a well-maintained one. As the driver, you are responsible for ensuring that everything about the vehicle you're driving is in good working order, particularly the steering, brakes, lights, reflectors, mirrors, speedometer, tyres, wipers, safety belts, horn, silencer and any roof rack or towing equipment used.

Not only is it unsafe to drive a vehicle that's not in proper working order, it is also illegal. As the driver, you are responsible for ensuring that everything is in good working order

This sounds like a lot, but it's not difficult to keep your car roadworthy. You can easily keep up with maintenance of all the parts and systems if you develop a habit of checking them regularly. Keep a service record, check over your vehicle whenever you fuel it and fix any problems immediately. These steps can all become a normal part of your driving routine.

When you care for your car properly, it becomes easier to maintain. This is because most problems are more obvious in a vehicle that normally runs properly, whereas a problem may not be noticeable with a vehicle that already runs poorly. Keeping your vehicle clean inside and out prolongs its life. Clean lights, windscreens and mirrors, add to safety by maintaining visibility. Finally, get your mechanic to check everything over whenever you have your car in for a service.

The Gardaí have the power to impound vehicles that are not roadworthy and that lack legally-required documentation such as tax, insurance, registration and NCT certificates. But the main reason to take care of your car is that a poorly-maintained vehicle may fail to respond as expected during normal driving or in an emergency, and therefore lead to a crash. You certainly don't want to find out that your brakes don't work when someone or something pulls out in front of you unexpectedly.

Keeping a service log

A service log may sound like a nuisance, but it's your ally in keeping your car roadworthy. Time and kilometres slip by faster than you realise, and it's easy to wait too long before checking your brakes, changing the oil or servicing the power steering. You can't always rely on your memory for these things, so keep a service log.

The owner's manual for your car usually has a section to record services and repairs. If it's missing with a second-hand car, buy a new manual. Keep it up to date so you can track what's been done to your vehicle and when. That way, you know when it's time for major or minor services, before problems occur.

Drivers who keep service logs have far fewer service-related problems because they get worn parts replaced before they become safety problems. As a side benefit, when you sell your car, a good service record shows prospective buyers that you've taken care of it. That makes it easier to sell than one with a questionable history.

Opening the bonnet

Many checks and regular maintenance require you to open your car's bonnet. If you've never done this yourself, you may not realise that there are *two*

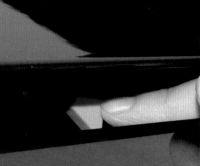

To open the bonnet, first release the catch which is located under the dashboard. Your fingers can then slide in under the bonnet to release the second catch

At or near the centre, you will feel the second release, which you pull or push

The design of these catches varies. Check your car handbook for exact details

releases on most vehicles. This double-catch system is important because if the bonnet were to release while driving at high speed, it would blow open and block your view through the windscreen. Two catches reduce the chance of this happening.

You'll find the first catch release inside the vehicle. It's typically a handle you pull, located under the dashboard. Pulling the handle opens the bonnet slightly, so that when you go to the front of your car, your fingers can slide in under the bonnet to release the second catch. At or near the centre, you will feel the second release, which you pull or push. Now you can lift the bonnet open and secure it with the support rod.

To close the bonnet, lower it so it is only a few centimetres open, then drop it gently, with your fingers clear. Press down on it if necessary to make sure it is fully closed.

You should lift the bonnet open and secure it carefully with the support rod

Changing light bulbs

Driving with burned-out lights is illegal, can be very dangerous and it's unnecessary because you can change most bulbs in a matter of minutes. Car manufacturers can usually supply replacement bulb kits with the correct bulbs for your make and model of car. If not, you can assemble a bulb kit yourself, storing the spare bulbs in a secure container with sponge or padding that separates and protects them.

You can change most bulbs in a matter of minutes, many modern cars allow you to remove the entire unit for easy access

You replace most bulbs by turning, pulling or unscrewing them. Check the owner's manual and make sure that you always have the correct bulb as part of your spares kit

You replace most bulbs by turning, pulling or unscrewing them – you can usually figure out which by looking at the base of the replacement bulb. If it's not clear what you should do, check the owner's manual (which is wise in any case). Make sure to replace blown bulbs with matching voltage and wattage.

Some vehicles have orange bulbs in their indicators instead of clear bulbs behind an orange-coloured lens. This is because orange bulbs are far less expensive than orange lenses. However, the colour coating on the bulb reduces its life because the coating fades over time. You must replace the bulb when it is no longer orange, even if it still works. Your car will fail its NCT if you have indicator bulbs that work, but that don't have a strong orange glow.

Keep your windscreen washer fluid topped up at all times and in winter make sure it is non freeze.

Changing windscreen wipers

Effective windscreen wipers allow you to see during rain, snow and other adverse conditions. The rubber wipers work effectively, but they wear out relatively quickly, even in climates where you don't need them often. Signs of wear include cracking, splitting or leaving streaks on the windscreen.

Fortunately, windscreen wipers are relatively inexpensive so you can change them often. Car shops and dealers supply new, ready-mounted blades

Rubber windscreen wipers work effectively but they wear out relatively quickly. Replacement wipers are not expensive so you should fit new ones regularly

with clip-on/clip-off brackets that vary according to the vehicle make and model. Many suppliers will fit them for you, but most people find it easy to do themselves by following the instructions on the box.

Keep your windscreen washer fluid topped up at all times and check it weekly. In winter make sure it is non freeze.

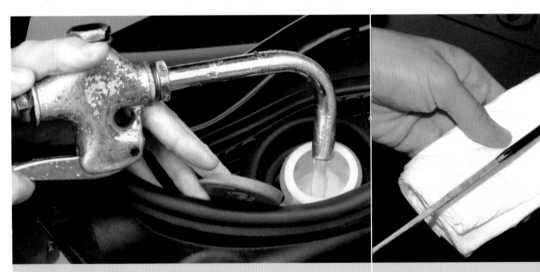

Don't let your screen wash reservoir run low. Keep it well topped up and in winter make sure that you have a non freeze additive

Check your oil regularly. If the level is below the minimum, add more. Be careful not to add too much because that can damage your engine

Checking engine fluids

In the last section, you learned that you use the engine dipstick to check the motor-oil level. As a rule of thumb, do this monthly, or even more frequently with an older vehicle.

- The car should be on a level surface and the engine allowed to cool before checking the oil level.

- Remove the dipstick and wipe the end with a paper towel or cloth.
- Reinsert the dipstick fully and then remove it again.
- Read the oil level based on the gauge marks on the end of the stick.
- If the oil level is below the minimum, add more. If necessary, check the owner's manual to find out how much or ask a garage attendant to help you. Be careful not to add too much because that can damage your engine. If necessary, add small amounts and recheck the dipstick until the oil level is within the acceptable range on the dipstick. With experience, you'll learn how much you need to add.

Check the engine coolant only with a cool engine. Never open the radiator while hot as coolant and steam can rush out and burn you

Check the engine coolant *only* with a cool engine. Opening the radiator while hot can allow coolant and steam to rush out and burn you. Consult the owner's manual for specifics; with many vehicles, you shouldn't open the radiator unless the coolant-overflow reservoir is completely empty.

You should also check the brake-fluid levels and the batteries when the engine is cool – again, consult the owner's manual. Wear eye protection when opening batteries to add water. You'll watch a demonstration and practise these checks yourself during Part Two of this course.

Never put anything but approved brake fluid in your brakes. Anything else can cause sudden brake failure.

Tyre pressure

To check your tyre pressure, you need a pressure gauge. You can buy small pen-sized models to keep in your car, and most petrol stations have a gauge integrated into the handle of their air pump.

- Park your car on level ground and apply the handbrake.
- Remove the dust cap from the tyre's valve stem.

To check your tyre pressure, remove the dust cap and press the filling nozzle firmly onto it

- Press the gauge or air-pump nozzle to the valve. A marked rod or dial will indicate the pressure. Compare the pressure reading to the pressure required according to the owner's manual and/or tyre markings. Pressure recommendations may also be on the inside of the fuel-cap door or the edge of the driver's door.
- If the pressure is low, use the air pump to add pressure.
- Remember that the pressure recommendations vary somewhat with the load you're carrying. Consult the owner's manual accordingly.
- Check tyre tread regularly, watch for signs of uneven wear.

You can read your tyre pressure by observing the reading in the gauge window. Be careful to check the pressure recommended for your tyres and load

Changing a tyre

If you properly maintain your tyres a flat should be a rare occurrence, but road hazards like nails, screws and debris will give you a puncture from time to time. It's not hard to change a tyre safely, but there are a few things you'll need to remember.

Park in a safe place, well off the road, away from traffic and on level ground. If possible, park where there is light at night-time. You don't want to drive any farther than necessary on a flat as doing so may make it irreparable. However, do not attempt to change a flat on a pronounced slope because your car could easily fall off the jack. If you can't find level ground, contact a service station to tow your vehicle to a place better suited for changing the tyre.

- Stop the car, turn off the engine and apply the parking/hand brake. Put the car in first gear if it has a manual gear box or in P (park) if it is automatic.
- Take out the spare tyre, brace, jack and a rag or gloves, if you have them, for your hands and put on your reflection vest
- Place the spare under the vehicle to provide extra safety in case the jack slips.
- Chock the diagonally-opposing wheel from the flat one. 'Chocking' means making a wedge to prevent the vehicle from moving. You can use stones, wood or whatever is to hand.
- Remove the hubcap if there is one. You may need to cut a plastic cable tie used to prevent accidental hubcap loss, or you may need a special tool kept with the jack and spare.

The safe way to change a flat tyre

Stop in a safe place, in gear and brake applied

Place a warning triangle 50m behind

Wear a high visibility safety vest

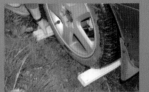
Lock the diagonally opposite wheel

Wear gloves and use a mat to kneel on

Lift out spare and place it near to hand

fit wheel brace and use key security adapter

Loosen nuts a half turn

Open the jack so it just fits under the car

Locate jack head in the correct jacking point

Carefully begin to jack up the car

Push the spare under car beside the jack

Raise the wheel to give a clearance of 50mm

Remove each nut with the wheel brace

Carefully place each nut on the mat

Lift off the punctured wheel

Lift the spare into place and locate on studs

Screw on all the nuts by hand

Hand tighten the nuts with the wheelbrace

Lower the car with the jack

Remove the punctured wheel from under car

Place the punctured wheel in the boot

With wheel on the ground, tighten nuts

Work diagonally around each nut

- Use the wheel brace to loosen the nuts but not remove them before jacking up the car because the wheel will simply turn if you try to loosen the nuts when the car is jacked up. Loosen opposite nuts in rotation – first, third, second and fourth – so you don't strain the nuts with uneven tension. If they're very tight, you may need to carefully stand on the brace to loosen them.
- Open the jack and place it into the jacking point near the flat tyre. Consult the owner's manual to be sure you're using a proper jacking point. Jacking in the wrong place may damage your vehicle, or worse, the vehicle may fall after you've lifted it. Be sure the jack is level and on firm ground.
- Raise the car using the jack. This is usually a matter of unscrewing/screwing the jack mechanism, though some cars have pump-action or lever jacks.
- Raise the car just beyond the height required to allow the flat to spin freely. A little extra distance gives you room to change the tyres. The spare will be slightly larger, because it is inflated.
- *Do not get under the vehicle or put any part of your body under the vehicle while it is on the jack.* Car jacks are not intended for anything other than brief tyre changes. Do not leave your car raised for an extended period.
- Remove the nuts and place them carefully to one side. Immediately lift off the flat and place it under the car and lift on the spare. For safety, minimise the time your car is elevated without a tyre in place.
- Replace the nuts and tighten them finger tight. Ease the car back down by lowering the jack.
- Tighten all the nuts alternately with the brace, but don't get as tight as possible in one go. Alternate tightening each one gradually until they are all fully tight.
- Put the flat, jack and other tools back into the car. If your spare is a compact tyre, drive to a service station not faster than 80 km/h. Compact tyres are intended for short distances and durations only, not for normal use. Check the spare's pressure at the first opportunity and replace it with your repaired full-size tyre as soon as possible.
- If carrying a spare is not practical, you can use a chemical tyre-inflation aerosol to repair most flats temporarily, long enough to reach a service station. These are also handy alternatives to changing a tyre in very poor weather or in unsafe areas.

You can have most flats repaired if the damage is a puncture into the tread. If you find the nail or other object that caused the flat, *do not* remove it. Leaving it in place makes it much easier to service because it identifies where the leak is. Damage to the tyre sidewall is, unfortunately, almost always impossible to repair. In this case, replace the tyre with one that matches your other tyres.

Preparing for the NCT (National Car Test)

In Ireland, cars require the NCT after the first four years and every two years after that. The NCT confirms that you're maintaining your vehicle in the minimum working order required for safe operation. However, having the NCT certificate does not relieve you of your responsibility to check and maintain your vehicle between NCT inspections.

To prepare for the NCT:

- Get a list of checks that will be performed at the test centre, or online at www.nct.ie.
- Arrange a full service check for your vehicle at least two weeks ahead so you have ample time for any necessary repairs. Note that if you're maintaining your vehicle and keeping a service log, there should be no major surprises here. Compare the service check to the test checks to be sure you cover everything.
- The day before and the morning of the test, check all the lights and make the other routine checks you've learned. Having spare bulbs can prevent last-minute problems if you need to change one.

In Ireland, cars require the National Car Test after the first four years and every two years after that

- Clean your car and remove anything unnecessary from the interior. Not only is this polite, but it gives the tester easier access to inspection areas. Remove the hubcaps and clear out the boot so the tester has easy access to the spare wheel.
- Schedule ample time for the test. Arrive early and give yourself room for delays if the centre is busy that day. Bring this book or the rules of the road to brush up on your own working order while you wait (think of this as your own personal NCT).

QUICK QUIZ

1 A poorly-maintained vehicle might fail to perform as expected, causing a crash.
T ☑ F ☐

2 When checking engine fluids, park so that the front wheels are uphill. T ☐ F ☑

3 When changing a flat tyre, it's important to do it on level ground with the parking brake on and to chock the opposing diagonal wheel. T ☑ F ☐

Answers: 1: T, 2: F, 3: T

Vehicle modifications

Aidhmeanna **OBJECTIVES** **3**

Look for, and highlight, the answers to these questions

- What is a 'vehicle modification'?
- Why might you modify your vehicle?
- What are examples of appearance, comfort, safety and performance modifications?

'Vehicle modification' is making any change to a vehicle's systems or accessories from the original factory design. This is, however, a very broad definition that ranges from adding a wide-angle mirror for better viewing to major engine modifications that increase power.

There are many ways to modify your vehicle and stay within the law, most people who modify their cars are motoring enthusiasts. You may modify your car to change its appearance, to improve comfort, to improve safety or to improve performance. Some modifications accomplish more than one of these. There is nothing wrong with responsible vehicle modification. It can be a good way to show that you take a pride in your vehicle.

There is nothing wrong with responsible, vehicle modification. It's a way of showing that you take a pride in your vehicle

Appearance modifications

Modifications to enhance how your car looks might include:

- Alloy wheels.
- Wider or lower wheels.
- Overlay on the wheel arches.
- Front-light projectors.
- Spotlights and under-lights.
- Stylised bumpers.
- Rear spoiler.
- Side-skirts (to make ground clearance seem lower).
- Suspension kit (actually lowers ground clearance).
- Partial or total re-spraying.
- Graphics.
- Sports steering wheel.
- Colour-coordinated trim.

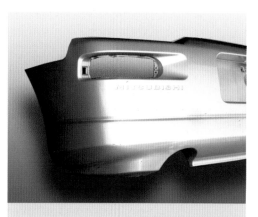

Some modifications, like a spoiler, enhance performance in theory, but not enough to realistically benefit you while driving responsibly in normal road conditions

Some of these modifications, like a spoiler, enhance performance in theory, but not enough to realistically benefit you while driving responsibly in normal road conditions. Therefore, the primary purpose is usually appearance, not performance.

Comfort modifications

Modifications to make driving more enjoyable might include:

- Upgraded seats (bucket, leather, heated, fluffy, *etc.*).
- Stereo.
- Video system (for backseat only) – may include DVD or games console.
- Satellite navigation.
- Tinted windows (in back of vehicle only).
- Padded safety belts.
- Air conditioner.

Safety modifications

Safety modifications might include:

- Additional mirrors front or rear to eliminate pedestrian blind spots or aid parking.
- Additional side-view mirror (passenger side).
- Extended side-view mirrors (for towing).
- Roll bars (for off-road vehicles).
- Reverse beepers to aid parking.

Performance modifications

Performance modifications change your vehicle's behaviour in some way. Some of these may be relatively trivial, (such as the sound it makes), whereas others affect power, fuel consumption or pollution emissions. These include:

- Removing or adding a catalytic converter.
- New silencer to change the engine sound.
- 'Chipping' (reprogramming the electronics to increase fuel intake per piston stroke).
- Upgraded leads and plugs for better combustion.

- 'Shaving the heads' to increase compression.
- 'Polishing the ports' to improve fuel/air mixture flow into the piston.
- Nitrous oxide gas induction kit (increases power by boosting combustion power).
- Changed wheel diameters.

Appropriate and inappropriate modifications

Aidhmeanna OBJECTIVES 3 — Look for, and highlight, the answers to these questions

- What are the potential problems of inappropriately modifying a vehicle?
- What kind of modifications are inappropriate for a vehicle?
- What is the best way to be sure modifications are appropriate and legal?
- What is an inappropriate driving attitude related to vehicle modifications?

Just as there are appropriate and inappropriate driving behaviours, there are appropriate and inappropriate modifications. Appropriate modifications are those that are within the law and do not compromise safety – the kind that is usually carried out by motoring enthusiasts. Many of these, such as a stereo, only require responsible installation. Other modifications require a TUV/EU standardisation certificate and you may need to declare them to the licensing authority and your insurance company. This typically applies to performance modifications; it's a good idea to determine what these requirements will be *before* you have the modification made.

Inappropriate modifications create several potential problems. The first, and most important, is that you may compromise safety – and it may not always be obvious when you have done so. This kind of modification is usually associated with boy and girl racers. A common example of this is tinted windows. During daylight hours, they seem beneficial and inconsequential,

If you want a modification so you can 'beat' other drivers on the road then you should reconsider having the modification made

but at twilight and later, heavy tinting can obscure visibility. Even during the day, tinting makes it hard or impossible for other drivers to see where you're looking so they can anticipate your actions. This is why heavily-tinted windows are illegal, and why you do not tint the front windscreen. Similarly, a video system is a useful comfort accessory, but if installed in the front seat it compromises safety by distracting the driver.

Another problem caused by inappropriate modification is poor performance. While some poor performance (such as altering how your vehicle handles on bends) can cause safety concerns, others, even when legal, primarily make your vehicle consume excess fuel, put out too much pollution, or unnecessarily irritate others.

The best way to be sure vehicle modifications are appropriate and legal is to consult a qualified mechanic and the applicable laws before making them. In particular, any bodywork or engine enhancements should be checked with a certified mechanic to be sure that the vehicle's safety has not been compromised.

Driving attitude and vehicle modifications

In Module Two, you learned that good drivers are co-operative and forgiving drivers who make their intentions known to other drivers. You also learned that novice drivers figure highly in crash statistics, and that it takes about five years' experience to reach average driving competence.

It's worth considering these facts alongside many vehicle modifications, especially performance modifications. If you're considering a modification

Heavily tinted windscreens and front side windows are illegal. At twilight and later, heavy tinting can obscure visibility

that markedly boosts engine power or similarly affects performance, it may be wise to ask yourself why – *and be completely honest with yourself because your safety is at stake.*

If, in being honest, you realise you want a modification so you can 'beat' other drivers on the road – to pull out faster or overtake rapidly, for example – reconsider having the modification made. What you've realised is that the modification relates to an inappropriate attitude that you've already learned about: competitive driving.

If, on the other hand, your modification couldn't be used competitively such as a stereo, or if you are *certain* that you would only use a performance modification on a proper race track (not while driving on the road), then the modification is compatible with a co-operative driving attitude. But be careful – it's easy to make a performance modification believing you won't abuse it, only to discover that you do in a weak moment when irritated or frustrated by another driver.

QUICK QUIZ

1 Potential problems of inappropriately modifying a vehicle include compromising your safety, increasing pollution and/or irritating other drivers. T ☑ F ☐

2 The best way to be sure a modification is appropriate and legal is to consult a qualified mechanic and the applicable laws. T ☑ F ☐

3 An inappropriate attitude related to vehicle modifications is modifying a vehicle so it is safer. T ☐ F ☑

Answers: 1: T, 2: T, 3: F

Breakdowns and personal safety

Aidhmeanna
OBJECTIVES **3**

Look for, and highlight, the answers
to these questions

- What is always the first priority in the event of a breakdown or other problem on the road?
- What are your priorities if you're driving when a breakdown or other problem occurs on the roadway?
- What should you do after you stop with a breakdown on the side of the road?
- Which way should you turn the vehicle wheels when stopped for a breakdown? Why?
- What should you do if you break down on a motorway or on a secondary road?

Like flat tyres, breakdowns are part of driving. However, if you maintain and check your vehicle properly, they should be rare occurrences. Regularly-maintained vehicles rarely break down but, because it can happen, many insurance companies, motor dealers and other groups offer breakdown and recovery services at low cost. These services greatly reduce the inconvenience and stress when breakdowns occur, so consider availing of one if you can.

When a breakdown or any other problem looms, your first priority is *always* safety – your own, your passengers' and that of other motorists. By being alert to potential problems, you should be able to get off the road before your car becomes difficult to control or no longer runs. It is always better to err on the side of caution and pull over somewhere safe at the first hint of trouble.

Breakdowns

The most difficult breakdowns to deal with are those that happen suddenly, with little warning while you are driving – especially on multi-lane motorways. Whether it is a flat tyre, power loss or complete engine failure, you may need to respond quickly to avoid a collision. You'll learn more about handling emergencies while driving in later modules. For now, let's look at the priorities, for dealing with a breakdown while moving.

Your first priority is to **control** the vehicle. Grip the steering wheel firmly, take your foot off the accelerator and use the brakes cautiously. Remember that cars with power-assisted brakes and steering will require more strength and pressure from you if the engine dies.

Your second priority is to **choose** the action to take. Do you try to stop immediately? Can you coast off the road? It will depend on the circumstances, and you may have to modify your choice as you manoeuvre the car.

Your third priority is to **communicate** your situation and intentions to other drivers, if possible. Put on your hazard lights, sound your horn or use your indicators as appropriate.

Remember – **control, choose** and **communicate,** in that order. In a problem situation, it reminds you what to do. All three are important, but you cannot choose what to do if you don't have enough control to carry out your choice. You can't communicate your intentions if you have not chosen what to do.

Breakdowns on the road

After stopping with a breakdown, put on your hazard lights and quickly assess the situation. Hopefully you made it safely off the road. In that case, quickly determine whether it's a simple problem you can fix – like changing a flat tyre – or whether you need professional help. If it's something you can do, consider where you are. Can you change the tyre safely, or would traffic endanger you? If in doubt, get professional help rather than put yourself at risk.

It's rare but not impossible to come to a stop so suddenly that you can't make it off the road. This can happen if the breakdown occurs in very slow, heavy traffic, or while climbing a hill. If it happens to you, put on your hazard lights. If there is traffic moving past you on both sides, such as on a busy motorway, remain in the vehicle with your safety belt on. Use your mobile phone to contact the emergency services and tell them where you are. If traffic is slow or intermittent enough, or if one side of the vehicle is against the roadside, exit the vehicle if you're confident you can do so safely, leaving the hazard lights and headlights on. Call the emergency services.

What you should do in case of a breakdown depends partly upon whether you're on a motorway or a secondary road.

For Motorway breakdowns, pull over as far as possible, do not attempt to place a warning triangle. Call emergency services from an emergency telephone and wait for help

If you have a breakdown on a motorway:

- Pull over on the left-side hard shoulder as far from traffic as possible.
- Put on your hazard lights.
- Turn your wheels to the left. This ensures the car will go off the road instead of into traffic if another vehicle hits it from behind.
- Get everyone out of the vehicle on the side furthest from the traffic flow.
- Wait for help well away from the vehicle. Climb up the embankment if possible.
- Call emergency services from an emergency telephone, if there is one at hand or from your mobile. On motorways, the direction to the nearest emergency phone appears on the back of the posts at the side of the road. When making a call, always face oncoming traffic. Tell the emergency operator if you feel threatened in any way, such as if you're a woman travelling alone.
- *Never* attempt to cross the centre median.

If broken down anywhere other than a motorway, place a warning triangle about 50 metres behind the vehicle

If you have a breakdown on a secondary road:

- Try to pull your vehicle as far off to the left as possible.
- Switch on your hazard and side lights.
- Turn your wheels to the left.
- Exit the vehicle if you can do so safely and call emergency services.
- Don't stand on the side of the car that faces oncoming traffic. This can block your warning lights from their view; also, if another vehicle runs into yours, you may be pinned between the two cars.
- If you have them, put on a reflective vest and place a warning triangle about 50 metres behind the vehicle. If there are dips or bends in the road, however, place the triangle on the far side of the dip or bend so that oncoming traffic can see it well before reaching your vehicle.
- If you were able to get your vehicle completely off the road so there is little danger of being struck by another vehicle, stay in the vehicle with the doors locked until emergency services arrive.

QUICK QUIZ

1 The first priority in the event of a breakdown or other problem on the road is avoiding penalty points and a fine   T ☐   F ☑

2 If you break down and come to a stop on a motorway and have traffic rushing past on both sides, you should exit the vehicle when it looks clear and run to the side of the road. T ☐   F ☑

3 Place a warning triangle at least 10m back from your vehicle.   T ☐   F ☑

Answers: 1: F, 2: F, 3: F

Managing breakdowns

Aidhmeanna
OBJECTIVES 3 ▷ **Look for, and highlight, the answers to these questions**

- What are the procedures for push-starting and jump-starting a car?
- What should you do if a warning light comes on?
- What should you do if you have a sudden flat tyre while driving?
- What should you do if your vehicle's engine catches fire?
- How do you re-enter traffic after sorting out a breakdown?

Push-starting and jump-starting

Now let's look at some breakdowns that you can often handle yourself, at least well enough to drive your vehicle to a service centre. Push-starting and jump-starting are two ways of handling a car that won't start, typically on a cold morning or after accidentally leaving the lights on for an extended period without the engine running. Cars that you can jump-start or push-start have a battery problem. If the problem is another electrical problem, push-starting or jump-starting usually won't work.

Push-starting is the simplest of the two methods, but you must have a manual gearbox and either have your vehicle facing down a hill, or be on level ground with several people who can help you with the pushing. Most vehicles with electronic control will not push-start even with a manual gearbox. Pushing the car helps to start an engine that won't start due to a dead battery; you use momentum to turn over the motor instead of the electric starter.

- Make sure the area over which you will push the car is clear of all traffic. Also, be sure there is an appropriate, safe place where you will be able to park the car if it fails to start.
- When ready to begin, turn the ignition to on, put the car into first gear and keep the clutch depressed. Begin coasting down the hill or have your helpers begin pushing.
- Remember that power steering and brakes require a lot of extra strength to use when the engine's not running.

- When the speed builds up. Gently ease off the clutch. You'll feel the car lurch a bit as the engine turns. Press the clutch immediately when the engine starts, stop the vehicle and shift into neutral. Let the car warm up a bit before driving because if it stalls in traffic, you won't be able to restart it as readily.
- Drive to a service station without delay to have the battery problem corrected.

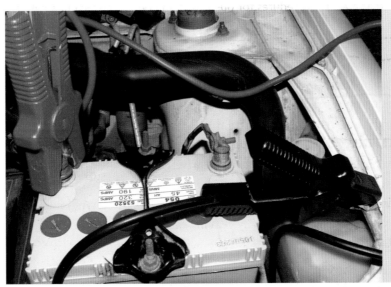

If your battery is flat you can start your car by "jump starting" from another vehicle or charged battery

If your car has an automatic gearbox or is not in a position where you can push-start it, you can attempt to jump-start the car. Jump-starting means using a vehicle with a good battery to provide enough power to start a vehicle with a bad battery.

- Position the donor vehicle with its battery as close as possible to the recipient vehicle's battery. You need to be close enough to use the jump-leads without stretching them too tightly.
- Turn off the donor engine.
- Switch off the lights, close the doors and turn off any electrical accessories in both vehicles. Put on both vehicles' hand brakes. Open the bonnets of both vehicles and remove the protector caps from both battery terminals on the donor car and the positive terminal of the recipient car.
- Put on eye protection if available. Sunglasses will work in a pinch.
- Connect the crocodile clip at one end of the red positive lead (+) to the positive post of the dead battery. Then, connect the other end to the positive post of the good donor battery.

- Connect the black negative lead (-) to the negative post of the good donor battery. Connect the other end of the negative lead to a solid metal part of the chassis of the recipient car – *not* to the negative lead of the dead battery.
- Leave the ignition turned to 'off' in the recipient car and start the donor engine. Allow the donor engine to run for a few minutes to boost the dead battery.
- Turn off the donor engine and attempt to start the recipient vehicle. It is best to shut down the donor engine because there is some danger of damaging the donor's electrical system due to a power surge when the recipient vehicle starts.
- If the recipient vehicle fails to start, turn the ignition off, reposition the leads on the posts to assure good contact, and then run the donor engine for longer before trying again.
- After the recipient vehicle starts, disconnect the leads in this order: negative lead on recipient vehicle, negative lead on donor vehicle, positive lead on donor vehicle, positive lead on recipient vehicle.
- If the car will not start after a few attempts, get professional help.

Warning lights

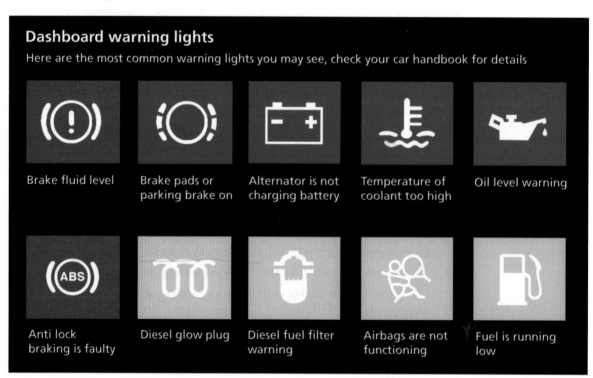

Dashboard warning lights

Here are the most common warning lights you may see, check your car handbook for details

Brake fluid level	Brake pads or parking brake on	Alternator is not charging battery	Temperature of coolant too high	Oil level warning
Anti lock braking is faulty	Diesel glow plug	Diesel fuel filter warning	Airbags are not functioning	Fuel is running low

Dashboard warning lights alert you to overheating, low oil pressure, ignition system problems, brake problems and other faults. The nature of warning lights is such that when they come on, the problem may be well advanced, so don't ignore them. If you continue to drive with a warning light on, you may permanently damage your car or incur very costly repairs. In some cases, you may lose an entire system, such as the brakes.

If a warning light comes on, immediately pull over in a safe manner, remember that safety is the priority. Turn off the engine and consult the owner's manual if you're not sure what the warning means. Based on what you learn in the owner's manual, you must decide whether you can drive the vehicle home safely or to a garage, or if you need help to come to you.

Besides warning lights, your indicator lights may alert you to a problem with a bulb. If the internal indicator blinks faster than normal, it means that the indicator bulb has blown and needs replacement. You may find that other motorists will flash their headlights to tell you that you have a blown headlight or that you've forgotten to turn your lights on. If you get either warning, pull over somewhere safe, check the bulbs and replace blown bulbs as soon as possible.

Puncture or tyre blowout

If you notice that the steering suddenly becomes sluggish or difficult to manage and/or you hear a thumping noise, you probably have a flat tyre. In the case of a severe blowout, you may hear a pop or bang that sounds a little like a gunshot. Remember to control, choose and communicate.

In the case of a severe blowout, you may hear a pop or bang that sounds a little like a gunshot. Remember to control, choose and communicate

- Grip the steering wheel firmly. Slow down, ideally by easing off the accelerator. If you must brake, do so as gently as possible. A car with a flat has impaired traction and tends to skid easily.
- Determine where you want to pull over off the road.
- As you slow, turn on your hazard lights (if you can release the wheel with one hand safely) and/or use your indicators to show where you intend to pull over.
- Allow the car to drift to a stop. If you can do so safely, try to stop in an appropriate place to change the tyre so you don't have to drive on your flat. However, do not compromise safety to do this.

Do not attempt to extinguish an engine fire unless it is very minor and you have a fire extinguisher. Car fires are one of the most common causes of permanent disfigurement

Engine fire

Engine fires are very rare in well-maintained vehicles. They most commonly occur in poorly-maintained ones. If you see or smell smoke coming from your engine:

- Pull over safely straight away.
- Get everyone well clear of the vehicle. Although cars rarely explode like you see on television, they burn quite fiercely.
- Call emergency services.

Do not attempt to extinguish the fire unless it is *very minor* and you have a fire extinguisher. In this case, release the bonnet but **do not** lift it open. Instead, open it just enough to give you space to aim the extinguisher under the bonnet at the fire. Stand well back and protect your hands and face.

Cars are expensive, but they are replaceable. You are not. Car fires are one of the most common causes of permanent disfigurement. If in doubt, stand back and wait for emergency services.

Re-entering traffic

After you've sorted out a minor breakdown on a roadside, you're ready to re-enter traffic. However, you may have to do this from a place that is not as ideal as a proper intersection or entry ramp. This is particularly an issue on a dual-carriageway or motorway.

Try to enter from a place with as clear a view of oncoming traffic as possible and ample distance to gain enough speed to merge. Often you can drive slowly along the shoulder until you reach a better place to enter the roadway. Time your entry to allow the greatest possible gap between cars and keep your indicator on throughout the manoeuvre to alert other motorists that you're coming back onto the road. Fellow cooperative drivers will usually slow down and help you enter if you give them enough warning of your intentions. But be cautious because you can't take common courtesy for granted.

After re-entering traffic, unless you're certain you've completely resolved the issue, you should go directly to a service centre or mechanic to assure your vehicle's roadworthiness.

QUICK QUIZ

1 If a warning light comes on while driving continue to drive to confirm the problem.
T ☐   F ☑

2 If you have a sudden flat tyre while driving turn the wheel hard to the left.   T ☐   F ☑

2 When re-entering traffic after sorting out a problem, try to do so from a place where you have ample visibility of oncoming traffic and sufficient distance to reach enough speed to merge.   T ☑   F ☐

Answers: 1: F, 2: F, 3: T

Summary points »»»»»»

In this module on understanding your vehicle you learned:

1. The chassis of your car is the frame that holds the vehicle together. It is an integrated structure with crumple zones that help protect the occupants. The shell is the outside structure that gives your car its look, style and aerodynamic qualities.

2. The suspension supports the chassis over the wheels for comfortable travelling and to properly transfer the load to the wheels and tyres so you maintain traction. The steering system links the front wheels to the steering wheel so you can control the car.

3. The engine transforms chemical or electrical energy into mechanical energy that moves the vehicle. The propulsion system includes systems that route fuel, electricity and gases to and from the engine, and that carry mechanical energy (power) from the engine to the wheels.

4. The brake system slows the car by using friction to convert momentum into heat.

5. Apart from accessories like a stereo, all your car's systems must be in good working order for safe driving.

6. Routine checks include checking lubrication/oil, the battery, coolant, indicators and lights, and tyres.

7. You need to keep your car roadworthy for safety, because the law requires it, to protect the environment and to save money. You can do this easily by making a habit of checking the systems regularly and keeping records of services performed on your vehicle.

8. Learn to handle basic procedures like fuelling, changing bulbs, opening the bonnet, changing windscreen wipers, checking fluids, tyre pressure and changing a flat tyre.

9   Prepare for the NCT by consulting the list of tests and having a full service check at least two weeks before your vehicle's test. Check all lights and make all other routine checks the day before and the morning of the NCT.

10   Vehicle modifications are any modifications for appearance, comfort, safety or performance that change a vehicle's systems or accessories from the original factory design.

11   Some modifications require special certificates. Inappropriate modifications have a negative effect on the vehicle's safety and/or performance. Consult a qualified mechanic and check local laws before making modifications.

12   Reconsider modifications that encourage you to be a competitive driver instead of a co-operative driver. Such changes may be appropriate for a race track, but not for the roads that you share.

13   Your first priority with any breakdown or problem is your own safety and the safety of your passengers and other motorists. In breakdowns remember to control, choose and communicate.

14   If you have a breakdown on the side of the road, turn your wheels to the left, turn on your hazard lights and stay clear of the vehicle while waiting for emergency services. Do not attempt to exit a vehicle if stopped on the road in fast-moving traffic. Place warning triangles, if available, at least 50 metres behind the vehicle, facing oncoming traffic and beyond any obstacles that may block other motorists' view of the triangle.

15   If you break down on a railway level crossing, exit the vehicle and contact emergency services. Only attempt to push the car clear if you can be absolutely sure there is no train approaching. If you see a train, get off the track. Do not attempt to judge how soon the train will arrive because the speed of a train is difficult to judge.

16 Know the procedures for jump-starting a vehicle. When jump-starting a car, do not connect the jump leads to the recipient car's negative battery terminal. Instead, attach it to a metal part of the engine. Wear eye protection if you can.

17 If an engine warning light comes on, pull over immediately but safely and stop the engine. Consult the owner's manual to identify the problem. Do not continue to drive until you sort the problem out because continuing to drive may be dangerous or cause serious, costly damage to the car.

18 If you get a flat tyre while driving, the steering will be sluggish and difficult to control. The car will skid easily. Grip the steering wheel with both hands to maintain control. Slow down, but avoid using the brakes if possible. Gently pull off the road with your hazard lights on.

19 If your vehicle catches fire, pull over immediately but safely. Get clear of the vehicle. You should only attempt to put the fire out if it is very minor, and then only if you have an extinguisher. Stay safe. If in doubt, stay away from the car and wait for the emergency services.

20 Cautiously re-enter traffic after dealing with a breakdown. Try to find a place where you can clearly see oncoming traffic and have ample room to reach an appropriate speed to merge. Take your vehicle directly to a service centre to confirm its roadworthiness.

4

'Just like alcohol, fatigue affects our ability to drive by slowing reaction time, decreasing awareness and impairing judgment. If you are over-tired, it can be just like being drunk behind the wheel.'

Mark Yakabuski

Attention

Introduction

You know that your attitude is the most important factor affecting your safety as a driver and also how important it is for you to take care of your vehicle and to understand and account for environmental and physical factors as you drive.

Safe driving ultimately boils down to you. With the wrong attitude or when you don't take care of your vehicle or you choose to disregard natural laws, you will not be able to drive safely. Safe driving requires you to think about what you're doing. By staying alert and paying close and continuous attention, you can receive and process the information you need to drive safely. Good driving requires more than just knowing what to think, it also requires knowing how to think.

Previously you learned that it takes about five years to reach average driving competence. You can protect yourself during this vulnerable period by understanding how safe drivers think – you can learn how to stay alert and aware while driving and to deal with influences that adversely affect your alertness, and therefore your safety.

In this module we will discuss...

- Alertness
- Information filtration
- Attention distribution

- Task fixation and switching attention
- Tunnel attention
- Fatigue and drowsiness

Alertness

Aidhmeanna **OBJECTIVES** **4** > **Look for, and highlight, the answers to these questions**

- What does it mean to 'be alert'?
- Why do you need to stay alert when driving?
- What kind of distractions affect your alertness when driving?
- What influences can have an adverse effect on alertness when driving?
- What can you do to remain alert despite these influences?

The first step in thinking like a safe driver is *being alert*. This means paying close and continuous attention to the task at hand – in other words, thinking about what you're doing. Just as you can daydream or sing while walking, once you develop proficiency with driving motor skills, it becomes possible to drive with your mind partially on something other than driving. It becomes possible, but it never becomes safe, because you're no longer fully alert to what's going on around you on the road.

As you've already learned, your safety as a driver depends upon constantly assessing what's going on around you. You need to be aware of where other road users are and their intentions. You need to note road conditions that affect traction; signals and signs; and other physical influences that affect your safety. You need to pay attention to your vehicle controls. You cannot do these unless you stay alert while driving.

Because a lot of your driving will become routine, even seemingly minor things can easily become distractions unless you make a conscious effort to concentrate and remain alert. A distraction is, in effect, anything you see, hear or otherwise perceive that draws your thoughts away from what is relevant for safe driving. Conversing with a passenger, playing music or looking at something at the side of the road (instead of the road itself) are examples of distractions that can divert your attention, making you less alert. Studies show that many more crashes occur in vehicles with passengers, the lesson is that when you give someone a lift, pay attention to driving first and conversing second. If your conversation requires your full attention, stop for a coffee or a bite to eat and then have a chat.

Here are some examples of other things that can compromise your alertness. Note that *anything that keeps you from actively paying full attention to driving adversely affects your driving alertness.*

You cannot give your full attention to the road and hold a conversation on a mobile phone at the same time. It is illegal to use a mobile phone without a hands-free kit. Pull over if you have to make or take a call

- **Alcohol and drugs.** In Module 1, you learned that these dramatically impair your ability to drive safely. One reason, though not the only one, is that they impair your ability to pay full attention to the road.
- **Mobile phones.** In Ireland, it's illegal to drive and use a mobile phone without a hands-free kit. However, even a hands-free mobile phone is a serious distraction. The only truly safe way to use a mobile on a journey is to pull over in a safe place to make or take a call, or to have a passenger take the phone for you (but don't let the passenger distract you).

If you need to use a map, either pull over or have a passenger check it for you. Don't attempt to read the map and drive at the same time

- **Using a map or following directions.** If you need to use a map, either pull over or have a passenger check it for you. Concentrating on directional signs can also reduce your alertness if you pay so much attention to them that it causes you to pay less attention to warning and regulatory signs and road conditions for example.
- **Emotions.** As you learned in Module 1, don't take extreme emotions into the car with you. When you're angry or in grief, you're not thinking about driving. This is why you offer a friend a lift after a traumatic event such as a death in the family. Your friend may be physically fine, but is not in a mental condition compatible with safe driving. Be sure you're in a calm state before you drive. If you aren't, either rest or get a lift.
- **Eating or drinking behind the wheel.** It's difficult to manage food and beverages while driving, especially when trying to change gears, steer, use your indicators and so on. There's a tendency to worry about spilling something on your lap instead of what's on the road. If you need to eat, stop the car. Use it as an opportunity to stretch and relax before resuming your journey.
- **Daydreaming.** Once driving becomes routine, it's easy to let your mind wander. Unfortunately, you are then unlikely to respond in time when something unexpected happens on the road. Train yourself to think only about driving while driving. You'll learn some helpful techniques later in this module and in Module 5.

 For long journeys, plan your route before you depart and list the road numbers on your dashboard for safe and easy navigation.

Having your route clearly displayed means that you don't have to constantly refer to a map

- **Fatigue or drowsiness.** In these states, you're physically unable to remain fully alert. You can train yourself to disregard distractions, but it is not safe to disregard drowsiness or tiredness. These are very serious impairments to safe driving, and we'll take a closer look at them shortly.

- **Roadside distractions.** As mentioned earlier, if you're not careful, you can pay too much attention to what's along the road instead of the road itself. Examples of this include looking at a crash someone else has had or at a billboard or shop window. You may be looking for a particular address or location and pay too much attention to what you're trying to find and too little attention to your driving.

- **Children.** In Module 1 you learned that children can be particularly distracting. When you become a parent, you will find that you're especially alert to anything that may threaten the well-being of your children, and that you are willing to take great risks on their behalf. Remember that whatever children may be fussing about in the car, your first priority – for their welfare and your own – is being a good driver. Ignore the fuss and stay calm until you can pull over safely and deal with it.

- **Pets.** For your safety as well as theirs, don't drive with unrestrained pets in the car. Not only are they distractions, but they could jump into your lap, block your field of view, get under your control pedals or become a flying missile in a sudden stop.

For your safety as well as theirs, don't drive with unrestrained pets in the car. Not only are they distractions, but they could jump into your lap, block your field of view, get under your control pedals or become a flying missile in a sudden stop

If a stinging insect is in the car, open the window and pull over before attempting to do battle

- **Insects.** It may surprise you to learn that many crashes occur because a bee or wasp is in the car. These and other insects tend to be very distracting because the driver fears getting stung or bitten – especially if allergic. If you discover a bee, wasp or other threatening bug in the car, open the window, pull over safely and deal with it. Don't continue driving while trying to do battle with an insect.

QUICK QUIZ

1 To 'be alert' means having proficient motor skills. T ☐ F ☑

2 You need to stay alert when driving because your safety depends upon constantly assessing what's going on around you. T ☑ F ☐

3 Anything that keeps you from actively paying attention to driving influences your alertness to driving. T ☑ F ☐

Answers: 1: F. 2: T. 3: T.

Information filtration

Aidhmeanna
OBJECTIVES **4** Look for, and highlight, the answers to these questions

- What is meant by 'information overload'?
- What is meant by 'information filtration'?
- What information should you consciously filter as (a) relevant or (b) irrelevant while driving.

Your brain can only process so much information at once. *Information overload* describes the situation when your brain cannot effectively process all the information it receives. Depending on the circumstances, information overload can make you confused, pay attention to the wrong thing, hesitate or panic – none of which is desirable while driving.

But even now as you read, your senses are sending thousands of messages to your brain at once. You're probably hearing, feeling, touching, smelling and seeing things beyond this page, and yet you aren't suffering from information overload (if you were, you wouldn't be able to concentrate on what you're reading). Your eyes alone take in 30 to 40 images per second. How is it that

As a driver, you need to learn to disregard the irrelevant and pay attention to the relevant. If the information relates to safe driving, it is relevant. Finding a restaurant is not

so much information comes into your brain all the time without constantly overwhelming you? The answer is *information filtration*. Through experience, you have learned subconsciously to filter out what is not relevant to the task in hand. Information filtration is the process by which your brain determines what information is important and what information to ignore. To varying degrees, this process requires experience. Have you ever noticed that when you go into a strange building for the first time, you hear, smell and observe details that you no longer notice when you're used to the place? This is because at first, your brain hasn't learned what is important or unimportant in that place but, through experience, it begins to filter out details that are irrelevant to your reason for being there.

Similarly, as a new driver, your brain is still learning to filter and select only the essential information your senses give it on the road. Since driving is still new to you, the filter isn't as effective as it will be after a few years of driving. However, remaining alert and consciously thinking about what you see, hear and do improves your information filtration. It takes practice, and you need it for safe driving.

As a driver, you need to learn to disregard the irrelevant and pay attention to the relevant. Although this gets easier over time, it will always be important to do this because no two situations on the road are precisely the same. It may sound complex, but it's easy to simplify if you remember what you learned in the last module: your first priority is always your safety, your passengers' safety and other road users' safety. So, if the information relates to safe driving, it is relevant; you must pay attention to it and act accordingly. If it does not, it is irrelevant and you can give it little or no attention.

Let's look at an example; Suppose you're driving home at dusk and you approach a junction that has cars and bicycles waiting to enter traffic. There are pedestrians on the footpath, cars parked on both sides of the road and several campaign posters and billboards. In addition, there are signs telling you the name of the road at the junction, that there's a reduced speed limit and that there are road works ahead. Inside the car, one passenger is complaining about being cold and asking you to turn up the heat. Another wants to know what your plans are for the weekend. Your stereo is playing a bit loudly.

Obviously, the cars, bicycles and pedestrians are relevant. The speed limit and the road works warning signs are relevant. The street name may or may not be relevant depending on how well you know the area. The campaign posters, billboards, passenger conversation and music are irrelevant. If the latter start to divert your focus too much, turn off the music and ask the passengers to be quiet for a moment.

After you pass the intersection and roadwork area, the traffic thins. There are no parked cars on the roadside and the signs say you can resume a normal, safe speed. Assuming no new circumstances present themselves, the demand for information filtering declines. While still remaining fully alert to what's on the road, it may be appropriate to turn the music back on perhaps at a lower volume, adjust the heating and discuss the weekend plans.

QUICK QUIZ

1 'Information overload' means thinking too much.
T ☐ F ☑

2 'Information filtration' means selectively processing the information. T ☑ F ☐

3 A wet patch of road ahead is an irrelevant piece of information and can always be filtrated out.
T ☐ F ☑

Answers: 1: F, 2: T, 3: F

Attention distribution

Aidhmeanna
OBJECTIVES **4** **Look for, and highlight, the answers to these questions**

- What is meant by 'attention distribution'?
- Why is it important for you to distribute your attention between information and different driving tasks?
- How do 'control, choose and communicate' relate to attention distribution?
- How can you be in control of your car but still not be driving safely?
- Why should you give navigation a lower priority in your attention distribution?

In the previous discussion, you learned that you must practice information filtration so that you manage and process only relevant information as you drive. However, you probably already recognise that this isn't enough. Although you've excluded the irrelevant information, not all relevant information is equally important or has the same priority. For example, suppose you approach a caution sign indicating an open ditch and a direction sign for a turn you need to make. Both are relevant, but the caution sign is more important. While it would be inconvenient to miss your turn, it would be disastrous to drive into the ditch. You therefore give priority to avoiding the ditch, and you only make the turn if you can do so safely.

Attention distribution is the skill you use to allocate your attention to all the relevant information your brain receives. That includes the information that relates to tasks you're already handling, such as steering and braking, along with the task of being alert for potential hazards, road conditions, signs and so on. Driving requires that you handle these tasks effectively as well as simultaneously, so it is important that you use attention distribution to keep from focusing too much or too little on any one task. Also, the amount of attention you must give a task changes depending on the circumstances.

You don't have the option of ignoring relevant information and tasks while driving, but you can and must prioritise them. The priorities of '*control, choose and communicate*' that you learned in Module 3 help you with attention distribution by giving you a way of prioritising information and tasks. Let's take a closer look at each.

Control, you've already learned, means keeping your vehicle under safe control. Control consists of the motor skills of driving (such as braking and steering), and includes responding to anything that affects your ability to control your car. For example, responding to poor road conditions and

Control

 Choose

 Communicate

slowing down as you approach a turn or hazard are part of control. Warning signs that relate to road hazards or safety, like speed limits, are part of maintaining control. When overwhelmed with choices, your first priorities are the control tasks.

Choose, you recall, means planning ahead to avoid or solve a problem. You maintain control so that you have more time to make the choice. Being alert to warning signs, approaching hazards, pedestrians, merging traffic and so on is part of maintaining control, but it is also part of choosing. For example, if you notice you're approaching ice, you may choose to slow on the dry part of the road where you still have traction before getting onto the icy patch. Or, you could choose to carefully stop on the dry area until the other lane is clear so you can then drive around the ice.

Choosing requires maintaining your *safety margin*. Time and space give you a safety margin while driving. The more time and space you have to respond to a problem, the more likely you are to respond (or choose) correctly and effectively. You maintain a safety margin by staying within speed limits, slowing down in poor conditions and not tailgating, for example. Going too fast or following other cars too closely will reduce your safety margin. Losing your safety margin takes away your ability to choose what to do in an emergency. Quite often motorists are in control of their cars as they crash. They have control, but they don't have time to choose what to do with it when something unexpected happens.

 Never confuse being in control with being safe. If you don't have a safety margin, you are not driving safely.

Never confuse being in control with being safe. If you don't have a safety margin – that is, enough time and space to respond – you are not driving safely. As driving becomes more difficult or if you're in any doubt, slow down so you have more time – a greater safety margin – to respond. We'll look at safety margins in more detail in Module 9.

Communicate means signalling your intentions to other drivers. Make sure that you have control and that you've made the right choice before you communicate. Communicating your intentions gives other road users the information they need to control and choose for themselves. They use your communicated intentions to help maintain their safety margins. In an emergency you may not have time to use an indicator or otherwise communicate, but most of the time you do, so make a habit of it.

Because the point of driving is to go somewhere, it may surprise you that you need to give navigation a *lower* priority in your attention distribution. As illustrated in the previous example of the ditch and the turn, safety is the priority. Unfortunately, people don't always drive that way. You've probably seen drivers make dangerous turns or lane changes because they suddenly discover they're about to miss a junction or exit slip road – a stupid decision that says, in effect, 'I'd rather be killed than be inconvenienced.'

Pay attention to navigation so you don't get lost, but don't act rashly if you're about to miss a turn or exit ramp that you come upon suddenly. Missing a junction is not an emergency. If necessary, drive past, turn around at the next safe opportunity and come back. This is far less inconvenient than a crash.

> **QUICK QUIZ**
>
> 1 'Attention distribution' is the skill you use to allocate your attention to all the relevant information coming to you. T☑ F☐
>
> 2 It is important for you to distribute your attention between information and different driving tasks so you avoid focusing too much or too little on any one task. T☑ F☐
>
> 3 Control, choice and communication relate to attention distribution by allowing you to disregard priorities. T☐ F☑
>
> Answers: 1: T, 2: T, 3: F

Task fixation and switching attention

> *Aidhmeanna*
> **OBJECTIVES** **4** ❯ Look for, and highlight, the answers to these questions
>
> ● What is 'task fixation' and what causes it?
> ● How do you avoid task fixation?

Task fixation is focusing your attention entirely or far too heavily on a single task. For drivers, this could mean concentrating so much on correct lane position while approaching a roundabout that you don't notice school children trying to cross at the same junction.

To avoid task fixation, take the time to develop your basic driving skills so that they become automatic and don't require conscious thought. This frees your attention for gathering information and making more complex conscious decisions

The primary cause of task fixation is lack of familiarity with the task. Think back to learning to ride a bicycle. At first, just staying up on two wheels took all your attention. Only after you became proficient at maintaining your balance could you devote your attention to other aspects of riding a bicycle. This is why it's best to learn to cycle in a relatively safe area where you can focus on balance without worrying about other vehicles or obstacles.

You will go through the same process as you learn to drive. Until you can locate and operate the controls with ease and confidence (and without looking at them), the simple actions of changing gear, using the clutch, braking and accelerating take all your attention. This is why you'll start in an open space where you don't have to pay much attention to signs, other vehicles or obstacles. After these basic driving skills become automatic, you can devote your attention to other tasks. As an example, suppose you notice a warning that the road ahead bends to the right. You decide to slow down as you take the curve. You consciously choose your action, but you don't *consciously* think 'take my foot off the accelerator and turn the steering wheel to the right'. You just do it automatically. Therefore, the first way to avoid task fixation is to develop your basic driving skills so that they're automatic and don't require conscious thought. This frees your attention for gathering information and making more complex conscious decisions.

Once you begin driving in traffic, you also avoid task fixation by developing your ability to constantly switch your attention. As you learned in the previous section, you have to distribute your attention to all the tasks

A good driver doesn't stay focused on one area too long. The driver maintains a global view of everything going on around the car

driving involves. Good habits help you do this. If you watch an experienced good driver, you'll notice the driver's gaze shift, perhaps first ahead, then briefly down to the dashboard gauges, back ahead, then briefly to the rear view mirror, then ahead, then to the side mirrors and so on. While looking ahead, the driver looks at the direction and condition of the road, then at signs, and then at other motorists. The process is endless, and a good driver doesn't stay focused on one area too long. The driver maintains a global view of everything going on around the car. Developing the habit of constantly switching your attention is a good way to avoid task fixation.

Tunnel attention

Aidhmeanna **OBJECTIVES** **4** ▷ Look for, and highlight, the answers to these questions

- What is meant by 'tunnel attention' and what are its symptoms?
- What causes tunnel attention?
- How do you avoid tunnel attention, or deal with it if it occurs?

Tunnel attention is similar to task fixation, though the two are not quite the same. Tunnel attention occurs when a driver becomes obsessed with a particular objective, such as getting somewhere on time or passing a slow vehicle. It can result in a collision when a driver's response proves ineffective and, rather than try something else, the driver simply repeats or continues the same ineffective response. With tunnel attention, the tendency is to focus only on the tasks and information directly related to attaining the objective or in some cases, a single task.

The cause of tunnel attention is emotion. Most commonly, the emotion is anger or frustration, although it can also be fear or panic. The symptoms include thinking about a singular objective repeatedly, usually accompanied by annoyance at traffic or another driver, for example. Symptoms also include

Tunnel attention occurs when a driver becomes obsessed with a particular objective, such as getting somewhere on time or passing a slow vehicle

a lack of attention to relevant driving information and a failure to switch attention regularly. Drivers with tunnel attention often resort to competitive driving behaviour.

Tunnel attention caused by panic occurs in an emergency. The symptom is choosing a single, ineffective response to the situation and then failing to try an alternative even though the initial response is clearly ineffective. A typical example would be 'standing on' the brakes when a driver turns a blind corner and finds stopped traffic ahead Even though the car is clearly not going to stop in time, the driver continues panic-braking instead of looking for a place to manoeuvre to avoid the collision.

When tunnel attention occurs due to anger, frustration or panic, the driver isn't thinking rationally. Prevention is far better, and more effective, than trying to cure tunnel attention. The best ways to prevent tunnel attention are to avoid the situations in which it can occur and to develop habits that keep you driving rationally rather than emotionally.

- When punctuality is important, leave early. A slow vehicle or a traffic jam won't cause you stress if you have plenty of time to reach your destination.

- Get in the habit of constantly and deliberately switching your attention like you learned in the last section. Don't allow yourself to focus on a single objective. You're less likely to become obsessed with something if you continually vary the focus of your attention.

- Think about typical situations ahead of time, when you have a clear head, so you will remain rational later when they occur. For example, suppose the speed limit is 100 km/h, you have 100 kilometres to drive and you get stuck behind someone travelling at 90 km/h. By how much will you be delayed if you're stuck behind them the whole way? Only about six minutes – certainly not worth getting angry about, much less risking a dangerous overtaking manoeuvre. Think about taking a sick child to the hospital. The child is crying and you're upset. How does rushing help in this situation? It doesn't help at all. All it does is endanger you and the child. Even if it is a medical emergency in which time is a factor and, for some reason, you couldn't summon emergency medical services to come to you a collision will make the situation far worse.

Look for a place to refuel while you still have a reasonable minimum left before you reach reserve

- Maintain your safety margin. Drive knowing that you can make mistakes – you can and you will. Tunnel attention due to panic in an emergency often results from not having another option after making an ineffective choice to begin with. By giving yourself time and space – a safety margin – you're more likely to make a good decision and to have time to implement it, evaluate its effectiveness and switch to another if necessary. Always use your indicators so other drivers know your intentions.

- Notice how efficiently you drive and how soon you reach your destination when you drive rationally, co-operatively and safely. Most of the time you arrive sooner than you would have if you'd rushed. This is because the most efficient driving involves flowing with traffic, not trying to 'beat it'. Remembering this will help you avoid frustration when things seem to be slowing you down. Calm, rational driving not only gets you there more safely, but also just as fast.

- Look for a place to refuel while you still have a reasonable amount left, ideally before you reach reserve. This reduces anxiety about getting stuck in heavy traffic or missing a junction because your fuel is so low you're afraid you'll run out.

- Disregard offensive driving behaviours by other motorists. If someone does something annoying – even when it was clearly on purpose – let it go. Slow down or pull over to let a tailgater pass you. Remember what you learned in Module 1: the best way to get even with such a driver is to not get even.

While it's best to prevent tunnel attention, do stay alert to its symptoms. If you find yourself experiencing tunnel attention, try the following:

- Remove the stressor. Tunnel attention results primarily from anger or frustration. If you're frustrated because you're running late, for example, have a passenger call ahead to explain the delay or pull over and do it yourself.
- Put distance between yourself and a rude motorist.
- Change your mood. Switch your stereo to some uplifting music. Make yourself reconsider the significance of the situation by asking yourself if you'll even remember what's upsetting you in a day or week from now. Think of something positive about the situation that's troubling you – for example, if you're stuck behind a slow driver, at least you won't have to worry about accidentally going too fast.
- If necessary, stop and take a break. Even a couple of minutes can help restore your perspective. You will seldom, if ever, encounter a situation on the road for which it is worth endangering yourself or others!

QUICK QUIZ

1 'Tunnel attention' is when a driver becomes obsessed with a particular objective. T ☑ F ☐

2 Tunnel attention can result from anger, frustration, anxiety or panic. T ☑ F ☐

3 If you begin to experience tunnel attention try to remove the stressor. T ☑ F ☐

Answers: 1: T, 2: T, 3: T

Fatigue and drowsiness

Aidhmeanna
OBJECTIVES **4** — **Look for, and highlight, the answers to these questions**

- What are the dangers of driver fatigue and drowsiness?
- What are the major causes of driver fatigue and drowsiness?
- What is the phenomenon of 'motorway monotony'?
- How do you avoid fatigue and drowsiness?
- What should you do if you become fatigued and/or drowsy?

Most influences that have a negative effect on your alertness are mental and emotional but, as you read earlier, fatigue and drowsiness are primarily physical. Fatigue and drowsiness are dangerous because they reduce your awareness and your ability to focus on driving. This substantially impairs your response to an emergency or to changing road conditions. Drowsiness is the state you enter just before you sleep, and it's commonly, though not always, caused by fatigue. You know the feeling: your eyes feel heavy and your head drops as you become more drowsy. The biggest danger of fatigue and drowsiness is falling asleep at the wheel.

Road collisions caused by drivers falling asleep are usually very serious and a major cause of fatalities.

The important thing to realise in dealing with fatigue and drowsiness is that they have many causes. If the causes are not related to being awake too long, then you can generally take steps to combat them. However, if you've been awake too long, it's a different story. You are physically unable to stay awake indefinitely. At some point, you will sleep, and there is nothing you can do to prevent it. Once you pass the point where you need to sleep, your alertness and driving ability will continue to decline until you sleep – and it will happen no matter what you're doing at the time.

The biggest danger of fatigue and drowsiness is falling asleep at the wheel

Highway Hypnosis is the effect of driving in relatively unchanging conditions so that road lines or lights seem to become constant and repetitive, especially on a straight road with no significant bends

The major causes of fatigue and drowsiness are:

- Driving very late or early, or after poor or insufficient sleep.
- Driving after a heavy meal.
- Driving for long periods without rest breaks.
- Driving in bad weather, poor light or in the glare of oncoming lights.
- Driving in a car that is uncomfortably warm or cold.
- Driving in a poorly-ventilated car. (Carbon dioxide from your breath builds up, causing drowsiness.)
- Dehydration. (Your body requires ample fluids for good circulation, which brings your tissues oxygen and energy, and carries away wastes.)
- 'Motorway monotony' or 'highway hypnosis'. This is the effect of driving in relatively unchanging conditions so that road lines or lights seem to become constant and repetitive, especially on a straight road with no significant bends. It creates a drowsy hypnotic state in which the driver operates the car almost entirely by automatic processes. In this state, the driver has dangerously low concentration and will respond poorly to emergencies or changing conditions. This drowsy state eventually leads to sleep.
- Driving the same route daily can lead to motorway monotony because the driver becomes so familiar with the route that it becomes repetitive.

There are several things you can do to avoid fatigue and drowsiness:

- Drive when fully rested after adequate sleep. Stop driving and sleep when you need sleep.
- To some extent, coffee, tea and other beverages with caffeine help you remain alert. However, don't overdo it and don't try to use caffeine as a substitute for sleep.
- Avoid heavy meals before driving. On long journeys, have several smaller meals when you take regular breaks.
- Take a break for 10 – 15 minutes at least every two hours.
- Keep your car at a cool but comfortable temperature with adequate ventilation.
- Stay hydrated by drinking enough water when you take breaks. Staying properly hydrated also helps because you'll need rest breaks to urinate – letting you take two anti-fatigue steps at once.
- Avoid motorway monotony by varying the focus of your attention, as you've learned. Don't stare at the road. Shift your position or adjust your seating slightly every few minutes. This is one time when a casual conversation with a passenger can help rather than hurt alertness.
- Vary your routine when possible.

If you begin to feel drowsy or fatigued, or if you notice related symptoms like cramping, irritability, sore eyes, lack of concentration or poor judgment, try the following:

- Stop, take a break, take a walk and get something, non-alcoholic to drink.
- Roll down a window if you think it may be a ventilation issue.
- Whatever you do, don't think you can win a fight with fatigue and drowsiness. You can't. If the previous steps don't overcome your fatigue and drowsiness, or if they return, you need to sleep. Pull over some place safe and sleep!

> **QUICK QUIZ**
>
> 1 The dangers of fatigue and drowsiness include; reduced alertness, loss of focus on driving, slow responses and falling asleep at the wheel.
> T ☑ F ☐
>
> 2 The major causes of driver fatigue and drowsiness are busy lifestyles, lack of sleep, poor ventilation and heavy meals. T ☑ F ☐
>
> 3 Motorway monotony describes the boring way houses are built near motorways. T ☐ F ☑
>
> Answers: 1: T, 2: T, 3: F

Summary points ⟫⟫⟫⟫⟫⟫⟫

In this module on attention you learned:

1 To think like a safe driver, you have to be alert. Your safety depends on you being alert as you drive.

2 Distractions like mobile phones, trying to read a map, eating, daydreaming and heightened emotions reduce your alertness. Fatigue, drowsiness, alcohol or drugs also make you less alert.

3 To remain alert, make a conscious effort to concentrate on your driving and the driving environment. Avoid distractions and don't drive when extremely emotional or when fatigued or drowsy. Never drive after drinking alcohol or taking drugs.

4 Your brain can only process so much information at once. Information overload occurs when your brain can't process all the information it receives. Reduce the overload by using information filtration, the process of disregarding irrelevant information.

5 Anything that relates to safe driving is relevant information. Anything else is irrelevant.

6 While driving, use attention distribution to vary the focus of your attention between the relevant information and the tasks required. It keeps you from focusing for too long on one task or piece of information.

7 Remember to prioritise 'control, choose and communicate' when distributing your attention.

8 Task fixation is focusing your attention too heavily on a single task. It is caused by a lack of familiarity with the task and a failure to vary the focus of your attention. Avoid it by developing your basic driving skills in safe conditions and by deliberately switching attention regularly as you drive.

9   Tunnel attention occurs when a driver becomes obsessed with a particular objective or, in an emergency, when the driver continues or repeats an ineffective response. It results from frustration, anger or panic.

10   Avoid tunnel attention by driving rationally, not emotionally. Avoid situations that cause these emotions. Do not let yourself focus on a single objective and remember to maintain a proper perspective. Maintain your safety margin so you avoid tunnel attention in an emergency.

11   Fatigue and drowsiness are dangerous because they reduce your alertness, lengthen your response times and impair your judgement. The worst danger is falling asleep while driving, which often results in fatal collisions.

12   Avoid fatigue and drowsiness by driving only when fully rested. Take a 10-15 minute break at least every two hours and avoid heavy meals before driving. Keep your car comfortable and adequately ventilated. If you are still fatigued or drowsy after a break, or if you become fatigued or drowsy again, pull over in a safe place and sleep.

5

'To become aware of, through the senses,--- Anything that might cause an accident, create danger or exposure to risk.'

Chambers English Dictionary

Hazard perception

Introduction

In the last module, you learned that you need to be alert and to think clearly so you can recognise and respond to problems. We looked at the need to filter out irrelevant information and how when handling a problem, your priorities are to control, choose and communicate. Thinking as a good driver means remaining rational and avoiding task fixation and tunnel attention. Part of doing this means training yourself to vary the focus of your attention so that you don't fixate on any one thing.

In this module, we'll take a closer look at how you perceive what's going on around you and how to make good decisions based on your perceptions. Good drivers use their senses to help build a full picture of the driving environment. They use this information to anticipate, recognise and avoid hazards.

Sight is the most important sense used in driving, so we will look at the different types of vision used and how to maximise your observations when driving.

In this module we will discuss...

- Sensory awareness
- Visual acuity
- Field of vision

- Scanning
- Anticipating and managing driving hazards

Sensory awareness

Aidhmeanna OBJECTIVES 5 > Look for, and highlight, the answers to these questions

- What is meant by 'perceptual skills'?
- What is the primary sense you use when driving?
- What is a driving 'hazard'?
- Why do you need to develop good hazard-recognition skills?
- What senses, other than sight, do you use as a driver?

Like most of the things you do, driving is a sense-based motor skill. That is, your senses give you information that you use to make decisions about starting, stopping, turning, slowing and so on. In the last module, you learned that your brain uses information filtration when you're driving to sort through what's important and what's unimportant to the task in hand.

Information filtering is a skill you learn. *Perceptual skills* are the processes of using your senses to find and gather relevant information from the world around you. The term is plural because even though vision is the primary sense you use when driving, your other senses play a part, too.

Remember that to maintain your alertness, you need to constantly switch your attention so that you know what's going on all around you. With experience, and by practising some of the techniques you learn in this chapter, you will learn to scan your surroundings for hazards systematically and habitually. Keep in mind that much of hazard recognition requires mental analysis – not simple recognition. Signs that indicate possible trouble can be subtle. For example, if a football rolls onto the street, an experienced driver will immediately slow down, become more alert and watch the roadside. Why? Because a child, or an adult, may be chasing the ball or at least playing nearby. One of the reasons it takes about five years to reach average driving competence is that you need experience to learn to recognise these clues.

If a ball comes rolling out onto the road it's likely that someone is going to follow

We've used the word 'hazard' a lot so far and it's only common sense to want to avoid hazards. However, it's worth stopping for a moment to define 'hazard', because it has a different meaning in the context of driving than it has in relation to other activities. Generally, a hazard is something that can harm *you*. In driving, though, a hazard is something that can harm *someone* – not necessarily you. For example, if a child chases a football out onto the street, that is a driving hazard. If you were to strike the child, the danger to you would be minimal, but for the child, the danger would be extremely high. Still, because it's better to strike a tree, wall, bush, parked car or almost anything inanimate to avoid the child, making an evasive manoeuvre may ultimately endanger you. So, a driving hazard is *anything* you need to avoid while operating a motor vehicle.

As you recall, your safety margin as a driver comes from *time* and *space*. Time not only gives you more time to respond – it also gives you more time to choose the *right* response. You need to develop good hazard-recognition skills because the more readily you recognise the clues that indicate a hazard, the more time you have to choose your response and the more space you have to put that response into action. This is one reason why good drivers tend to become more conservative with experience – they recognise possible problems that inexperienced drivers may not even notice.

Although you use sight as your primary sense in driving, as a driver you will use *all* your senses, except taste. Hearing, touch, smell and balance all give you information that help you to steer clear of problems.

- **Hearing.** Besides the obvious sounds like car horns or the screech of tyres, you can hear other things that help you drive safely. A strange sound can alert you to a mechanical problem. The hiss of tyres on the road may tell you that a car is coming up alongside yours. The sound of children suggests that youngsters are in the area and may be near the road. A siren that's getting louder warns that you may need to give way to an emergency vehicle. This is why it's important to keep your radio low enough to hear what's going on outside the car. If you drown out all the other sounds, you deprive yourself of important information. In conditions like fog, increase your safety by partially rolling down your window and turning off all music so your ears can help compensate for low visibility.
- **Touch/feel.** As you become more experienced, you get a feel for the road. You feel resistance in your steering wheel and different vibrations from different road surfaces. You feel centrifugal force and cross-fall as you take a bend, thanks to your sense of balance, and you feel when you're starting to take the corner too fast. A rough engine reverberates through the vehicle, suggesting a possible service issue. Rumble strips call your attention to an approaching stop, corner, edge of the road or a reduced speed limit.
- **Smell.** Your nose may pick up the odour of coolant or burning rubber, warning that you have engine problems. The smell of wet asphalt or tarmac may call your attention to changed road conditions.

Your senses work in harmony as well as independently. Your sense of speed is based on what you see, the sound of the road and how the road feels. You see a strong crosswind bending trees and grass, you feel it push the car to one side and you hear the gust buffet you. By learning to pay attention to all your senses and by letting them work together, you become a better driver, with a greater awareness of what's going on around you.

QUICK QUIZ

1 Perceptual skills are the processes of using your senses to gather information. T ☑ F ☐

2 The primary sense you use when driving is hearing. T ☐ F ☑

3 You need to develop good hazard-recognition skills so that you have more time and space to respond to hazards. T ☑ F ☐

Answers: 1: T, 2: F, 3: T

Visual acuity

Aidhmeanna
OBJECTIVES **5** **Look for, and highlight, the answers to these questions**

- What is 'visual acuity'?
- What is the law regarding vision for driving?
- When driving, from what distance should you be able to read a number plate?
- At a minimum, how often should you have your vision checked?

Since vision is the primary sense you use while driving, how well you see is not just a safety issue, but also a matter of law. Visual acuity is the measure of how well you see. It's based on how much detail you can see from a given distance.

When you apply for a provisional driving license, you must include a satisfactory eyesight report. This is defined as having visual acuity, with glasses or contact lenses if necessary, of not less than 0.5 using both eyes together. (Most people have their best acuity using both eyes).

When you drive, you should be able to read a number plate from approximately 20 metres. If you can do that, whether with or without glasses, you should have sufficient acuity to read road signs and spot potential hazards. Have a vision test at least every two years to ensure that your vision meets the minimum standard.

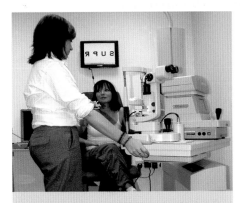

Good eyesight, with or without prescription lenses, is essential for safe driving

QUICK QUIZ

1 Visual acuity is a measurement of how far you can see in the dark. T ☐ F ☑

2 You should be able to read a number plate from a distance of 20m while driving. T ☑ F ☐

3 You should have your vision checked every five years. T ☐ F ☑

Answers: 1: F, 2: T, 3: F

Field of vision

Aidhmeanna
OBJECTIVES **5** Look for, and highlight, the answers
to these questions

- What is 'field of vision'?
- What is the difference between central vision and peripheral vision?
- How frequently should you use your mirrors? In what particular situations will you use them?

Along with visual acuity, you also need to be concerned with your *field of vision*. Field of vision is the broad area that you can see, from the far left to the far right and the topmost point to the lowest. Typically, a person's field of vision is 90 degrees to either side, which means you can see about 180 degrees from right to left. Your up/down field is not quite as broad.

Within the total area you can see, you have *central vision and peripheral vision*. Central vision comprises an area of approximately three degrees, directly ahead and this area gets your full attention. When you look at

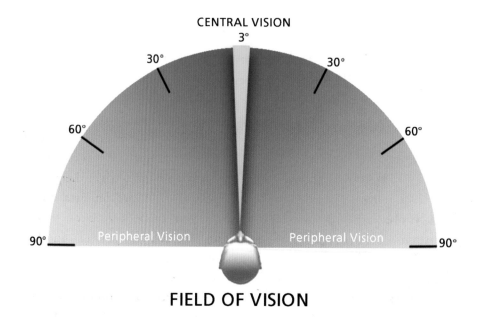

CENTRAL VISION
3°
30° 30°
60° 60°
90° Peripheral Vision Peripheral Vision 90°

FIELD OF VISION

something, you focus so that your central vision falls upon the object. Peripheral vision comprises the remaining area in your field of vision. Your brain subconsciously monitors this area and diverts your attention to anything that it perceives as important. Your peripheral vision is especially sensitive to motion. This is why peripheral vision enhances your sense of speed as objects pass by your car windows. It also makes you aware of other motorists coming toward you from the sides.

Because your field of vision does not extend behind you, your car has mirrors to allow you to see what's going on behind the car. Most cars have three mirrors: the side-view mirror on the driver's side; the rear-view mirror that's mounted on the windscreen; and the side-view mirror on the passenger's side. Some of the mirrors may be convex, wide-angle or split to broaden your view. Convex mirrors show a wider angle of view but they make things appear farther away than they really are. Be aware of the difference between the apparent and true distance with convex mirrors.

You use your mirrors by looking directly into them with your central vision, but they're also in your peripheral vision, alerting you to approaching cars. With experience, you will know exactly where other cars and objects you see in the mirrors are without having to think about it consciously. Get in the habit of checking your mirrors every seven to 10 seconds, even on a clear, straight road.

Get in the habit of checking your mirrors every seven to 10 seconds, even on a clear, straight road.

Some mirrors are convex, wide-angle or split to broaden your view. Convex mirrors can make things look further away than they really are

This is part of varying the focus of your attention regularly, as discussed in the last module, which helps you to stay alert. More importantly, it helps you to be aware of what's going on around you so another vehicle doesn't come up behind you unobserved. Mirrors are so important to your ability to drive safely that you should be sure they're de-iced and clean before driving, just like the windscreen.

1 Field of vision describes how well you can see in a field. T ❑ F ☑

2 Central vision is the central three degrees and peripheral vision covers approximately ninety degrees to either side. T ☑ F ❑

3 You should use your mirrors: every seven to 10 seconds, before changing lanes, before moving off and before turning. T ☑ F ❑

Answers: 1: F, 2: T, 3: T

Apart from checking the mirrors regularly as you drive, you'll also need to use them to manoeuvre. You should use them before moving off, overtaking, changing lanes, slowing down, stopping, speeding up, turning or before you or passengers exit the vehicle. However, avoid looking into your mirrors for too long. You can't afford to keep your eyes off the road for more than a moment when you're moving, even when driving relatively slowly.

Blind spots

Aidhmeanna OBJECTIVES 5   **Look for, and highlight, the answers to these questions**

- What is a 'blind spot'?
- What are some common blind spots, and which one is generally the most dangerous?
- How should you check blind spots before carrying out a manoeuvre?
- What considerations should you have with regard to other drivers' blind spots?
- What external objects and conditions can obstruct your field of vision?
- What should you do if something restricts your view of the road?

Although you have broad peripheral vision and mirrors, you still have to deal with *blind spots*. A blind spot is any area outside your vehicle that you cannot readily see from your position while driving. They are caused by parts of the car, passengers, luggage or other items that block your view. Some vehicles have more or larger blind spots than others. Your mirrors help reduce blind spots, *but they don't eliminate them*.

In most vehicles, you have blind spots just behind your field of vision, to the left and to the right. You also have blind spots in the front and rear below the level of the bonnet and boot, which is why you have to be cautious before moving off when small children or pets are nearby.

Probably the most dangerous blind spot is behind your right shoulder.

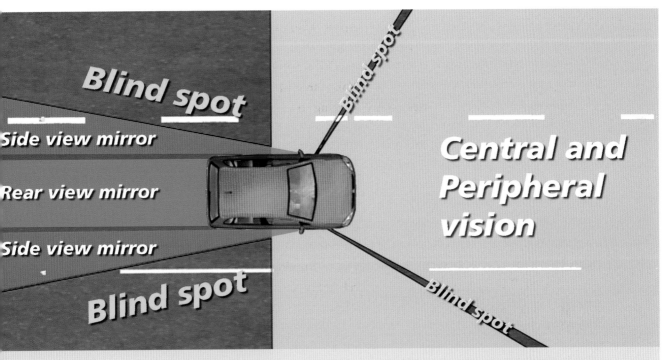

Blind spot

Side view mirror

Rear view mirror

Side view mirror

Blind spot

Blind spot

Central and Peripheral vision

Blind spot

A blind spot is any area outside your vehicle that you cannot readily see from your position while driving

In this spot, it is possible for a vehicle to be too close to be visible in your side-view mirror. You would collide with the car if you were to move into its lane. It's important to check this and other blind spots by quickly turning your head to look rather than relying on your mirror. You can see around most, though not all, blind spots by quickly turning your head, leaning forward or leaning back momentarily, with and without using your mirrors.

Remember that anything between you and the world outside is a potential blind spot. Even your rear-view mirror can create a blind spot, such as when you approach a left-side junction on a downward slope. Hanging things from your mirror and putting stickers on the rear windscreen are generally bad ideas because you're creating unnecessary blind spots. Other blind spots can be temporary, such as a passenger's head or poorly-stowed luggage. A windscreen that's fogged up is

Hanging things from your mirror is a bad idea because you're creating unnecessary blind spots. Can you spot the truck?

an obvious visual impairment, but even a small fog patch can create a blind spot, especially if it's in front of a side-view mirror.

To drive safely, be aware of where your blind spots are, and then do what you can to see around them before executing a manoeuvre.

You must also be mindful of other drivers' blind spots. Most drivers will have similar blind spots so it helps to think of where those blind spots are, and to then try manoeuvring to a place where you know the other driver is more likely to see you. Trucks and other large vehicles, such as tractors and vehicles towing trailers, typically have blind spots directly behind them and directly in front. When behind such a vehicle, remember that if you can't see the vehicle's mirrors, the driver can't see you. When in front or when overtaking remember that if you can't see the lorry's windscreen through your rear-view mirror, the driver may not be able to see you.

External objects and conditions

Along with blind spots in your car, you need to be cautious of external objects and conditions that block your view. Perhaps the most obvious of these are rain and snow, which greatly reduce how far you can see and also obscure the parts of the windscreen that aren't cleared by the wipers. The sun can be just as bad when you drive toward it in the morning or evening, or when it reflects off wet roads or other vehicles, creating glare. It's a good habit to keep sunglasses in your vehicle.

Rain and spray greatly reduce visibility and obscure the parts of the windscreen that aren't cleared by the wipers

Blinding sunlight can obscure your view of the road ahead. Slow down, use your visor to shield your eyes and always keep sunglasses in your vehicle

When you drive at night, you have two considerations: seeing and being seen. Your car's lights serve both purposes, which is why you need to replace burned-out bulbs immediately. Your headlights provide a lit area on the road and, along with streetlights, ensure that other cars can readily see you in the dark. This may be obvious, but it's still important to remember: because of their headlights, you can see other cars coming from a greater distance than you would in the daytime. How you drive should be determined in part by how far you can see clearly with your own headlights, keeping in mind that you may need to stop or manoeuvre suddenly. We discuss night-driving in greater detail in the module on Risk Management.

Your lights allow you to see and be seen which is why you must replace faulty bulbs immediately

Like weather conditions and the time of day, physical obstructions can also affect visibility. Trees, bushes, signs, buildings, large vehicles and countless other objects can block your view or limit how far you can see.

You can't drive safely if you can't see well enough to properly recognise and respond to hazards, read road markings and signs, or keep an eye on traffic. If something restricts your view of the road, you need to sort out the problem immediately – how you do so will depend on the nature of the problem. It may mean pulling over and cleaning the windscreen or putting on sunglasses. It may mean waiting for a vehicle to move out of your way so that you can see. It may mean taking a break until weather conditions improve. It may mean slowing down to whatever speed is appropriate to reduce your stopping distance. It may mean reversing or nudging forward slightly so you can see around something. Do whatever it takes to drive safely.

QUICK QUIZ

1 You don't have to worry about blind spots if you use your mirrors. T ❑ F ☑

2 Always check your blind spots before carrying out a manoeuvre. T ☑ F ❑

3 You do not need to concern yourself with other drivers' blind spots because they will deal with them themselves. T ❑ F ☑

Answers: 1: F, 2: T, 3: F

Scanning

Aidhmeanna
OBJECTIVES 5 >

**Look for, and highlight, the answers
to these questions**

- What is 'scanning'?
- How does scanning contribute to safe and effective driving?
- How do you scan while driving?

In the last module, you learned that you need to constantly change focus, never paying too much attention to a task for too long. You've also learned that you need to check your mirrors and look around the car every seven to 10 seconds. You can put all this together in one driving technique known as *scanning*. Scanning is just what it sounds like: checking around your vehicle regularly and methodically so you know what's in your area, what you're approaching and what's approaching you. Scanning makes driving safer and more effective because it helps you to anticipate what will happen, or what could happen, in the next few seconds. A 'few seconds' may not sound like much time, but seconds often mean the difference between having a collision and avoiding one.

When you're driving, you never stop scanning. The keys to effective scanning are to never concentrate on one place for too long and, though it is primarily a visual technique, to bring all of your senses into play.

Don't follow too closely, not just because you may not be able to stop in time, but so you can see beyond the vehicle in front

- Shift your visual focus from one place to another, including your mirrors so you know what's happening around you at all times. Look across both sides of the road.

Good scanning helps you detect and respond to hazards in plenty of time

- Pay particular attention to potential trouble spots, such as approaching junctions, competitive drivers and children on the footpath.
- Scanning includes watching the vehicle directly ahead of you, but also well beyond it, further down the road. Don't follow too closely, not just because you may not be able to stop in time, but so you can see beyond the vehicle in front. Don't rely on drivers ahead of you to spot trouble in time. With good scanning, you may respond to road hazards before drivers who are ahead of you and closer to the hazard.
- Pay attention to what you see, hear, smell and feel.

- Scan before you move off at a junction. You may have the green light, but check that the cross traffic has stopped so you don't pull out in front of someone who breaks the red light.

QUICK QUIZ

1 Scanning means checking around your vehicle regularly and methodically.
    T ☑ F ☐

2 Scanning contributes to safe and effective driving by alerting other drivers to your presence. T ☑ F ☑

3 A quick scan before you move off when the traffic light turns green is a waste of time. T ☐ F ☑

Answers: 1: T, 2: F, 3: F

Anticipating and managing driving hazards

Aidhmeanna OBJECTIVES 5 > **Look for, and highlight, the answers to these questions**

- What are the four categories of driving hazards? What are some examples of each?
- What thought processes and skills do you apply when you anticipate and avoid a driving hazard?
- What is the difference between *perceiving* and *observing*?
- What are examples of common hazards that you will need to anticipate and address?
- What is the almost universal response to all hazards, and your best response when you're uncertain?

Earlier, you learned that a driving hazard is anything you need to avoid when driving, to prevent harm to yourself or to anyone else. We can classify four basic types of driving hazard.

- **Static hazards.** As you may expect, these are physical hazards that don't move. They include bends, potholes, junctions and road debris. Once you negotiate a static hazard, that particular hazard is behind you until you come that way again. When you drive in the same area frequently, you become familiar with many of these and learn the best ways to avoid them. However, remember that new ones can appear and that you don't have the advantage of familiarity when driving in a new area.

- **Moving hazards.** Anything that may enter or move in the vicinity of your vehicle is a moving hazard. This includes other vehicles, pedestrians, animals and sometimes objects. You can anticipate some of these hazards based on location (e.g., approaching cars at junctions or pedestrians near a shopping centre), though your response may need to account for where they will be as they move. A moving hazard may travel with you, such as a cyclist heading the same way when you're in slow traffic.

- **Road hazards.** These include temporary repair surfaces, loose chippings, mud, steep hills, dips, hollows and other surface conditions that might impair your ability to control your car.

Static hazard

Moving hazard

Road hazard

Weather hazard

- **Weather hazards.** Hazards caused by weather include snow, ice, frost, flooding, wind, wet leaves and rain, all of which affect traction and control. Fog, bright sunlight, rain, snow and condensation can affect visibility. Weather hazards differ from other hazards in that you usually have to contend with the particular condition for most if not all of your journey.

By now, you realise that to drive safely, you must recognise hazards and problems and respond quickly and correctly. You know that in the face of a problem, your priorities are control, choose and communicate, and you know that by giving yourself a safety margin – time and space – you're more likely to choose the correct response and put it into action. You get this time by slowing down when needed or when you are unsure, and by learning to anticipate and recognise driving hazards.

Anticipating and avoiding driving hazards involves several thought processes and skills. First, you must perceive the hazard with your senses. Second, your brain must correctly filter the information and identify the hazard. Third, through training and experience, you must anticipate the potential consequences of that hazard based on the circumstances such as: where it is, what it is doing, where you are, how fast you are going and the road conditions. Fourth, you must choose the best response to avoid the hazard. Fifth, you must then carry out your chosen response. Finally, you must repeat these steps during your response and adjust or change the response based on new information, as appropriate.

Notice that the first three steps depend on *observation*, not simply perception. *Perceiving* involves your senses detecting something and passing the information to your brain. *Observing* means that you not only perceive something, but you *analyse* what you perceive – that is, you filter the information and draw conclusions. Your ability to analyse increases as you gain experience, especially during your first five years of driving.

You must also learn to apply your conclusions to the circumstances, and to do so frequently, *without conscious thought*. That is, you must learn to observe a hazard and correctly avoid it without having to say to yourself, 'Ah-ha, there's a hazard. Hmmm. Maybe I should...' Rather, you just do it – you see, you understand and you act. This is why learning to control a car is relatively easy, but learning to make quick, correct choices when faced with hazards takes years.

Here are some examples of common hazards and how you might anticipate and respond to them. Notice that *slowing down* is an almost universal response to all hazards. It is also your best response when you're not sure about possible hazards or the circumstances. **Remember, slowing down gives you more time and space, and time and space give you a safety margin.** There will certainly be times when speeding up is the best response such as to get clear of an impending collision but when in doubt, slowing down is the best bet.

Your ability to analyse potential hazards increases as you gain experience, especially during your first five years of driving

- If you see a playground, ball, sports gear, toys or the like, there's a strong possibility that children are in the area. Slow down enough so that you can stop short if a child darts in front of you. Be especially alert for children stepping or running onto the road from between cars parked along the roadside.
- In a car park or when driving along a road with parked cars, drive slowly and watch for vehicles moving off into traffic in front of you or backing into you. A car by the side of the road may pull out suddenly. Scan for drivers in the vehicles and for brake lights and reversing lights.
- Scan for pedestrians and cyclists at junctions and on footpaths. A cyclist at a junction may be planning a right turn in front of you, so stay back until you know the cyclist's intentions.
- At a junction, an approaching vehicle with a flashing indicator may not make the turn. The driver may have left the indicator on by mistake, or may be making another turn beyond the junction. Similarly, a vehicle may turn without using an indicator. Don't rely on indicators alone. Pay attention to the road; whether or not the car is slowing down; and driver behaviour. Assume a hazard until the driver's intentions are clear. School signs and buses with children getting on or off always demand caution. Slow down. Remember that children don't always have good judgement when it comes to road safety.

- Watch the brake lights of vehicles that are well ahead for sudden braking, especially on a fast-moving main road. If you have to stop unexpectedly on the main road, put on your hazard lights to warn traffic behind you.
- When in the overtaking lane on a dual carriageway or motorway, watch for vehicles in the travelling lane that fail to see you and abruptly pull into the overtaking lane.
- On narrow country roads, watch out for pedestrians and cyclists as you go around blind bends, especially to the left. You may have to drive close to the margin on narrow roads, but that's where pedestrians and cyclists will be, and you may have little time to avoid them or stop if you're going too quickly. Therefore, be sure to slow down before you go around blind bends and turns particularly at night time.
- A stopped bus anywhere should alert you to the possibility of people trying to cross the road either in front of or behind the bus. Again, slow down.
- The noise of wind can affect a cyclists' or pedestrians' ability to hear a car coming, especially if the car is coming from downwind (that is, the direction the wind is blowing to). Cyclists may wobble or be blown across the road by a gust of wind, so slow down when approaching cyclists in windy weather.
- Be aware that different vehicles have different performance characteristics. Motorcyclists generally stop more quickly than cars because they have less weight and momentum, *provided* they have good tyres and a dry road. Therefore, don't drive too closely behind a motorbike. However, in wet conditions or on ice, for example, motorbikes typically need more room to stop because with only two wheels on the road, they have less traction than a car. Therefore, assume a motorbike will need more room to stop in these conditions and drive accordingly.
- Adverse weather creates many hazards, some of which you've learned about already. You'll find out more about these in Module 10, 'Risk Management'. Once again, your first response to weather hazards is almost always to slow down.
- Motorcycles can easily travel as fast as cars but they are much less visible, therefore you need to pay particular attention and be alert for their presence, especially in heavy traffic in order to accommodate and facilitate their needs.

QUICK QUIZ

1 The four categories of driving hazards include; static, moving, road and weather hazards.
T ☑ F ☐

2 Anticipating and avoiding driving hazards involves perceiving, identifying and braking suddenly in that order. T ☐ F ☑

3 Slowing down is almost always your best response to a hazard.
T ☑ F ☐

Answers: 1: T, 2: F, 3: T

Without a doubt, you could fill an entire book with example scenarios like these. Fortunately, learning to anticipate and manage hazards is not about memorising examples, but about developing skills.

The SIDE rule and multiple hazards

Aidhmeanna OBJECTIVES 5

Look for, and highlight, the answers to these questions

- What are the four parts of the SIDE rule?
- What should you do when you encounter more than one hazard at the same time?
- What priorities do you generally apply when you encounter more than one hazard at the same time?

As a new driver, you can use the SIDE rule to learn the thinking processes and skills you need to use to drive safely. SIDE stands for:
Scan, Identify, Decide and Execute.

For example, suppose you're driving through a residential area and you see (Scan) a dog dart across the road with its lead hanging from its collar. You conclude (Identify) that it may have escaped from someone who may be chasing it. You determine (Decide) that the best response is to slow down and be extra alert for someone crossing the road ahead. You do this (Execute) by easing off the accelerator and scanning ahead, looking in your mirrors and listening. You're also prepared to stop if someone appears (Decide).

Note that the SIDE rule summarises everything you do during 'control, choose and communicate'. You can let the SIDE rule shape your thinking as you drive and whenever you want to make a manoeuvre. For example, when you want to change lanes, first scan to check where the other traffic is, and then identify any hazards that would prevent you from making the manoeuvre. Next, decide on your best option and finally, execute the manoeuvre if it is safe to do so. You will learn more about putting the SIDE rule into practice during your driving instruction in part two of this course.

S.I.D.E. rule

Scan

Identify

Decide

Execute

Multiple hazards

Driving would be easier if you could count on hazards coming up one at a time, but that's not how it is in reality. Often, you'll have to manage multiple hazards at once. For example, suppose you're approaching a pothole while driving in the rain and you notice a cyclist slipping on mud just ahead. To prepare for a situation like this, you can use the SIDE rule to help you to manage the situation based on your best judgement and experience. Part of your decision-making will be based on how *immediate* a hazard is (what you have to deal with first) and the *consequences* of a hazard (how bad will the outcome be if you hit it). Internalise the following priorities now so they will guide your thinking when you encounter hazards. It's important to internalise them now because you won't have time to sort through them consciously during the split second when you are dealing with a serious problem.

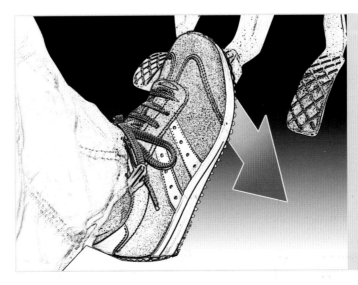

Manage your safety margin by slowing down when needed or when you are unsure and by learning to anticipate and recognise driving hazards

- **Slow down, slow down, slow down.** The more you have to deal with, the more time you need to give yourself. In the above example, you should already be going more slowly than usual because it's raining. Upon seeing the pothole, you should have slowed a bit more.

  You should already have a good safety margin when you see the cyclist, but it's still a good idea to slow down even more. This gives you control as well as time to choose how to respond. The sooner you slow down, the more likely you are to be able to avoid all the hazards and to not have to choose which one to hit.

- **Sacrifice property and animals before endangering people.** If the worst happens, people take priority. If the only way you can avoid hitting the cyclist is to hit the pothole, then hit the pothole and accept that your car will be damaged. Similarly, if a dog runs out in front of you suddenly, try to stop *safely* if you can. But if you have to swerve or stop abruptly, you endanger other motorists and yourself. The best choice, while regrettable, is to hit the dog.

- **Put protected people at risk before unprotected people.**

  You're better prepared to survive a collision protected by your car than are unprotected pedestrians or cyclists. If a person suddenly runs in front of your car and you can't stop, you may need to swerve off the road to avoid them. If the way isn't clear, try to hit something at a glancing blow and try to hit something that gives, rather than something unyielding. Similarly, if you have to choose between a pedestrian and another vehicle, the other vehicle would be the better choice, *provided it is not a head-on collision.* The other vehicle affords its occupants at least some protection.

Don't ignore hazard signs, they are well placed to give advance warning of particular dangers ahead. Slow down in good time

- **Risk few versus many.** In the worst instances, you may need to choose how many people you endanger. For example, if there is a crowded footpath on the left and high-speed oncoming traffic to the right, you can't swerve if a cyclist suddenly falls in front of you. Going either way endangers many people instead of a single cyclist. All you can do is hope you can stop in time. But as a good driver, of course, you would already be driving slowly in this sort of situation, so stopping should be possible.

These are generally useful priorities, but even so the best decisions aren't always clear cut, and you have to use common sense. For example, if you have no other choices, is it worse to hit an unprotected pedestrian or a bus full of children? The answer may depend on how fast you and the bus are going. At 10 km/h, there's probably little risk to the children. At 120 km/h, the risk is unacceptable. Here's an example of how common sense applies to choosing between hazards. The scenario is extreme and unlikely to occur, but makes a clear point: if you're travelling at 2 km/h, it would not make sense to drive off a 100-metre cliff to avoid hitting a pedestrian. The speed is so slow that the risk to the pedestrian is minor, but the fall would probably kill you.

QUICK QUIZ

1 The four parts of the SIDE rule are Scan, Indicate, Determine and Evade. T ☐ F ☑

2 If you encounter more than one hazard at the same time, you should only worry about the most immediate hazard. T ☐ F ☑

3 If you encounter multiple hazards, your priorities are generally to slow down; sacrifice property and animals before endangering people; put protected people at risk before unprotected people and risk few versus many. T ☑ F ☐

Answers: 1: F; 2: F; 3: T

Summary points ⟫⟫⟫⟫⟫

In this module on hazard perception you learned:

1   Perceptual skills are the processes of using your senses to find and gather relevant information from the world around you. You use sight, hearing, touch, balance and smell to perceive the driving environment. The primary sense you use when driving is vision.

2   A driving hazard is anything you need to avoid while driving.

3   You need to develop good hazard-recognition skills to maximise the time you have to respond to a hazard. You use all your senses while driving (except taste).

4   Visual acuity is how well you see. Irish law requires acuity of not less than 0.5 using both eyes. You should be able to read a number plate from a distance of 20 metres and you should have your eyesight checked at least every two years.

5   Field of vision is the broad area you see. Central vision comprises the three degrees or so straight ahead. Peripheral vision comprises the remaining area. Mirrors help you see what's behind you. You should check your mirrors every seven to 10 seconds and before the manoeuvres of moving off, overtaking, changing lanes, slowing down, stopping, speeding up, turning or before anyone exits the vehicle.

6   A blind spot is any area outside the car that you can't readily see from your position while driving. In most vehicles there is a blind spot just behind your field of vision to the left and to the right. Probably the most dangerous blind spot is behind your right shoulder. Check blind spots by turning quickly to look, by leaning forward or by leaning back to see around them. Try to stay out of other drivers' blind spots as much as possible.

7   Objects like signs and trees, and conditions like rain or reflected sunlight, can obstruct your field of vision. If something restricts your view of the road, sort out the problem before continuing.

8   Scanning is looking around regularly and methodically so you know what's in your area, what's approaching you and what you're approaching. It makes driving safer by helping you to anticipate what will happen or what could happen in the next few seconds. You scan by shifting your visual focus regularly, with attention to potential trouble spots. Use your sight, hearing and your sense of smell, balance and touch.

9   Driving hazards include static hazards, moving hazards, road hazards and weather hazards. To anticipate and avoid a hazard, you must perceive the hazard, identify it, anticipate the possible consequences, choose the best way to respond, take action and then monitor and modify your response based on what happens.

10 Perceiving is when your senses detect something and pass the information to your brain. Observing means perceiving something and analysing it.

11 The almost universal response to all hazards is to slow down. Slowing down gives you time and space, and time and space give you a safety margin.

12 The SIDE rule helps you learn the thought process for anticipating and handling hazards. SIDE stands for Scan, Identify, Decide, and Execute.

13 You will encounter multiple hazards at the same time. You must deal with these based on how immediate each hazard is and what the consequences of hitting the hazard would be.

14 When facing multiple hazards, slow down. Sacrifice property and animals before endangering people. Generally, put protected people at risk before those who are unprotected, and risk few versus many, in that order.

MODULE

6

'We are inclined to judge ourselves
by our ideals; others, by their acts'

Harold Nicholson

Evaluation

Introduction

Avoiding hazards requires anticipating and identifying risks and responding appropriately. You learned previously that often you have to use your judgement to determine the best response when faced with multiple hazards. Now you'll learn more about developing your judgement as a driver. In particular, we'll focus on your ability to evaluate risks when choosing a course of action and how to apply good judgement as you interact with other road users.

It takes time and experience to develop good judgement. This course will help you to start thinking in ways that lead to good judgement, but there is no real way to teach judgement. It comes with experience – one of the reasons why it takes about five years to become competent. Fortunately, you can develop good judgement more quickly and reduce your risk during those first five years of driving by learning from and applying what others have already experienced. That's really what driver education is about - helping you to develop and learn from the experience of others without having to make the mistakes yourself.

In this module we will discuss...

- Risk assessment
- What other road users expect of you
- What you should expect of other road users

Risk assessment

Aidhmeanna OBJECTIVES 6

Look for, and highlight, the answers to these questions

- What driving factors should influence your evaluation of risk?
- What personal factors can influence your evaluation of risk?
- How can personal factors cause drivers to underestimate or overestimate risks?
- What are 'safe gap' and 'safe-gap acceptance'?
- How do you evaluate whether or not you have a safe gap?
- What is the one and only factor that you can truly control when driving and why is controlling it the secret to safe, effective driving?

Driving requires that you not only anticipate hazards, but that you also evaluate the level of risk associated with those hazards. Your ability to accurately assess risk directly affects your ability to choose the right response. In addition, you must constantly evaluate risk while driving. Driving and even being a passenger always involves some risk; the only way to avoid all driving risks is to avoid using the road at all, which is obviously not practical. Your goal as a new driver is to learn good judgement when evaluating risks so that you can minimise your chances of having a collision.

Driving requires that you evaluate the level of risk associated with multiple hazards. The only way to completely avoid driving risks is to avoid using the road at all

A child or ball on the road are hazards that you wouldn't want to hit. Hitting the child is not an option

In the last module, you learned that you use perceptual skills to gather available information and that, based on your experience, you use information filtering to sort out what is and isn't relevant. Using the relevant information, you then determine and execute an appropriate course of action. However, not all hazards present the same level of risk and assessing the differences between them is part of the risk-assessment process. For example, a child or ball on the road are hazards that you wouldn't want to hit. If you hit the ball it would be annoying; if you hit the child, it would be devastating.

Coming to this conclusion requires that you use your judgement. In assessing risk, you are doing at least one of two things: (1) you're evaluating the consequence of hitting a hazard, and (2) you're evaluating the probability of hitting a hazard under the circumstances. You probably recognised – without needing to dwell on it – that hitting the child is not an option. This illustrates that you already have a basic foundation for good judgement, which is something you can build on. Not all hazards are as easy to assess, though. We'll now look at some factors that influence how you appraise a hazard, but keep in mind that many other factors come into play; it's impossible to list them all. Also, there will be times when you'll need to deal with several factors at once, and determine the relative significance of each in the circumstances.

Physical structure. When faced with a hazard, its size, weight and strength affect the level of risk. It may be too big to manoeuvre around, such as a stalled lorry that's blocking the entire road. It may be small but unyielding, like a concrete post, or it may be small, light and therefore inconsequential, like the ball.

Distance. The closer the hazard, the more immediate it is and the harder it is to avoid. The sooner you note it, the sooner you can take evasive action. In applying your judgement to this factor, it is useful to figure out what you *would* do if something that is not presently a hazard suddenly becomes one. For example, when you see someone walk toward a junction, you slow down, check that the other lane is clear and think, 'If he steps into the roadway in front of me, I'll brake or

If a pedestrian steps into the roadway in front of you, would you be able to brake or change lanes to avoid them?

Moving hazards give you less time to respond than stationary ones

be able to change lanes to avoid him'. This prepares you to respond if the pedestrian does step onto the road. If you don't consider this until you reach the junction, it would likely be too late to avoid hitting the pedestrian.

Speed reduces the time it takes to reach a stationary hazard. You'll have even less time if the hazard is moving toward you, such as another car, because your speeds effectively combine. As you learned in Module 2, momentum results from speed and weight. The faster you're going and the faster the hazard is moving, the greater the combined momentum and the greater the danger of physical injury or death.

Road conditions directly affect risk evaluation by interfering with your ability to respond to hazards. Reduced visibility, caused by conditions like rain, fog and glare, will prevent you from spotting hazards farther ahead. A wet or icy road will also impair your ability to stop quickly. A hazard that you assess as low-risk in ideal driving conditions may become a serious risk in poor conditions.

Control helps you to deal with a problem. Remember that your priorities, in order, are control, choose and communicate. The less control you have over your vehicle, the greater your exposure to risk. With less control it will be more difficult to avoid a hazard and you will also lack alternatives in dealing with it. Control is also an issue in an unfamiliar vehicle because you won't be sure how well it takes corners or stops, for example. Vehicle control is a risk factor because if you don't have control, other risks that would not otherwise matter can become significant.

Suppose you're approaching a two-way bridge that is too narrow for both cars to cross at the same time. If there is a car on it already you must wait your turn, allowing the car on the other side of the bridge

The less control you have over your vehicle the greater your exposure to risk

When approaching a bridge that is too narrow for two cars to cross at the same time, you must wait your turn. Whichever car reaches the bridge first has priority

to cross before driving onto the bridge yourself. Whichever vehicle reaches the bridge first has priority.

Using your judgement, and what you've just learned, assess the risks in the following scenario. Use a scale of 1 to 10, with 10 representing a serious risk and 1 representing almost no risk.

Driving Factor	Risk (1–10)
The bridge is 100 metres away	
The bridge is 30 metres away	
You are travelling at 50 km/h	
You are travelling at 80 km/h	
You can see if traffic is approaching the bridge from the other side	
You cannot see if traffic is approaching the bridge from the other side	
It is a dry, fine day	
It is raining heavily	
It is raining heavily and it is dark	
You are driving according to your vehicle's capabilities	
You just bought your vehicle and are unsure about its capabilities	
The bridge is 30 metres away, you are travelling at 80 km/h, it is dark, raining heavily and you're unsure about your vehicle's capabilities	

How did you rate each risk? It's likely that you and a friend might not give everything exactly the same score, but you should have similar answers with a consistent trend of high- and low-risk ratings. It is not hard to judge objectively how the driving factors listed earlier influence risk. But when it comes to more complex scenarios like the one above, you'll find that accurate risk assessment requires experience that you can only gain over time.

Unfortunately, assessing risk involves more than driving factors such as speed and control. *You* are also a key factor. Emotions, value judgements, self-image and inexperience are four personal factors that can make your ability to evaluate risk more subjective and less accurate. Personal factors can make a driver under- or overestimate risk by influencing the driver to make choices based on considerations that have nothing to do with driving safely.

Emotions such as anger and frustration can make you a competitive driver. In this frame of mind, you may decide to do something despite a high risk. If you're anxious, you may overestimate risk and become so cautious that when a problem comes up, you freeze and do nothing out of fear you'll do the wrong thing. Being late can cause task fixation and tunnel attention, making you oblivious of risks. If you're feeling euphoric, you may feel invincible. If you've been waiting for a space to enter traffic, impatience may lead you to 'put the boot down' rather than wait any longer. All of these feelings distort your perception of risks, leading to poor judgement and bad decisions.

Time pressures can cause task fixation making you oblivious of risk. Give yourself plenty of time when punctuality is important

Asserting your 'rights' on the road almost always leads to poor decisions. You may have priority, but that doesn't mean you should create a risk when another motorist doesn't give way.

Value judgements. Asserting your 'rights' on the road almost always leads to poor decisions. You may have priority, but that doesn't mean you should create a risk when another motorist accidentally or intentionally refuses to give way. Driving in an unyielding, inflexible manner because you think the other driver ought to be doing something different does not reduce risk. The rules of the road exist to minimise risk and allow traffic to flow smoothly, but you should be accommodating when other drivers don't follow those rules.

Self-image. As you learned in Module 1, peer pressure and the media's glamorisation of reckless driving can lead drivers to make irrational choices. As we've mentioned before, media portrayals, while entertaining, are not realistic. Responding to peer pressure is childish. Nonetheless, you need to remember that at times these influences will be present. You raise your risk

Be careful not to overestimate your driving ability. Remember it takes about five years to reach *average* driving competence

when you allow *what you think others will think about you* to determine what you do when behind the wheel.

Inexperience. To repeat what you've read many times, new drivers require about five years to reach average driving competence. If you believe you're as knowledgeable about driving as you will be in five years, you're increasing your risk. This is because you're not being conservative enough to allow for hazards that you have not yet learned to recognise.

Here are some examples of thoughts that might go through a driver's mind in different driving scenarios. In each, determine what personal factor(s), if any, is or are affecting the driver's exposure to risk.

1   'I'm driving a bright red car which must be visible to everyone. There's no way that cyclist can avoid seeing me.'
   Personal factors _____

2   'There's no need to use my indicator for this lane change because there's no one within a kilometre. Besides, my friends will think I'm an eejit if I do."
   Personal factors _____

3   'That car had better not pull out in front of me or I'll run them off the road. I have priority, so it would serve them right after the way they cut me off a while ago.'
   Personal factors _____

What factors did you assign to each? For number one, you should have cited **inexperience. Self-image** and **inexperience** are the influencing factors for number two. For three, **emotion, value judgements** and **inexperience** are at work. Note that inexperience is a factor in all three scenarios. If you didn't include inexperience for all three, that's not surprising because, as a new driver, you *are* inexperienced.

Inexperience is a factor in all three scenarios because an experienced driver would realise that the assumptions the drivers make in each scenario are wrong. You can't assume the cyclist will see you. Experienced drivers know that people fail to see things all the time. You can't assume that you don't need to use indicators just because you think no one is nearby. Experienced drivers know that it's easy to cut in front of someone you didn't see, perhaps because they're in your blind spot, and that this is the kind of situation in which indicators help the most. You can't assume that someone won't pull in front of you just because you have priority, nor can you assume that that person will be able to avoid a collision after realising their mistake. Experienced drivers know that people fail to give way all the time, and that they often don't even realise they've made a mistake.

How might the following personal factors cause a driver to evaluate risk incorrectly?

Reason to make an under– or overestimation of risk	Under– or overestimation of risk?
Feeling anxious and being unable to determine the distance to a hazard	
Being emotionally upset while driving	
Being angry because the driver behind you is tailgating	
Having to drive at night and feeling scared	
Securing a new job and feeling on top of the world	
Feeling very confident with your driving, having just passed your driving test	
Being late for a job interview	
Showing the driver in the flashy car that your car is better	

Notice that in most cases, personal factors tend to make you underestimate or even disregard risk. Being over cautious is only a problem when it leads to indecision and you end up responding without thought. That is not the same as being cautious and conservative as a reasonable response to conditions, hazards and your lack of experience.

Safe-gap acceptance

When it comes to evaluating risk and using judgement, one of the most important concepts you must learn is the *safe gap*. The safe gap is the minimum acceptable distance between you and any object, whether moving or stationary, that you need to avoid while driving. It has no set length because it varies depending on your

Learning how to judge the safe gap is one of the most important concepts to master

Safe-gap acceptance

Speed of lorry 60 km/h (16.66 metres per sec)
Speed of car 75 km/h (20.83 metres per sec)
Time to complete overtake - 15 seconds
Safe gap required - 490 metres

If you were travelling at 75 km/h and you wanted to overtake a lorry travelling at 60 km/h then you would need a minimum safe gap of 490 metres to safely complete the manoeuvre. You would have to be certain that you could see that at least this distance was clear before you attempted to overtake

490 metres

speed, the speed of the other object, your direction relative to the object, the road conditions – such as traction and visibility – and the minimum amount of room required to avoid a collision. *Safe-gap acceptance* is the minimum safe distance that you should allow based on your evaluation of all these factors.

Certain factors can have a substantial influence on the safe gap. For instance, suppose you're travelling at 75 km/h on a two-lane road and you want to overtake a lorry that's travelling at 60 km/h. (Note that a speed of 75 km/h is equivalent to 20.83 metres per second and 60 km/h is equivalent to 16.66 metres per second.) Allowing for the length of the lorry, the speed at which it is travelling and a safety margin of two seconds between you and the lorry, the overtaking manoeuvre will take approximately 15 seconds. Because your speed is 75km/h, you will travel over 490 metres in that time. This is a sizeable distance and it will increase as the vehicles' speeds increase. You must be able to see that the road ahead is clear for the total distance before you start the overtaking manoeuvre. When the view is obstructed by bends and dips, or for other reasons, it is not safe to overtake.

If another car is coming towards you, the scenario becomes more complicated. Suppose the car is travelling at 60 km/h. The gap between you and the car closes at a rate of 135 km/h or 37.5 metres per second. (Remember, combine the speed of the two cars: 60 km/h + 75 km/h = 135 km/h which is equivalent to 37.5 metres per second.) This means the gap between you and the car is reduced by 562 metres in the 15 seconds your overtaking manoeuvre takes. Now, to that distance, add the 490 metres needed for the manoeuvre: you find that you need to be over one kilometre away from the other car to have enough room to overtake the lorry safely. In general, assuming you want a typical margin for error – or a greater one to allow for inexperience – then you must start the overtaking manoeuvre when the other vehicle is no less than 1,050 metres away. This calculation assumes that the other car is not going any faster than you think, which isn't easy to judge; that it doesn't speed up; and that the lorry doesn't speed up or do anything unexpected. If in doubt, hold back, maintain a safe following distance and wait until a safe overtaking opportunity arises.

You can use mathematics to determine the safe gaps for lots of different situations. You can figure out how quickly you would close the gap with a lorry stopped 300 metres ahead of you, or if you can enter the road and accelerate with a safe gap if a car is 250 metres away and coming toward you at 30 km/h. While the maths is interesting, it's not what you'd do in real life. Even if you're a whiz who can do the numbers in your head, you don't know how fast other cars are going, the actual distances or the changes that will take place as you close the gap. The numbers aren't really useful when you're on the road.

So, the way you learn to judge safe gaps is, once again, through experience. It's common sense that the faster a gap is closing, the larger it has to be before you can move into it or through it safely. Here are the steps experienced drivers use to maintain safe gaps that can help you as you gain experience:

- **Observe before acting.** In many situations, you can watch the traffic and note the gap length before you act. Before trying to overtake, watch how quickly oncoming cars close the distance between you and them. If queuing up at a junction, watch the size of the gap that the cars ahead allow when pulling onto the road. If the oncoming traffic had to brake, then perhaps the gap allowed was too small. If there's no queue, you can take a moment to watch some cars go by to help you better judge the gap.

- **Be patient.** As mentioned earlier, impatience can affect how you assess risk. If you've had to wait at a junction, you may be tempted to reduce your safe gap, especially if you think motorists behind you are impatient. Don't let this happen. If you think you're wasting time behind a slow lorry or getting through a junction, think how much time you'll waste if you have a collision.

- **Go another way.** Your goal is to reach your destination safely, but the shortest distance isn't always the fastest or most efficient. If you can't get onto a road because you're unable to get a sufficient safe gap, try to find an alternative. For example, suppose you can't make a right turn across lanes during heavy traffic without waiting a long time or else having to turn in a gap that's too small, risking a collision. You may save time by going left and then doubling back at the next roundabout or by turning around at some other place.

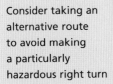

Consider taking an alternative route to avoid making a particularly hazardous right turn

The only factor you can control

Up until now in this module, you've been learning about evaluating risk and some of the factors that affect risk assessment. Realise that there's a difference between *evaluating* and *controlling*. In driving, you don't control most of the factors. Rather, you control *yourself* and behave in a way that minimises the risk that other factors may present. For example, you can't control whether or not it will rain, but you can control whether or not you slow down, use your wipers and increase your safe-gap acceptance. You can't control whether or not another driver will stop at the junction ahead as the sign says, but you can control whether or not you anticipate the possibility that he won't stop and you can be prepared to respond appropriately.

If you learn nothing else in this course, learn this: you can only fully control one factor when you're on the road and that is *yourself*.

There is absolutely nothing else you can fully control – not even your vehicle. Fortunately, controlling yourself is the most important thing you need to control anyway. It is the secret to safe driving because only by controlling yourself can you minimise all the other risks you face on the road. If you fail to control yourself, nothing but good luck and the best intentions of other imperfect people stand between you and misfortune.

Non alcoholic drinks are the only option if you drive your car to a social occasion

When evaluating risk, remember that it begins with you. *You* account for driving factors. *You* do not let personal factors affect your decisions. *You* must drive conservatively and remember to allow for your inexperience. *You* drive co-operatively instead of competitively. *You* abstain from alcohol and drugs before driving. *You* scan and check your blind spots and *you* must keep your car in good working order. Ultimately a clean driving history will be your reward – or a string of collisions and penalty points will be the price you pay. The choice is yours. It's that simple.

QUICK QUIZ

1   Personal factors can cause drivers to under- or overestimate risk by influencing the driver to make choices based on considerations that have nothing to do with driving safely.   T ☑   F ☐

2   The safe gap is the minimum acceptable distance between you and any object you need to avoid while driving. Safe-gap acceptance is the minimum safe distance that you tolerate, based on your evaluation of the driving factors and personal factors in play.   T ☑   F ☐

3   You are the only factor you can truly control while driving.   T ☑   F ☐

Answers: 1: T, 2: T, 3: T

What other road users expect of you

Aidhmeanna
OBJECTIVES **6**   **Look for, and highlight, the answers to these questions**

- Why do various road users perceive situations differently?
- How do other road users expect you to act?
- What are the possible consequences of acting contrary to other road users' expectations?
- What should you do if you realise you have failed to make your intentions clear?
- Why should you be courteous?

In Module 1, you learned that a good driver is co-operative and courteous. You also learned that this isn't simply a matter of being a nice person, but that it's essential for your safety and for moving efficiently through traffic. You probably recall that competitive drivers make the road more dangerous for everyone, and that the only reason that they don't cause more collisions is because other drivers, like you, modify their own driving to compensate for competitive drivers' selfish behaviour. You also learned that because no one is perfect – including you – good drivers try to make their intentions clear and to allow for other road users' mistakes.

Let's return to the concept of co-operative driving as it relates to evaluating hazards and risks. In this section we'll look at what other road users expect from you. In the next section, we'll look at what you should expect from them.

Being co-operative and courteous is essential for everybody's safety and for moving efficiently through traffic

Different users, different perceptions

When it comes to understanding what other road users expect of you, the first thing you need to realise is that different people may perceive the same situation in different ways. It isn't always a matter of the right perception versus the wrong one. Different road users perceive situations in varying ways because they have different points of view with respect to the hazards and the measures they should take to avoid them.

For example, suppose someone drives through a residential area at 20 km/h above the speed limit. Driving conditions are ideal and the road is clear, though narrow. The driver has a full view of the road and the roadside. Here are some possible perceptions of the scenario:

- The driver believes there's nothing wrong with going faster than the speed limit in this case, because he or she can stop the vehicle easily and has full control.
- Pedestrians on the roadside feel that the driver is going too quickly on the narrow road. The wind draft buffets them. They think the driver is inconsiderate.
- A parent with children playing nearby, but well back from the road, perceives the driver as inconsiderate and dangerous. In the parent's mind, the driver has no idea how quickly a child can run unexpectedly onto the road.
- A Garda doesn't care how much control the driver thinks they have, and pulls them over to issue penalty points for exceeding the speed limit.

It is impossible to know exactly how all road users perceive all situations, but if you treat the road as a *shared* resource, you will probably address most people's concerns. Other road users expect you to:

Using and regarding the road as a shared resource is the best way to accommodate the needs of others

- Drive within the law.
- Drive in a way that accommodates their needs.
- Make your intentions known.

Or, to say it another way, *put yourself in their shoes.* Let's look at the previous example again to see what difference this approach can make. This time you're driving, you're within the speed limit and you're thinking about how other road users perceive the situation.

- Although you're within the speed limit, you slow down as you approach the pedestrians. You time it so that the other lane is clear as you pass, which also allows you to move over to give the pedestrians more space.
- You resume a safe speed, but ease off the accelerator again when you see children close to the road.
- The Garda watches you pass, sees no threat and turns his or her attention to the next vehicle.

Do the pedestrians think 'What a courteous driver'? Does the parent think 'It's nice when young drivers know how to drive safely'? Does the Garda note that you're a good driver? Maybe, but probably not. With information filtration, our brains tend to pay less attention to things that happen the way we expect and more attention to things that are unexpected. Others will notice that you're driving safely, but if they don't remember sharing the road with you a bit later, that's usually a good thing. It means you met their expectations. You only stand out when you drive exceptionally well – or if you drive in a manner that's dangerous, selfish and inconsiderate.

Merging and changing lanes become hazardous when drivers fail to understand the intentions and needs of the others

Merging into the traffic flow on a dual carriageway or motorway requires good communication and observation

Consequences

You may be confident about what you intend to do in a given situation, but you must communicate your intentions and meet the expectations of others as you carry out a manoeuvre. This is particularly important when you and the other party both have intentions that would result in a collision if you both carry them out without communicating. One or both of you needs to adjust to avoid this. You can't expect others to accommodate for your needs or mistakes if they have no idea what you're trying to do.

Imagine how you would react, or what the outcome might be, if the following were to happen:

- The driver ahead of you is travelling at 80 km/h when he suddenly realises that he needs to turn left a short distance ahead. Without using the indicator, he brakes hard to make the turn.
- You're on a long stretch of uncongested motorway and are slowly coming up behind another car in your lane. You change lanes to overtake and, as you get close, the car pulls out in front of you without signalling.
- You're travelling at a speed of 60 km/h and are approaching a junction. You noticed a car waiting at the junction from some way off. The driver has passed up large gaps to enter the road, but suddenly pulls out in front of you into a much smaller gap.

In all these scenarios, you will have little or no time to respond. At best, you will be lucky but annoyed. At worst, you will have a collision due to the other driver's failure to meet your expectations. Here are some possible consequences of failing to meet the expectations of other road users:

- **Inconvenience.** If other drivers don't know what you want to do, they can't help you do it. If you want to change lanes, for example, they won't be able to widen the gap to help you move over unless you use your indicator. This means you might miss an exit or junction.
- **Retribution.** Unfortunately, people tend to respond in much the same way that they're being treated. Although it's wrong to respond in this way, realise that people sometimes do. (We'll learn more about this in the next section.) If you do something unexpected or something that is perceived as inconsiderate, others may respond with anger, ranging from blowing the horn to stopping abruptly in front of you. This is especially true when your action forces them to brake or manoeuvre to avoid a collision.
- **Collision.** The worst consequence of not meeting expectations is a collision. It can happen when your behaviour is too sudden or unpredictable for others to accommodate or when another road user doesn't meet your expectations.

If you don't meet the expectations of other road users you are heading for a collision. Make your intentions clear at all times

Check you indicators have cancelled as you may be communicating the wrong message

Indicating that you are about to turn but not completing the manoeuvre may encourage a driver to pull out in front of you

Because your safety rests partly on meeting the expectations of other road users, it's important to consider what you should do when you realise that you have failed to do what other road users were expecting. Consider this scenario: you're overtaking on the outside lane of a dual carriageway when you realise that you need to take the upcoming left turn. You're travelling at 100 km/h, so you take your foot off the accelerator, turn on your indicator and drop your speed to slip in behind the car you were going to overtake. However, the turn is coming up quickly and there's only a small gap to move into. To make the turn, you'd need to pull into this small gap and then brake hard. What should you do?

You should forget about making the turn. You have not adequately communicated your intentions to other drivers. Trying to make the turn will be at best dangerous and annoying and, at worst, cause a severe, multiple-vehicle collision. Instead, drive past the turn, get back into lane safely and then turn around at the next safe opportunity. Yes, it's inconvenient – but wouldn't you rather be inconvenienced than killed?

This is the general rule: if you find that you have failed to make your intentions clear, do what other road users expect you to do, even if it means not doing what you originally planned.

Along with making your intentions clear, you must also ensure that you don't accidentally communicate an intention that you don't plan to carry out. At best, this can be a distraction; at worst, it can lead to a collision.

For example:
- Indicating right when you plan to take the second exit – *i.e.*, the exit directly ahead – off a roundabout.
- Leaving your indicator on after completing a manoeuvre.

- Flashing your hazard lights to thank a motorist for allowing you to pass. This may be mistaken for an emergency signal.
- Flashing your headlights to greet a pedestrian as you pass. This may dazzle or distract other drivers.
- Using your fog lights in wet conditions. This creates a blinding glare on the road.

Courtesy

Someone once said that manners are the oils of society – they help everything run smoothly. That's certainly true on the roads. It only takes a moment to quickly wave 'thanks' when someone accommodates you or to say 'sorry about that' when you make a mistake. Similarly, it's no great inconvenience to let someone take a place in front of you in a long queue, or to give way when it's not clear who has priority. Being courteous has a tangible effect on your safety:

- Showing courtesy is often connected to communicating your intentions.
- Courtesy breeds courtesy. By being courteous, you're encouraging those around you to behave in the same way, which means more drivers will try to accommodate each other. That adds up to safer driving and more efficient traffic flow.
- Courtesy dispels anger. When you make a mistake that inconveniences another driver, a wave that says 'sorry' may calm someone who might otherwise become angry.
- Courtesy helps to keep your emotions in balance. Psychologists tell us that emotions can shape behaviours, but that behaviours can also shape emotions. It's hard to be angry or deeply upset and be courteous at the same time. If you commit to being courteous – especially when you don't feel like it – it helps to keep any distracting emotions under control.

Courtesy breeds courtesy. By being courteous, you're encouraging those around you to behave in the same way, which means more drivers will try to accommodate each other

When you think about it, you can't call yourself a co-operative driver unless you're also a courteous driver. Here's a word of caution regarding courtesy, however: when saying 'thanks' or 'sorry' – or anything else – be brief and don't communicate in a way that could be confusing or cause a distraction.

Contrary to the rules of the road, you will find that many drivers follow an unofficial etiquette that includes a quick flash of the hazard lights to say 'thank you' or a momentary flash of headlights to allow another driver to enter a lane in front of them. Always be cautious if using your lights in this way because the message may be misinterpreted.

QUICK QUIZ

1 Various road users perceive situations differently because they have different points of view with respect to the hazards and the measures they should take to avoid them.
T ☑ F ☐

2 Retribution and collision are two possible consequences of acting contrary to another road user's expectations. T ☑ F ☐

3 If you realise you have failed to make your intentions clear to other drivers, you should go ahead anyway because you've already committed to a manoeuvre. T ☐ F ☑

Answers: 1: T, 2: T, 3: F

What you should expect of other road users

Aidhmeanna 6 **OBJECTIVES** ▶ Look for, and highlight, the answers to these questions

- What expectations should you have of other road users?
- What is 'attribution bias'?
- How can attribution bias lead to bad driving decisions?
- What's wrong with blaming the road or other drivers for collisions, close calls and other unfortunate situations you experience while driving?

In the last section, you learned that much of your safety while driving depends on meeting the expectations of other drivers. It's important that you let them know your intentions so that they can adjust accordingly. They have the same obligation to you and to other road users. You might think, then, that you can expect other drivers to drive according to the law, to reasonably accommodate your needs and intentions, and to always let you know what their intentions are. Unfortunately, you can't count on it.

Before you say that this is unfair, stop and think. What is the only factor you can truly control on the road? It's yourself. Relying on other road users to do what they're supposed to do means relying on something you can't control. You can *hope* they will do the right thing, and we can be thankful that most drivers do, most of the time. But as a good driver, you must allow for the unpredictable nature of other road users' actions. While you can't control what they do, you can prepare for the unexpected. Here are some common situations similar to those you will encounter every day on the road:

- In an urban area, a pedestrian suddenly steps out in front of your car.
- A cyclist or motorist goes through a roundabout but fails to indicate which exit they intend to take or indicates incorrectly.
- A bus driver pulls out from a bus stop without indicating.
- A lorry is parked on the hard shoulder near a petrol station, blocking your view as you attempt to enter the road.
- Someone drives very close behind you while talking on a mobile phone, completely unaware that they're tailgating.
- A driver indicates before an upcoming junction but drives past the junction without turning.
- A driver approaches an upcoming junction without indicating and turns anyway.

You need to control how you react to the behaviour of other road users. This is important because it allows you to remain level headed rather than get angry or frustrated

This isn't to say that you face chaos on the roads. Generally most people drive safely and predictably; if they didn't, safe driving would be impossible. Even so, so you should never take it for granted. Remember, always maintain a safety margin because it gives you time to respond to the unexpected.

Attribution bias

Besides being prepared for the unexpected, you also need to control how you react to what other road users do. This is important because it allows you to remain level-headed rather than get angry or frustrated. It also keeps you from making the wrong decision based on incorrect conclusions.

Attribution bias is the term for our tendency to explain a person's behaviour based on our assumptions about that person. If your assumptions are wrong, then it's likely you will also be wrong about what's motivating someone. Attribution bias tends to be negative and critical, leading to emotions like anger and frustration.

Let's look at an example. You're stopped at a traffic light and there is no crossing traffic. Suddenly a sports car pulls out from behind you and dashes through the junction, even though the light is still red. It pulls away at high speed. What goes through your mind?

- 'What an inconsiderate and dangerous driver.'
- 'Anyone who drives a car like that is obviously a total idiot.'
- 'There is absolutely no justification for such behaviour.'

You feel angry and resentful. After all, you're a considerate driver who stays within the law, and it's annoying and dangerous when others don't do the same. The light changes and you proceed. A few kilometres up the road, there's the same car stopped with a flat tyre. 'Serves them right,' you think. Still angry, you're inclined to pass and let them stay stuck for a while, but the driver waves at you to stop. 'Please help!' the driver shouts. 'I need to get my baby to the hospital!' Without waiting for an answer, the driver opens your passenger door and jumps in, carrying an infant who is obviously very ill.

Does this change your perspective? Of course, there are better ways to drive in such an emergency, but this isn't some inconsiderate person who thinks they own the road. It's a desperate person with a completely different motivation than you assumed – trying to save a child. Most of the time your assumptions in this situation might be right – there are plenty of reckless drivers out there – but in this case attribution bias would have led you to the wrong conclusions. As a result, you would be angry, resentful and reluctant to stop and help.

Attribution bias doesn't always occur in such dramatic circumstances. Suppose you are driving too close to a vehicle whose driver keeps putting on the brakes to cope with the bends on a winding road. As a result, you have to use your brakes a lot, which makes you angry and frustrated. You might think that the driver ahead is entirely at fault rather than acknowledge a problem with your own driving. If you dropped back a little and stopped tailgating, your driving would be much more relaxed, in control and safe.

The point is that it's best to accept that you do not know why another driver does something unlawful, unexpected, unsafe or inconsiderate on the road. Remember that you can't control them but you can control yourself. By giving other road users the benefit of the doubt, you're much less likely to let negative emotions affect your decisions. This will make you a safer driver.

I'm not sure why this lorry is moving so slowly. Before I do anything, I'm going to wait until I can be sure there's nothing in front of it

Let's look at an example of the different ways of thinking:

Situation: Another driver tailgates you on a rural road, even though you're travelling at the speed limit.

Attribution-biased thinking: 'What an idiot! I'm going at the speed limit. They can just wait.'

Possible results: The other driver might try to get revenge due to frustration and anger. There might be a collision if you stop suddenly, or a three-car collision if the other car crashes while making a dangerous manoeuvre such as overtaking.

Sensible thinking: 'I'm not sure why that car is on my tail. Maybe they have a good reason, or maybe they don't, but the safe thing to do is get out of the way.'

Result: You allow the driver to overtake at the first safe opportunity and remove the hazard of having him or her follow you too closely.

Another problem with attribution bias is that it can lead you to make poor judgements about road conditions or hazards. Suppose you're driving on a main road and the car ahead of you slows down suddenly for no apparent reason. The prudent response is for you to slow down too, because that driver has probably spotted a road hazard beyond your view.

If you see that the driver is elderly, however, attribution bias may lead you to assume that he or she slowed down because you believe that all older drivers like to drive slowly. Based on this assumption, rather than slowing down, you might overtake, only to find yourself going at full speed toward a road hazard. When you think rationally, however, you disregard the driver's age and evaluate every driving situation on its own terms.

Here's an example of the difference:

Situation: A lorry is travelling at 20 km/h below the speed limit, blocking your way on a two-lane road.

Attribution-biased thinking: 'This lorry is driving slowly because it's big and loaded. Fortunately, I can easily overtake.'

Possible results: There may be a collision as you try to overtake and find that the lorry is going slowly because there's a queue of slow-moving cars ahead, leaving you no place to pull back in.

Sensible thinking: 'I'm not sure why this lorry is moving so slowly. Before I do anything, I'm going to wait until I can be sure there's nothing in front of it. Travelling at 20 km/h below the limit might make me late, but it's not as inconvenient as having a collision.'

Result: You confirm that the way is clear in front of the lorry before overtaking safely, or you discover that it isn't clear and wait until it is.

To ensure that attribution bias doesn't lead you to make bad choices, make a habit of giving other road users the benefit of the doubt. Until you find out exactly what's going on, always assume that you don't know the whole story.

The problem with blame

Attribution bias and being annoyed when other road users don't do what you expect both lead to negative thinking and blame. You begin to blame collisions, near misses and other incidents on other road users. From there, it's easy to blame the wet road conditions, the car manufacturer's bad design, the faulty tyre tread or the sun on the windscreen. It's easy to blame everyone and everything but yourself.

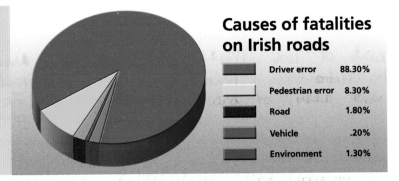

Recently published figures from an Garda Síochána show that human error is by far the greatest cause of fatalities on Irish roads

Causes of fatalities on Irish roads

Driver error	88.30%
Pedestrian error	8.30%
Road	1.80%
Vehicle	.20%
Environment	1.30%

Blame has no place in driving, and the research proves it. The Garda Síochána statistics show that 88.3% of road fatalities result directly from the actions or inactions of drivers. Errors made by pedestrians account for 8.3%. Only 1.8% of the fatalities can be reasonably blamed on the road, 1.3% on the environment and only 0.2% on the vehicle. This demonstrates that driver behaviour needs to change, and that human error is the primary cause of collisions and fatalities.

You may have noticed that this course doesn't use the word 'accident'. Back in Module 1, we described how accidents are the *statistically inevitable* outcomes of poor driving behaviours. Often the media call them 'accidents', but that implies randomness and infers that the incident was unavoidable. In truth, most so-called 'accidents' are a fairly predictable consequence of human behaviour.

The problem with blaming the road or other drivers for collisions, close calls or any other incident you experience while driving is this: it takes your focus off the only thing you can truly control – yourself. You have to accept responsibility for your safety on the road. When you blame other people or things, you're looking to external factors for safety – things you can't control. That's why you must not fall into the blame game.

As you read earlier, your driving history will be either be a credit to you or an embarrassment. It's wrong to suggest that a good driver would never have an unavoidable collision, but it is reasonable to say it would be exceedingly rare. You can drive safely with few if any incidents for decades by controlling yourself.

QUICK QUIZ

1   You should be reserved in your expectations of other road users and always be prepared for the unexpected.   T ☑   F ☐

2   Attribution bias means using observations and logic to determine what motivates someone to do something.   T ☐   F ☑

3   You should blame the road and other drivers for collisions, close calls and other incidents you experience while driving, otherwise the Gardaí will automatically assume it is your fault in the event of a crash.   T ☐   F ☑

Answers: 1: T, 2: F, 3: F

Summary points >>>>>>>>>

In this module on evaluation you learned:

1. The physical structure of a hazard, your distance from it, your speed, the road conditions and the control you have over your vehicle all influence your evaluation of risk.

2. Personal factors can lead you to over- or underestimate risk. These include emotions, value judgements, self-image and inexperience. Most of the time they cause you to underestimate risk.

3. The 'safe gap' is the minimum acceptable distance between you and any object that you need to avoid while driving. 'Safe-gap acceptance' is the minimum safe gap that you allow based on your evaluation of all the factors in the circumstances.

4. You learn to judge safe gaps through experience, by observing before acting and by being patient. Finding another route may be an alternative to waiting for a safe gap.

5. The only factor you can control on the road is yourself.

6. Various road users perceive situations differently because they have different points of view with respect to the hazards and the actions they need to take to avoid them. Other road users expect you to drive according to the law, to reasonably accommodate their needs and intentions, and to make your own intentions known.

7. Failing to meet the expectations of other road users can lead to inconvenience, retribution and collisions. If you discover you have failed to make your intentions clear, do what other road users would reasonably expect you to do, even if it's not what you originally planned.

8. Being courteous on the road means communicating your intentions. Courtesy also encourages others to be courteous, helps dispel anger and helps keep your emotions in balance.

9   You should be conservative in your expectations of other road users.
     Maintain a safety margin and expect the unexpected.

10   Attribution bias is the term for our tendency to explain a person's behaviour
     based on our assumptions about that person. It tends to be negative and critical,
     leading to negative emotions that can affect your driving. Attribution bias can
     also lead you to make wrong judgements about road conditions or hazards.

11   Blame has no place in driving. The vast majority of fatalities result from poor
     driving decisions. Blame takes your focus off the only thing you can truly
     control – yourself. Accept responsibility for your safety on the road.

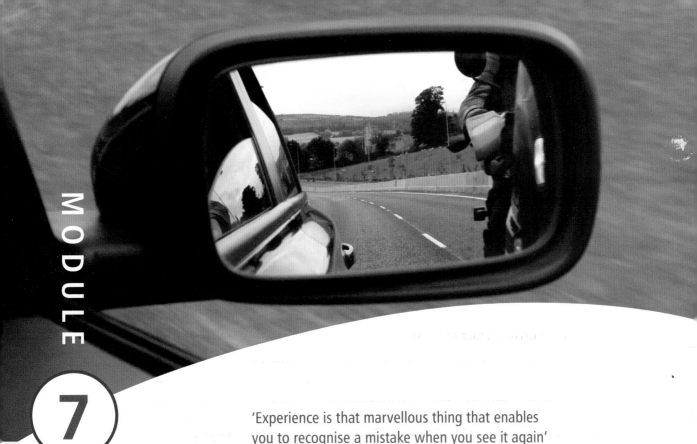

7

'Experience is that marvellous thing that enables
you to recognise a mistake when you see it again'

Franklin P. Jones

Making decisions

Introduction

Drivers who learn how to operate a vehicle but who never become good decision makers are likely to be over confident and end up as part of crash statistics. You've read repeatedly that it takes time and experience – typically five years – to reach average driving competence. The majority of this time is needed to learn how to make good decisions.

You have already learned about making certain choices, what sort of attitude you should have and how to handle emotions that can lead you to make bad decisions. This module takes you further into the decision-making process and the choices you must make as a driver, both before facing a hazard and when one arises.

In this module, you'll start by looking inward and examining your values and attitudes about risk taking, and how you may need to change your attitude if you intend to drive well. Then you'll learn about your thought process when measuring the benefits and risks of a decision. Finally, you'll see how to apply these concepts while driving.

In this module we will discuss...

- Risk acceptance

- Benefit-to-risk and response selection
- Review, retry and abort

Risk assessment

Aidhmeanna **OBJECTIVES** **7** > **Look for, and highlight, the answers to these questions**

- What is 'risk acceptance'?
- Why is judging personal risk-acceptance level important to you as a driver?
- How do you judge your personal risk-acceptance level?
- What factors can raise risk acceptance while driving?
- What *illusory* benefits can influence risk acceptance?
- How can your risk acceptance be raised or lowered by your way of thinking?
- What situations justify deliberately taking risks?
- Why is your personal risk acceptance while driving not a choice you can freely make?

Driving involves risk. The only way to avoid all driving risk is to stay off the road. You obviously believe that the risk is acceptable or you would not be taking this course. This means that you generally consider the risks to be within your *risk acceptance* – that is, within the risk levels that you are prepared to tolerate.

While you consider driving within your risk acceptance, you may have different levels of risk acceptance to other drivers. Two centimetres of snow on the road may be within the risk acceptance of an experienced driver who's used to a cold climate with long winters, but it will be an intolerable risk for someone from a tropical climate who has no experience of driving in snow. In this case, the drivers' different risk tolerances are based on an honest assessment of their own skills and experience.

Being aware of your own risk acceptance is a matter of being honest with yourself. Do you take more or less risks than others?

Being able to judge your personal risk acceptance is important because it will influence the decisions you make when driving – and how you'll make them. It is also important because inappropriate influences may raise your risk tolerance, leading you to accept risks that you shouldn't which results in poor decision making on the road. Your decisions determine how much risk you face when you drive.

This leads to the question, 'How do I know my risk-acceptance level?' In general terms, it's not always an easy question to answer, partly because the answer is subjective and partly because most people's risk-acceptance level tends to depend on the activity in question. In fact, risk acceptance *should* vary when you recognise that the relationship between risks and benefits differs significantly in different situations.

For example, you might have a high risk acceptance for paragliding, rock climbing or another adventure sport, but a low risk acceptance on the road. This makes sense because adventure sports tend to mitigate risk through highly specialised training. Also, participants accept the risks because they're inherent in the sport – and in any case, the risk applies only to the person who chooses to participate and accept the risk. By contrast, there are no *real* benefits to high risk acceptance while driving, driving in a high-risk manner endangers others who have not chosen to accept the same risk level that you have.

Determining your own risk acceptance is primarily a matter of awareness and being honest with yourself.

Adventure sports tend to mitigate risk through specialised training, usually the risk applies only to the participant who chooses to accept the risk

- Start by evaluating your attitudes to risks in general. Do you take more or less risks than most people?

- Are you willing to accept some risks but not others? Consider the risk of personal injury, financial loss or humiliation. This can help you understand how a high risk acceptance can be inappropriate while driving. If you have a high risk acceptance for personal injury and a low one for social risk, you might be more likely to make a dangerous manoeuvre to avoid embarrassment.

- Are you able to weigh risks separately according to activity? It's great if you can, because part of being mature is being able to judge when it is and when it isn't appropriate to accept a risk, as the previous example of paragliding versus driving shows.

- Are you conscious of how much you know about risks or how much you need to learn about them? One reason young people figure so highly in collision and fatality statistics is that they make poor driving decisions because they fail to recognise or fully appreciate the risks. They have a high risk acceptance simply because they don't *understand* the risks involved in driving.

Drive at the appropriate speed, as slow as conditions require and well within the speed limit

Now, in relation to driving alone, ask yourself how closely the following statements represent how you feel or what you do:

1 'I drive at the appropriate speed, which is either as slow as conditions require or at the speed limit – whichever is less.'

2 'I keep my car in first gear at red lights so that I can be first to get away when the light changes.'

3 Overtaking a slow-moving car on a two-lane carriageway requires an adequate view of the other lane and what's ahead of the slower car. Otherwise, I should be patient.

4 'A pint or two doesn't affect me. It won't affect my driving either.'

5 There's nothing wrong with slowing down when you're uncertain about a hazard ahead or a change in conditions.

6 People judge my social status by the car I drive and by how I drive it.

7 'My driving doesn't change even when there's a Garda behind me.'

8 It's OK to use my mobile phone while driving if the road's not busy.

9 'I always pull over when I need to read a map.'

10 'I drive at the appropriate speed, which is not necessarily as slow as the speed limit.'

Be honest with yourself. Which statements are close to your thinking and behaviours, and which are not? If your thinking is like the statements with odd numbers, then your risk acceptance for driving is about right. If you think along the lines of the statements with even numbers, however, then your risk acceptance is probably too high. In that case, *lower it*. Your level of risk acceptance is not fixed. It is a *choice*. Remember, the only factor you can truly control is yourself. Just being aware of your risk acceptance will help you to change it.

Novice drivers do not yet have the necessary experience to recognise and access all hazards

Unless you decide to keep your level of risk acceptance in check, you'll be vulnerable to factors that can lead you to accept even greater risks:

- Competition – such as having a faster car or wanting to be a 'thrilling' and more daring driver.
- Inexperience. The less experience you have, the less skilled you are in recognising and assessing hazards.
- Youth. This is associated with less experience, and younger people generally tend to have a high risk acceptance.
- Peer pressure.
- Anger – like doing something to 'get even' with another motorist.
- Thrill seeking – for example, enjoying the adrenaline rush from a dangerous manoeuvre.

You may admire Formula One but don't imagine yourself as a racing driver when you take to the road

- Fantasy – such as imagining you're a racing driver.
- Time pressure – for example, when you're late for an appointment or work.
- Habit. When you keep getting away with a risky driving behaviour, you no longer perceive the risk.
- False sense of security. This means believing – wrongly – that something offers you complete protection from risk, such as an airbag.

Again, you have a choice. For example, even though younger people have a higher risk acceptance in general, there are many young people with the appropriate level of risk acceptance who display good driving to match.

Illusory benefits

People wouldn't do risky things if they didn't think they benefitted in some way – and some risks *do* confer real benefits. For example, driving is only possible if you accept some level of risk. Adventure sports involve greater percieved risks than driving, but the rewards are excitement and fun. Starting a business or speculating in the stock market risks money and time, but it can be lucrative if it works out. You cannot succeed in life without taking risks.

Speculating in the Stock Market, risks money but it can be lucrative if it works out. You're headed for trouble, though, when you start taking risks because you perceive benefits that are not real

You're headed for trouble, though, when you start taking risks because you perceive benefits that are not real. We call these *illusory* benefits – that is, driving behaviours that seem beneficial but actually are not. Here's a list of some of the illusory benefits of high risk acceptance while driving – along with a dose of reality to help you avoid falling for them.

Illusory benefit: 'Showy' driving impresses people – especially your friends.
Reality: No, it doesn't. Does it really impress you? Some people may say they're impressed, but those lacking maturity frequently say what they think they're supposed to say instead of what they really believe. Pay attention to whom your friends pick when they want a lift, especially your female friends, who are generally more cautious. The 'showy' drivers who take unnecessary risks are seldom the popular choices.

Illusory benefit: Imagining that not being conservative while driving shows that you're confident behind the wheel and capable of taking care of yourself or thinking that it's a mark of maturity.

Reality: Not being conservative while driving shows you have poor discretion or a lack self-discipline – or both. It says you're more concerned with what others may think than you are with thinking for yourself and driving safely. It's actually a mark of immaturity.

For the sake of a few minutes gain... how many lives are you prepared to risk?

Illusory benefit: Driving in a competitive manner saves time because you get ahead of the slow people.

Reality: Competitive driving seldom saves you much time; in the long run, it wastes time. In heavy traffic, you will not save more than a few minutes by trying to beat the normal traffic flow. In exchange for just a few minutes at best, you substantially increase your own and other drivers' exposure to risk. Often, you increase the risk but don't save time at all. Exceeding the speed limit on a motorway may save time if you maintain the higher speed on a journey that's hours long, but consider this: if you get stopped and fined, you will waste more time than you saved when you count the time spent in court and the time needed to earn the money to pay the fine. Competitive drivers also tend to start and stop more aggressively, so they spend more money and time on brake maintenance and petrol. Co-operative drivers save the most time overall.

Illusory benefit: Competitive driving is exciting.

Reality: It can be, right up to the moment when it becomes terrifying, expensive and/or tragic. If you enjoy competitive driving, that's fine – but take a rally driver's course and keep your racing on the track, where it belongs.

Taking a rally driver's course is a good way of keeping your racing on the track where it belongs

Why do people still believe that these illusory benefits are real? The ideas are kept alive by a combination of social convention, media representation, peer pressure and a failure to give them any serious thought. *You* can now choose to be among the drivers who realise that these perceived benefits are an illusion.

While reading the scenarios above, you may have noticed a conspicuous difference between the thought processes that cause you to lower your risk tolerance and those that cause you to raise your risk acceptance while driving. *Rational* thinking tends to lower your risk acceptance while *emotional* thinking tends to raise your risk tolerance. Research shows that good drivers are rational and not emotional while behind the wheel.

When to take risks

You recall from Module 5 that when you have to deal with multiple hazards, there may be circumstances in which it is difficult to avoid a collision. Even though you're driving conservatively and maintaining an ample safety margin, you may have to take a risk to avoid doing something even more dangerous. Here are some examples:

To avoid one risk you may have to expose yourself to other risks

- A child suddenly falls off their bicycle in front of you. You can't stop, so you swerve into the other lane.
- You come around a blind corner. Even though you had slowed down because you could not see clearly, you are surprised to discover a lorry coming toward you in your lane. You must swerve off the road onto the hard shoulder to avoid a head-on collision.

As you would expect, good driving habits reduce the chances of situations like these becoming even more serious. Also, if you're in the habit of scanning, you'll have a better sense of your alternatives. You don't really have time to think when these things happen so, the sharper your awareness of the road, the more likely you are to pick the manoeuvre with the least severe consequences.

Not your choice alone

In many situations, your risk acceptance is your choice. If you want to take up an adventure sport like snowboarding, rock climbing or scuba diving, then your decision to accept the risks involved primarily affects you. The right to accept risks is important to human progress and to having challenging and rewarding purposes in life.

Follow someone too closely exposes them to unreasonable added risk

You *do not*, however, have the right to expose others to risk without their consent. Yet that's exactly what a bad driver does by driving in a high-risk manner. If you follow someone too closely, you expose them to added risk without their consent. If you're walking on the side of the road and someone drives by very close to you or at a high speed, that person has put you at risk without your permission. When someone drives competitively and without caution, that person raises the risk for every road user around them. Don't be that driver.

QUICK QUIZ

1 Emotional thinking often increases your risk acceptance whereas rational thinking decreases your risk acceptance. T ☑ F ☐

2 There are no situations that justify deliberately taking risks. T ☐ F ☑

3 You cannot freely choose a high risk acceptance while driving because you will expose other road users to an increased risk without their consent. T ☑ F ☐

Answers: 1: T, 2: F, 3: T

Benefit-to-risk and response selection

Aidhmeanna OBJECTIVES 7

Look for, and highlight, the answers to these questions

- What is a 'benefit-to-risk assessment'?
- How do you use benefit-to-risk assessments to make appropriate decisions?
- How do you prepare yourself to choose the best response in an emergency?
- Why is indecision often worse than a bad decision?

Even though you maintain a low risk acceptance when driving, you still face risks. As you've seen in numerous examples so far, you constantly make decisions based on both the risks and benefits while you're driving. The process of evaluating risk and benefit is called a *benefit-to-risk assessment*. Applying common sense, you realise that the greater the benefit and the lower the risk, the more likely it is that your decision is a good choice. On the other hand, the greater the risk and the lower the benefit, the more likely it is that the decision is a bad choice. Using your indicators is an example of a good choice, whereas running a red light is an example of a bad one.

Low-benefit, low-risk decisions tend to be easy choices. In the context of driving, this may mean something simple like deciding to turn on the radio. In contrast, high-risk, high-benefit decisions are the most difficult. These often arise in emergency situations – for example, driving an injured person to hospital during a storm.

You make benefit-to-risk assessments constantly while driving. When you spot a hazard, you sort through your options, weigh the risks and benefits and then choose the best option. Fortunately, the majority of driving decisions don't require a lot of thought because the benefits and risks are fairly clear. *Often, the primary benefit of a decision is avoiding the risks associated with an alternative decision.* For example, suppose you're approaching a red traffic signal. Here are some possible benefit-to-risk assessments.

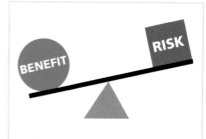

The greater the benefit and the lower the risk, the more likely the decision is a good one

Running a red light may benefit you by saving a little time, but you risk: collision, fines and an increased stress

- Running a red light: The benefit is that you might save a little time. The risks are a high probability of collision, being fined and increased stress levels.
- Stopping and waiting for the light to change: The benefit is that you'll avoid a collision or other negative consequences. The risk is losing a small amount of time.

In a situation like this, you don't even think about the benefit-to-risk assessment. That's because you make many of these assessments long before you need them. You know from your training that obeying traffic regulations is the better benefit-to-risk choice. You didn't even think about running the red light because you had long decided not to break the law intentionally.

Still, when you're on the road, you'll face decisions that you had not considered before. You use the benefit-to-risk assessment to guide your driving decisions by applying the principles in unfamiliar situations. The greater your safety margin, the more time you'll have to respond – which means you're more likely to reach the best decision.

For example, suppose you're on a two-lane rural road and you spot a horse and rider about 50 metres ahead. Choose from these options:

- Slow down as you approach and pass by with care.
- Maintain your speed and assume the horse and rider will move onto the verge.

- Blow your horn to warn the rider to get out of the way.
- Pull over to the side and wait for the road to clear.
- Drive toward the horse, brake suddenly and then swerve quickly to overtake.

When approaching a horse and rider, slow down and only pass when it is safe to do so

Even though you may never have been in this situation or thought about it before, you probably picked the first option without much conscious thought. It is low-risk and high-benefit – that is, you avoid the hazard without much delay. The second, third and fifth options are high-risk and low-benefit. In all three options, the only benefit is saving a little time – a few seconds. The fourth option lowers the risk compared to the first, but with a considerable waste of time. Since the risk in the first option is low and you also avoid the hazard, it has the best benefit-to-risk assessment.

Here are some pointers for using benefit-to-risk assessments to make the right decisions:

- Apply what you learn in this course. Safe-driving principles are based on data from hundreds of thousands of good and bad benefit-to-risk assessments that other drivers have made in the past.
- Beware of illusory benefits. Perceiving a benefit that isn't real tilts the 'scale' when you make assessments. Use logic rather than your emotions.
- Maintain your safety margin to maximise the time you have to make benefit-to-risk assessments in the face of multiple options.

Responding in an emergency

The choices you make while driving usually aren't difficult. With good driving habits, such as maintaining your safety margin, scanning and not allowing distractions, you'll have the time, space and information you need to determine the best response in most situations. Experience will back you up even more, so that over time it becomes still less likely for anything to take you by surprise.

While good driving habits will help you fare better in a hazardous situation, there are circumstances in which you may have very little response time through no fault of your own.

There is no way to tell you how to choose the best response in an emergency because you won't have to time to think about it. You'll simply do whatever you can. But there is a lot you can do before you face an emergency so that doing 'whatever you can' is a good, reasonable choice. It all boils down to one important principle: **develop and maintain good driving habits.** This is crucial because *in an emergency, you will fall back on your habits and they will determine your response.* Consider these examples:

Even the best of drivers can get caught out by unforeseen events!

- If you're in the habit of easing off the accelerator and slowing down when you spot a potential problem, you will do the same automatically when an emergency occurs.
- If you're in the habit of constantly scanning and being aware of your surroundings, you will know where you could move to in an emergency – and you'll be able to go there.
- If you're in the habit of braking carefully when road conditions are poor, you will automatically do the same in an emergency.
- If you're a conservative driver who's in the habit of following the rules, then you will already have the necessary safety margin and ability to manage risks at the moment you most need them – in an emergency.

Develop and maintain good driving habits because in an emergency you will fall back on your habits and they will determine your response.

Indecision can be a very expensive lesson

You can't decide to change how you drive in the middle of an emergency. You must decide long before you ever face one. And here's the irony: a competitive driver is not only *more likely* to face an emergency due to poor driving habits, but is also *less likely* to be able to handle the emergency well, for the very same reason. No one can guarantee that good habits will protect you from every eventuality on the road. But you can guarantee that you will minimise the probability of facing an emergency and that you'll handle it well should an emergency arise.

Indecision

Whether you're facing an emergency, assessing a hazard or just driving normally, indecision is probably the worst offence. Indecision is usually worse than a poor decision because it means you fail to communicate your intentions (which can cause the problem in the first place). If you're indecisive in an emergency, you do nothing to help the situation.

With a poor decision, you've at least done *something* to reduce the effects of the hazard or emergency. While it's possible that a poor decision could make things worse, *no* decision is generally more likely to lead to the worst possible outcome. With any decision, you may be able to modify your response, so at least doing *something* gives you a starting place.

Remember the priorities of 'control, choice and communication'? You learned this so that you will act. Indecision isn't a result of choosing not to decide – it stems from being paralysed by fear because you don't know what to do. With 'control, choise and communicate', you know what to do: first control your vehicle, next think about options, and then communicate your intentions. Keeping these simple priorities in mind means you're less likely to freeze in an emergency.

Review, retry and abort

Aidhmeanna OBJECTIVES **7**

Look for, and highlight, the answers to these questions

- Why is it a good idea to have a second option after you make a decision in driving and why is this not always possible?
- What does it mean to 'review and retry'?
- How do you prepare to review and retry in an emergency?
- How does it benefit you to think through other possibilities after you've dealt with a hazard?
- In what situations would abort options be particularly useful?

Review and retry

Driving is like everything else in life in that your first decision won't always turn out to be the best one. If that happens, you need to be prepared to try something else. It's a good idea to have an alternative in mind when you make a decision because you won't always have enough time to come up with another idea should your first choice fail. Let's go back to the concept of benefit-risk assessment and the example of the horse and rider 50 metres ahead to see how this works.

The best option is to slow down and carefully pass the cyclist. It's likely that you'll be able to drive on without a problem. But suppose the cyclist swerves out suddenly to avoid a pot hole. If there's no traffic coming the other way and you can see a reasonable distance, you could respond by driving into the other lane to make a wide pass. If traffic is approaching, you might decide to slow down even more or stop if necessary.

Unfortunately, you don't always have time to come up with a second option in this way – particularly in an emergency. This is because there's no time to think of one. Having good habits makes all the difference because in circumstances where you only get one chance to solve a problem, you need to be able make the right decision immediately.

Whatever the hazard you don't always have time to come up with a second option

However, in some emergency situations there may be time to come up with a second option if you don't blindly stick with your first choice. The most typical example of this is an emergency stop from high speed. As you brake hard, the distance closes and you pay close attention to the rate at which you are slowing and how fast you're closing the distance to the hazard ahead. If it looks like you're not going to be able to stop in time, you must maintain control and make another choice. Check what's on either side of you – you may have to choose to go off the road or into the other lane. You may even have to decide that a collision is the best choice because there are pedestrians on either side of the road, for example – but you are at least making a choice.

You prepare yourself for emergency situations by mentally rehearsing options that you may apply should the need arise

The process of evaluating your decisions and trying new ones if they don't seem to be working is called *review and retry*. With experience and training, review and retry becomes automatic.

For instance, suppose you hit an ice patch and your car goes into a skid. You respond incorrectly by gently braking and steering in the direction of the skid. It turns out you have even less traction than you thought and you begin to skid even more as you tap the brakes. In this brief instance, you'll be able to review the situation. Your second response is to continue steering, but to take your feet off both pedals so that you regain control and slow down. That's the 'retry' – trying out your second response.

You prepare yourself for these situations by mentally rehearsing options that you may apply should the need arise. Sometimes you encounter a hazard and deal with it, but later you realise that your response would have failed or needed modification if any number of things had changed. Even though you've already dealt with the problem, think through the possibilities and the appropriate responses. Once you do this mental rehearsal, you'll be ready to respond more easily and quickly if the situation ever comes up again.

Abort

In many situations, a good alternative is to abort the attempt to manoeuvre. This is particularly useful when you run into trouble during a standard manoeuvre such as overtaking. For example, suppose you're preparing to overtake a slow-moving lorry. You check your mirrors, move out a little to check that the way is clear, and proceed into the other lane to begin the overtaking manoeuvre. At that moment, you notice that the road makes an

Aborting a maneuver is sometimes the safest move

unexpected bend and you can no longer see oncoming traffic, so you slow downand pull back in behind the lorry. You've wisely chosen to abort the manoeuvre because you're not sure about the risks. Instead, you wait until it's safe to try again.

In this example, you don't wait until you pull out to decide how you will abort. Instead, you decide beforehand that you will check the conditions again when you pull out and pull back in immediately if they've changed. With practice, planning to check and abort as part of such manoeuvres will become a habit that keeps you out of trouble.

QUICK QUIZ

1 It's a good idea to have a second option in mind when you make a decision because your first decision may not work and you may not have time to think of a second decision in the moment. T ☑ F ☐

2 'Review and retry' means you assess the results of your decision as you apply it, and modify or change your decision if the original one isn't successful. T ☑ F ☐

3 It helps to think through other possibilities after you've dealt with a hazard so that you learn from the experience. T ☑ F ☐

Answers: 1: T, 2: T, 3: T

Summary points ⟩⟩⟩⟩⟩⟩⟩

In this module on making decisions you learned:

1 Risk acceptance is how much risk you're prepared to tolerate. As a driver, your personal risk acceptance level is important because it affects how you make decisions.

2 It's important to determine your own risk acceptance for driving and to lower it if it's inappropriately high. Risk acceptance is a choice you make.

3 Factors that tend to raise your risk acceptance are competition, inexperience, youth, peer pressure, anger, thrill seeking, fantasy, time pressure, habit and a false sense of security.

4 Illusory benefits are benefits you perceive that aren't real.
These include the false beliefs that 'showy' driving impresses people, that not being conservative shows control and maturity, and that competitive driving is exciting and saves time. Believing that illusory benefits are real leads to poor decisions.

5 In driving, rational thinking usually reduces your risk acceptance, while emotional thinking usually raises your risk acceptance.

6 In some situations, you may have to take a risk to avoid a more dangerous situation. An example is swerving into another lane to avoid a pedestrian.

7 Driving with a high risk acceptance is wrong because you do not have the right to expose others to risk without their consent.

8 You do a benefit-to-risk assessment to weigh the pros and cons of a decision. To put this into practice while driving, drive safely based on what you have learned in this course. Beware of illusory benefits and maximise your safety margin so you have time to make assessments.

9 You prepare for responding to emergencies by maintaining and developing good habits. What you do by habit is what you will do in an emergency.

10 Indecision is almost always worse than a poor decision. Remember to control, choose and communicate so you don't fail to make a decision.

11 Whenever you can, plan a second option to use in case your first decision isn't effective. 'Review and retry' is the process of assessing your decisions and attempting new ones if your original choice doesn't seem to be working.

12 A useful second option is often to abort. This is particularly useful when you run into trouble during a standard manoeuvre. Think about how you would abort a manoeuvre before you begin it.

8

'It is our choices....that show what we truly are, far more than our abilities.'

J.K.Rowling

Motor skills

Introduction

So far, you've been learning a lot about behaviour, attitude, the physical environment and the decision-making process – because when you think like a good driver, it's more likely that you will be able to drive well and safely in the way that good drivers do. Armed with this knowledge, you're now ready to look at some of the specific physical skills you will use when driving.

The skills you use while driving are called *motor skills*. 'Motor skill' is a general term: sitting up, nodding your head and walking are all motor skills. Your mind communicates with your skeletal muscles to move them in a co-ordinated way, sometimes consciously but mostly subconsciously. Some of the motor skills you use when driving are steering, changing gears and using the pedals.

The best way to learn a motor skill is simply to do it. The good news is that once you master a motor skill, you'll be able to remember it even if you haven't used it in a long time. Just like riding a bike, you can usually get back into it with a little practice.

The best way to learn the motor skills for driving is to picture yourself at the wheel. Imagine yourself executing the skill as it's described when you read about it or watch a demonstration. Then get into your car and practice the skill in an area that affords you some room for error. When you begin driving in an open area where there are few obstacles, there's less stress and distraction – and less to bump into if you don't get it right the first time.

Driving motor skills are integrated skills, which means you have to do more than one thing at a time. You have to steer, operate the pedals, use the controls and scan, all at the same time. It sounds complex, and it is – but with practice and experience, the skills become routine and habitual, and you no longer have to think about them consciously. Soon they will be as natural as nodding your head.

In the last module, you learned that what you normally do by habit is what you will do in an emergency. With this in mind, the most important thing to do when learning motor skills is to get into the habit of doing them correctly from the start. Bad habits are difficult to change later. Mastering the skills and forming good driving habits early will not only stand to you in an emergency, but they will also make your whole driving experience smoother and more efficient. Overall, you'll be a safer road user.

The optimum driving position within the lane your are driving in is the centre of the lane

In this module we will discuss...

- Acceleration and speed control
- Controlling deceleration
- Steering
- Error correction

Acceleration and speed control

Look for, and highlight, the answers to these questions

- Why do you use the same foot to control the accelerator and the brake?
- What are the benefits of smooth acceleration and steady driving speeds?
- How do you accelerate smoothly?

More than likely, you already know the basics of how to operate a car. Over the years, as a passenger, you've probably grasped the difference between the accelerator and the brake. In this module, you'll learn some of the specific things you need to know that may not have been obvious just from watching. Remember that the goal is to develop good driving habits from the start.

Acceleration and deceleration control

A vehicle with an automatic gearbox, which is often called an automatic, has two pedals: the accelerator pedal on the right and the brake pedal on the left. A vehicle with a manual gearbox, which is known as a manual, has three: the accelerator pedal on the right, the brake pedal in the middle and the clutch pedal on the left. This is a worldwide standard, even in countries where the steering wheel is on the left-hand side of the car. This makes it safer and easier for everyone who wants to drive in another country.

Always use your right foot to control *both* the accelerator and the brake and, in a manual, use your left foot for the clutch. Usually you control the clutch with your left foot while simultaneously controlling the accelerator

Automatic cars have an accelerator pedal on the right and a brake pedal on the left

Manual cars have an accelerator pedal on the right, a brake pedal in the middle and the clutch pedal on the left

Use your right foot to control the accelerator

or brake with your right foot. Even in an automatic, it is important to use *only* your right foot for the accelerator and brake because it prevents you from pressing the accelerator and brake at the same time in an emergency. It will also help you to form good habits should you need to drive a manual in the future and allow you to change from automatic with less difficulty.

Another good habit is to keep your foot *completely off* the pedals that you're not using. Avoid the habit of resting your foot gently on a pedal. It may not seem to be doing anything, but the brake lights come on easily, which sends a false message to vehicles behind you. When you 'ride the brakes', the gentle pressure transmits through the pedal and causes excess wear in the braking system.

Use the right foot to control the brake

Use your left foot for the clutch

By accelerating smoothly and maintaining a steady driving speed, you'll have a more relaxed and comfortable journey. It's easier for other motorists to have time to respond and to anticipate what you're going to do when your actions are smooth rather than abrupt. Steady acceleration and driving is less wearing on the propulsion system and more fuel efficient.

In an automatic, accelerating smoothly and driving steadily are easy. Just press on the accelerator slowly to gradually come up to the appropriate speed. Once you reach that speed, ease off the accelerator and hold just enough pressure to maintain speed. Give the engine more acceleration and fuel to climb a hill and ease off as you go downhill.

Getting to a stage when you can change gears smoothly in a car with a manual gearbox takes a little more practice, but it quickly becomes second nature. As a passenger you will have seen drivers do this many times, but let's look at the steps involved in a little more detail. Assume the engine is running with the gears in neutral and the parking brake is on.

The parking brake is operated by the left hand

- With your foot on the brake, press the clutch and move the gear stick to the first-gear position.
- Now, do the following in one smooth motion: move your right foot from the brake to the accelerator and press down on the accelerator gently while steadily letting the clutch out with your left foot, when you reach biting point the engine noise will change.
- Hold the clutch steady in this position, while you release the parking brake.
- Let the clutch out a little more while simultaneously applying a little acceleration. The vehicle will start to move forward, let the clutch out all the way and take your foot off the pedal.
- As you gather speed, release the clutch pedal entirely.
- Shift or change gears when you begin to hear the engine pitch rising. This sound indicates that the speed is getting too high for that gear – that is, the engine is turning much faster than the wheels. Ease off the accelerator, press the clutch and shift into second gear. Begin pressing the accelerator again while smoothly easing the clutch pedal out again.
- Repeat the gear-changing procedures until you reach the appropriate cruising speed.
- When you slow down or stop, you need to depress the clutch to prevent a stall and shift to a lower gear or neutral.

Automatic transmissions vary from car to car so check the handbook for each model

Here are a few pointers. If you give insufficient acceleration or if you let the clutch out too fast, the car will lurch and stall. If this happens, don't panic – put your foot on the brake, shift into neutral, turn off and then restart the engine and try again. With a little practice, you'll become proficient at gear changing and you'll be able to do it without having to think about it. While driving, you constantly shift gears to maintain a comfortable engine speed that's neither too high nor too low. You'll notice when you shift too early because you won't be able to accelerate and the engine will 'chug'. On the other hand, if you wait too long to shift gears, the engine will whine as it races too quickly for the gear.

Practice helps you become proficient at gear changing - it soon becomes smooth and seamless

When you want to slow down, gradually ease off the accelerator and, as you slow, shift down to the lower gears exactly as you did when shifting up – depress the clutch, shift gear and ease the clutch out. As you come to a stop, you need to press the clutch to disengage the engine while you apply the brake. Otherwise, the engine will stall. As you come to a stop, gently ease off the brake pedal just a bit so that you stop smoothly instead of abruptly. If you're not super smooth the first few times, it's not a big deal. Smoothness will come with practice.

In terms of the rate at which the car's wheels turn, reverse gear is virtually the same as first gear, except that it allows you to go backwards. You must be fully stopped before you attempt to engage the reverse gear or the engine will stall and may be damaged. If you park on a hill, it's good practice to put the car into gear after shutting down the engine and applying the hand brake. Use the reverse gear if facing downhill or first gear when facing uphill. This reduces the chances of the car rolling down the hill when no one's in it.

QUICK QUIZ

1 Using the same foot to control the accelerator and the brake prevents you from accidentally pressing both pedals at the same time. T ☑ F ☐

2 The benefits of smooth acceleration and steady driving speeds include: safety, comfort & fuel efficiency. T ☑ F ☐

3 In a manual vehicle you begin moving by smoothly and gradually pressing the accelerator while gradually letting out the clutch. T ☑ F ☐

Answers: 1: T, 2: T, 3: T

Handling characteristics

Aidhmeanna
OBJECTIVES **8**

Look for, and highlight, the answers to these questions

- What qualities give different vehicles different handling characteristics?
- What elements affect weight distribution and traction during a manoeuvre?

Vehicles feel different depending upon their design, the load they're carrying and their mechanical condition. Cars built for performance accelerate more quickly and manoeuvre well but have less towing and hauling capacity. Lorries and other work vehicles accelerate more slowly and are more cumbersome, but they can carry or tow more cargo. Most vehicles fall somewhere in between.

Alongside major design differences are some less obvious differences that affect handling. For example, you can accelerate more quickly and easily in a rear-wheel-drive car than in a front-wheel-drive car. This is because the force of acceleration tends to shift weight toward the rear of the vehicle. With a front-wheel-drive car, this shifting can cause a loss of traction.

Another example is four-wheel-drive vehicles, which are generally built for power rather than speed. They are balanced during acceleration but, because they're designed for off-road use, they tend to be elevated. This results in a higher centre of gravity, which means it's easier to roll the vehicle if you attempt a sharp turn even at relatively slow speeds – especially if there is strong cross-fall in the roll direction.

Four wheel drive vehicles tend to be elevated and present a greater risk of rolling if you attempt too sharp a turn

The most important aspect of vehicle handling relates to traction. In Module 3, you learned that the suspension system helps maintain the correct distribution of weight between the wheels as the weight shifts during steering, acceleration and deceleration. This is a very important consideration. When you're driving on a level road in a straight line, the wheels grip the road equally, with the weight distributed fairly evenly between all four wheels for maximum traction. We say 'fairly' evenly because the distribution of passengers, luggage and the like can alter the centre of gravity and affect the weight distribution to some degree. The effects of turning, speed changes, momentum and centrifugal force all have a bearing on the weight distribution, the centre of gravity and ultimately the stability of the vehicle.

When you accelerate, the weight tends to shift to the back due to inertia. This increases traction on the rear tyres and reduces it on the front tyres. Deceleration, on the other hand, shifts the weight forward. When you steer, the weight shifts to the side opposite the direction of the turn – that is, to the left if you're turning right and to the right if you're turning left.

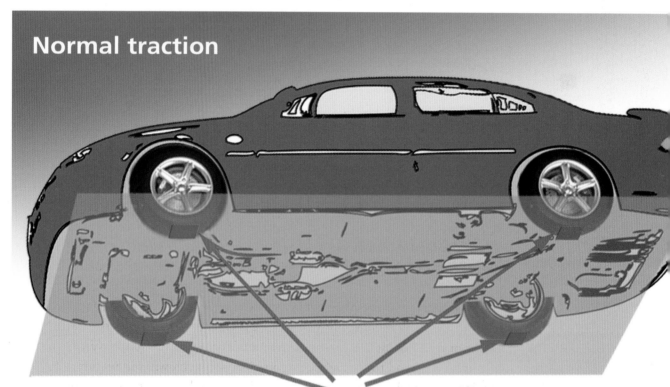

Normal traction

When you're driving on a level road, in a straight line, the wheels grip the road equally, with the weight distributed fairly evenly between all four wheels for maximum traction.

When you combine braking and turning, or accelerating and turning, the weight tends to go to the forward or rear corner that's opposite the direction of the turn. Each of these manoeuvres therefore increases traction on the area receiving the extra weight and reduces traction on the opposite side or end of the vehicle that's temporarily bearing less weight.

Effects of braking

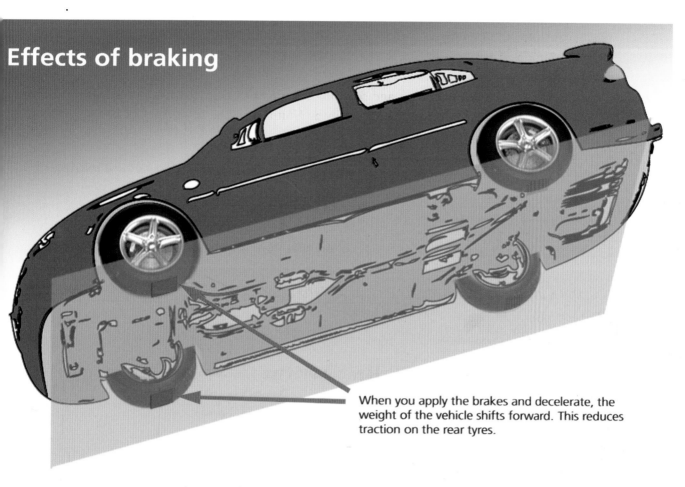

When you apply the brakes and decelerate, the weight of the vehicle shifts forward. This reduces traction on the rear tyres.

Higher speeds also reduce traction because air passing under the vehicle creates lift, much like it does on an airplane, reducing the weight that's pressing on the tyres.

Think about the variables that affect the traction of a vehicle for a moment....... Now think about what happens when other variables such as weather or road conditions also affect traction. For example, suppose you're going around a bend to the right and you hit a wet patch without warning. To maintain control, you reduce speed by easing up on the accelerator, but *not* by braking. This slows you down so you have less centrifugal force pushing you to the left and it helps to even out the traction. If you were to brake in this situation, you would force more weight onto the front left side of the car, further reducing the traction on both rear tyres – especially the right-hand tyre. That could amount to enough traction loss to start a skid, which is why you shouldn't use your brakes. If you have to use your brakes to avoid a collision, use them cautiously and as lightly as possible.

While you have to be aware of and understand the forces that affect your driving, you don't have to think about all of the variables constantly as you drive. By learning about these forces now, you will be in a much better position to keep your car under control in different driving conditions in the future. You also need to get a feel for each vehicle you drive and recognise that different vehicles perform differently with respect to traction and handling.

QUICK QUIZ

1 Factors that affect vehicle handling include: weight distribution, vehicle height and centre of gravity and whether the vehicle is front-, rear- or 4-wheel drive. T ☑ F ☐

2 Factors that affect weight distribution and traction include: Acceleration, speed, braking and steering T ☑ F ☐

3 The faster you travel the more weight the vehicle has therefore it will have more traction and stop more readily. T ☐ F ☑

Answers: 1: T, 2: T, 3: F

Controlling deceleration

Aidhmeanna **OBJECTIVES** 8 ➤ **Look for, and highlight, the answers to these questions**

- What are the benefits of smooth, gradual deceleration?
- How do you decelerate and accelerate when going around a bend or making a turn?
- What causes rear-end collisions?
- How do you determine the safe stopping distance between you and the car you're following?
- How does your safe stopping distance change when the road is wet?
- When does 'wheel lock' occur and how can you avoid it?
- What is different about anti-lock braking systems?

Smooth deceleration and braking

Decelerating and braking smoothly can matter more than smooth acceleration because usually you have a fixed distance in which to stop. Even in an emergency, when you're trying to stop as quickly as possible, you still need to stop as smoothly as you can to maintain control. Like all motor skills, this is something you'll learn with practice.

When you want to slow down, you ease off the accelerator. In an automatic car, you simply let the car slow down, gently using the brakes to come to a smooth stop. In a manual car, you shift down through the gears as you slow. Keeping the engine engaged while slowing provides additional slowing power and helps you maintain control. It's generally a bad idea to keep the clutch depressed or to *coast*, as it's known, except just before coming to a stop because you have less control while coasting.

Due to traction and other physical forces, it's easiest to brake safely on a dry, straight road. Therefore, whether on a dry or wet road, it's much more effective and easier to maintain control if you slow as you *approach* a bend rather than as you go through it. This avoids the problems of weight transfer and loss of traction associated with braking and steering that you've already learned about. Then you can accelerate a little as you come out of the bend to resume or maintain your speed. You'll get a feel for this with practice.

Rear-end collisions

Whenever you decrease speed, you need to pay attention to other road users, especially those behind you. Although your brake lights go on to alert other drivers when you touch the brake pedal, you can't assume that the driver behind you sees the lights or has allowed enough space to stop safely. Remember, don't take anything for granted and be prepared to manoeuvre or lengthen your stopping distance if it looks like the driver behind you isn't going to be able to stop in time. If you are being followed too closely, begin slowing and stopping well before you need to so that the other driver can stop under control. A tailgater may collide with you if you stop quickly – or even if you come to a normal stop. The safest action is to stop slowly and gradually and pull over in a safe place to let a tailgater go by.

If you are being followed too closely, begin slowing and stopping well before you need to do so

Tailgating is a common cause of rear-end collisions, where one vehicle follows another too closely. To avoid this, you need to determine your safe stopping distance. The distance you allow between you and the car in front of you has to account for two things: first, the time it takes to recognise that you need to stop and second, the time it takes to respond and come to a stop. The faster you're going, the farther you travel during the time it takes to recognise that you need to stop and the more distance you'll need to decelerate. This means the faster you're going, the more space you need to leave. If the road is wet or affected by another traction-reducing condition, you need more stopping distance – which is another reason why you should drive more slowly in poor conditions.

Let's look at some examples to see just how much these variables can affect the stopping distance. A typical car travelling at only 50 km/h on a dry, straight road has a stopping distance of 25 metres. When the road is wet, the stopping distance is 30 metres. Doubling the speed to 100 km/h, more than doubles the stopping distance in both cases, to 70 metres when it's dry and 125 metres when the road is wet. Try pacing these distances to get an idea how far they are. 125 metres is equivalent to the length of about 31 saloon-type cars.

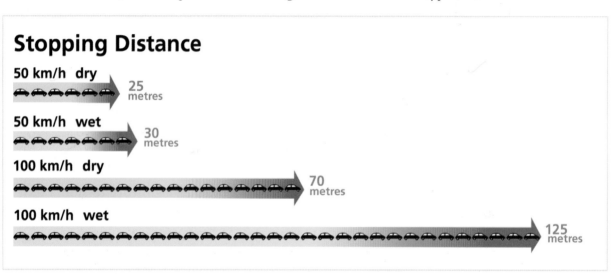

Stopping Distance

50 km/h dry — 25 metres

50 km/h wet — 30 metres

100 km/h dry — 70 metres

100 km/h wet — 125 metres

While it's not easy to estimate distances while driving, it's very easy to estimate time. You can use the 'two-second rule' to determine your safe stopping distance on a dry road. When the car ahead passes a stationary object like a lamppost, say 'only a fool breaks the two-second rule' or count 'one-one-thousand, two-one-thousand'. The time it takes to say each of these is about two seconds. If you reach the lamppost within two seconds, you're too close to the car in front. In wet conditions, do the same thing, but double distance by saying the two-second rule twice or by counting four seconds.

The Two Second Rule can be used to calculate a safe distance between you and the vehicle ahead

In wet conditions you should leave a space of four seconds between you and the vehicle ahead

Always give yourself plenty of space when roads are wet or greasy. There should be a gap of at least four seconds between you and the vehicle in front

You'll quickly notice that using these rules automatically makes your safe-distance gap vary with your speed and the conditions. With practice, you'll get a feel for the proper distance to leave, but develop the habit of measuring the space by reciting the rule now and then. When you're not sure if you're leaving enough room, leave more. You can go just as fast as the car in front of you whether it's 20 metres ahead or 200 metres ahead.

Emergency braking

As you learned in Module 3, when braking in an emergency, you want to avoid locking the wheels. Wheel lock can happen when you brake hard and continuously, resulting in skidding. Not only does this compromise control, but you actually take longer to stop, even on a dry road. If your car doesn't have an antilock braking system (ABS), you should use cadence braking in an emergency stop situation. This means you press and slightly release the brake in a rhythm when you are coming to a sudden stop, to avoid locking your brakes.

ABS brakes, you recall, have a system that automatically prevents lockup. ABS brakes use electronics to do what you do manually with cadence braking. They also monitor the wheel speeds and divert braking power based on which wheels have the most traction. When using ABS brakes in an emergency, you just press the brakes hard and let them do their job. This is more natural than cadence braking, and ABS brakes are far more responsive than a person will be in this situation, which makes them a definite safety advantage.

You'll notice a pulsing sensation when you brake hard with ABS brakes; the system is automatically adjusting the stopping power as you come to a stop. Keep in mind that even cars with ABS brakes can skid, especially on a wet or slippery road. It is still up to the driver to drive more slowly and decelerate over a longer distance when traction is likely to be compromised.

QUICK QUIZ

1 Smooth, gradual deceleration helps maintain control and makes slowing down more comfortable. T ☑ F ☐

2 When going around a bend, you should accelerate going into the bend. T ☐ F ☑

3 Rear-end collisions are caused by one car following another too closely. T ☑ F ☐

Answers: 1: T; 2: F; 3: T

Steering

Aidhmeanna
OBJECTIVES **8** ➤ **Look for, and highlight, the answers to these questions**

- How should you sit and hold the wheel for steering? Why?
- How do safety belts help prevent collisions?
- How do you hold the steering wheel as you drive?
- How does power steering affect steering characteristics?
- How do you prevent over-steering?
- How does steering differ in small, large and multi-wheeled vehicles and in vehicles towing trailers?

Position for steering

As a new driver, it's very easy to develop bad habits in how you sit and hold the steering wheel. You may not have noticed the subtle aspects of how a good driver sits and steers.

'Ten to Two' hand position

'Nine to Three' hand position

'Eight to Four' hand position

For the best control, grip the wheel evenly on both sides, with your left hand at about 10 o'clock and your right at about 2 o'clock. If your car has an airbag in the steering wheel, then a 9 and 3 or 4 and 8 o'clock position is safer. Next, bring your seat forward and sit up straight. Recline the seat only slightly if necessary – just enough to provide a natural upright position. Sit close to the wheel, but not so close that your legs push up against the wheel or dashboard. Check the minimum space the manufacturer requires when air bags are fitted. Your reach to the steering wheel and to the pedals should feel natural. After adjusting your position, remember to adjust the mirrors before beginning to drive. Some driver's seats can also be adjusted for height to give you the optimum view.

Your position is important for staying alert and maintaining control of the car. On a long journeys in particular, drivers tend to slump. You should avoid slumping because as you slide lower into your seat, you relax and become less alert and it can cause back problems. Sitting lower also reduces your field of view. Safety belts are just as important for preventing collisions as they are for surviving collisions because they help keep you in the best position for driving. When worn snugly they combine with the seat to provide back support.

Your seating position is important for staying alert and maintaining control

Slumping can affect your alertness and your view of the road

Holding while steering

As you drive, keep *both* hands on the wheel as much as possible. If your car is an automatic, your hands should be on the wheel almost all the time, except to operate controls like the lights or windscreen wipers. When driving a manual, remove one hand only when necessary to shift gears or to operate controls.

While driving, control the car by pushing and pulling the wheel to feed it through your hands with neither hand going past the 12 o'clock or 6 o'clock position. Maintain maximum control by avoiding crossing your hands to the opposite sides of the wheel, except in tight manoeuvring situations in which you have no choice. As you complete a turn, allow the wheel to shuffle back through your hands as you straighten out.

Cars with power steering require much less steering effort so, if you're used to driving a car with manual steering, you may tend to over-control and be too forceful until you get used to power steering. You've already learned that you should avoid turning the steering wheel when the car is stationary because it strains the steering system and wears down the tyres.

Over-steering is a symptom of trying to over-control, and it usually occurs in an emergency. The typical scenario is when the driver gets distracted and stops watching the road momentarily. Suddenly the driver notices a hazard and steers abruptly, going off the road. To avoid this, the important step is obviously to keep your eyes on the road.

Motor skills tend to co-ordinate with eye movement. Suppose someone says 'go right' but instinctively looks and points to the left. The direction in which they pointed is most likely correct and the verbal direction wrong because the eyes and hand coordinate. Similarly, in an emergency, you tend to steer where you look – so by looking to your chosen path you may avoid the hazard and the danger of over-steering. Look *primarily* at where you want to go, not at what you want to avoid. We say *primarily* and not *exclusively* because you also need to stay aware of what's happening around you, such as where other vehicles and pedestrians are. Next time you see a footballer on television, note how he scans and looks at the area of the goal – not just at the ball or the obstacles in his way.

The best players scan and look at the area of the goal - not just the ball or the obstacles in their way

Because of the various physical forces at work, a lorry is more likely to skid when making a turn and towing a trailer

Steering and vehicle size

A vehicle's handling characteristics depend to a large degree on its size, shape and weight. A small vehicle with a short distance between the wheels will have good manoeuvrability and stability, provided the body doesn't extend far beyond the tyres to the sides, front or rear. Large vehicles with longer distances between the front and rear wheels have less manoeuvrability. One reason lorries have more than four wheels is to improve their ability to manoeuvre.

Articulated lorries and vehicles with trailers have even less steering control. When driving in a straight line, the drag that the trailer puts on the towing vehicle tends to reduce traction on the towing vehicle's front tyres. When stopping, the trailer tries to push the towing vehicle forward, thereby shifting the weight forward and reducing the traction of its rear wheels.

Because of the various physical forces at work, a lorry is more likely to skid when making a turn and towing a trailer. This is because the lorry and trailer tend to move independently of each other due to inertia. The leading part of the vehicle has to change direction first and then pull the rear part, which resists due to inertia, around the turn. The trailer's momentum pushes the rear of the truck in the original direction, which can cause a skid if the momentum exceeds the lorry's rear tyre traction. Lorries often have extra wheels to provide the added traction needed to resist the trailer's momentum. In a sudden stop the trailer's momentum can overcome traction and 'jack-knife' the lorry.

This doesn't mean that articulated lorries and vehicles with trailers are a menace to other motorists. If that were they case, they would not be permitted on the road. Rather, be aware that driving these vehicles requires extra care, skill and training. As a co-operative driver, you should be considerate and help such vehicles to manoeuvre safely when you can. You'll help to make the roads safer by opening a gap or by staying well clear when a lorry is trying to manoeuvre, even if you have priority.

QUICK QUIZ

1 For best control, grip the steering wheel evenly on both sides. T ☑ F ☐

2 Safety belts help prevent collisions by helping you to stay in the best position for driving.
   T ☑ F ☐

3 To prevent over-steering in an emergency look primarily at where you have chosen to go.
   T ☑ F ☐

Answers: 1: T, 2: T, 3: T

Lane position

Aidhmeanna
OBJECTIVES 8

Look for, and highlight, the answers to these questions

● What is the optimum lane position?
● What are the dangers of lane weaving?

'A driver must drive as near to the left-hand side of the road as is necessary to allow approaching traffic to pass and following traffic to overtake on the right.' That's from the official Rules of the Road, and this keep-left rule applies even when driving on multilane roads. The optimum driving position within the lane that you are driving in is the centre of the lane. You may need to move toward the outside of that lane or to an outside lane to allow a safe distance from cyclists or pedestrians, or you may need to move to the inside when another vehicle overtakes you. On roads with no dividing line, keep well to the left and slow down, especially when going around blind bends – but you must still be prepared to make room for pedestrians or other hazards that may not be visible on your approach.

On roads with no dividing line, keep well to the left and slow down when traffic is approaching

On dual carriageways and motorways, drive in the left lane, only moving out temporarily to overtake. Lane weaving is not effective driving. Weaving creates unnecessary risk for you and other road users, and it slows down the general traffic flow. Rapid lane changes reduce traction, balance and control, and they make it difficult to respond to unexpected hazards. If you're constantly switching lanes, you're not meeting other drivers' expectations, leading to an increased risk of collision. As you've already learned, this kind of driving seldom saves you much time anyway.

It is illegal to overtake on the left. The only exception is in lines of heavy, slow-moving traffic where the traffic in the left lane is moving more quickly than the traffic on the right.

Error correction

Aidhmeanna
OBJECTIVES **8**

Look for, and highlight, the answers to these questions

- What is lost when you go into a skid?
- What causes a skid?
- What are the three main categories of skids?
- What can you do to recover from a skid?
- What is the danger of regaining traction too abruptly?
- What should you do after a skid?
- When is it appropriate to drive on the hard shoulder?

No driver is perfect, so even experienced drivers occasionally lose control of their vehicle. As you've learned, almost 90 percent of crashes result from driver error, which includes drivers not recognising or allowing for factors such as poor road conditions, vehicle problems and road hazards. If you lose control of your vehicle, your ability to recover it quickly will most likely determine whether or not you have a collision.

Cause of skids

Skids are the most common reason for loss of vehicle control. Skids occur when you've lost traction and your tyres no longer grip the road, resulting in reduced or very little ability to steer or brake. A skid can involve some or all of your wheels, but typically it's either both front wheels or both rear wheels.

Following a skid, drivers often try to blame road conditions, poor tyres and so on for the incident, but this is seldom justified. Skids most commonly result from an error the driver has already made. A typical example would be failing to slow down when the road has reduced traction due to rain. In an emergency braking situation, the wheels lock and the car skids out of control because momentum overcomes traction. Had the driver slowed down to account for conditions, the skid would not have occurred.

It's important to remember, then, that the *primary* cause of a skid is nearly always driver error. This means that by controlling how you drive, skidding should be a rare event. However, no driver is perfect so it's important to understand what to do if you do have to deal with a skid.

Skids normally result when you lose traction either on a turn or while braking hard, or both. As you recall, braking and turns tend to change the

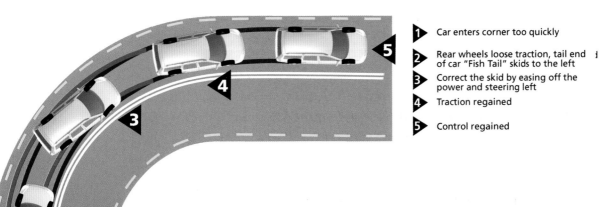

1. Car enters corner too quickly
2. Rear wheels loose traction, tail end of car "Fish Tail" skids to the left
3. Correct the skid by easing off the power and steering left
4. Traction regained
5. Control regained

weight distribution in the car, thereby affecting the traction of the tyres. For example, when a driver brakes while steering to the right, weight tends to shift to the left and forward – left due to centrifugal force and forward due to braking. This reduces the rear traction, particularly on the left-hand side of the vehicle. If you are driving too fast on a wet road and suddenly have to brake going around a bend, the combination of centrifugal force and inertia may overcome traction on the rear tyres. While the front of the car continues around the turn, the rear keeps going straight on because the rear tyres no longer have sufficient grip. The result is a rear-wheel or 'fishtail' skid.

It can be worse. Entering a bend too quickly can result in all four tyres losing traction. When the momentum substantially outweighs the available traction of all the tyres, it can force your car to keep moving in its original direction, which may be off the road or across the other lanes of traffic, totally out of control. On top of this, the rear tyres often lose traction just before the front ones, causing the vehicle to spin as it slides out of control.

Skids can be divided into three categories depending on what errors and conditions cause you to lose control. A single incident may fit into all three categories.

Driving-related skids result from driving too fast, braking too harshly, accelerating too quickly or steering and cornering at too fast a speed. Bad driving can cause skids even with ideal road conditions.

Road-and-weather-related skids result from ice, snow, rain, mud, oil, gravel, leaves or anything else that makes the road slippery.

Vehicle-related skids result from poor maintenance that contributes to skidding. These include insufficient tyre tread, poor and uneven brakes and uneven tyre pressure.

Recovering from a skid

To get out of a skid, you need to regain traction. This may be as simple as removing the cause. For example, if you are not going too fast and you start to fishtail as a result of using the brake while going around a bend, simply taking your foot off the brake may restore control. The sooner you recognise that you're beginning to skid and the sooner you take corrective action, the more likely you are to regain control. The longer you delay, the less likely you are to recover control. Again, slowing down reduces the chances of a skid but, if a skid happens, a slower speed makes the skid easier to deal with.

If you go into a skid, take your foot off the brake and turn in the direction of the skid. That is, if the rear of the car is skidding to the left, steer to the left. You want to keep the front of the car pointed in the direction the car is going in the skid. If you must brake because you're trying to avoid a collision, pump the brakes if you don't have an ABS system. In a rear-wheel skid, doing this will usually restore control, but you will likely slide farther in a four-wheel skid. As you regain control, avoid trying to return to your intended direction too harshly or abruptly. If you regain traction too soon on one side of the car while you have a lot of momentum, the vehicle may roll. This is particularly important when driving a vehicle that has a higher centre of gravity, such as an SUV.

After you've dealt with a skid, you'll probably have a pounding heart, an adrenaline rush and perhaps mild shock. This is a normal part of your body's survival mechanism, but you need to give yourself time to calm down. After a skid, pull over in a safe location and take five or ten minutes to relax and calm down before you resume driving safely. Think about what happened and use it as a lesson to keep it from happening in the future.

Again, if you stay alert, maintain a safety margin and slow down when necessary, skids should be unlikely because you will avoid harsh braking and manoeuvring. In situations where you must take evasive action to avoid a collision, use 'control, choose and communicate' to help avoid skids. For example, to maintain control, you may choose to drive onto the hard shoulder rather than brake or steer harshly. Choosing the appropriate action will depend on the situation, of course, but by driving well you can avoid skids even when the unexpected arises.

QUICK QUIZ

1 Most skids result from poor road conditions.
   T☐ F☑

2 Recover from a skid by braking as hard as possible.
   T☐ F☐

3 You are in danger of rolling the vehicle if you regain traction too abruptly. T☑ F☐

Answers: 1: F; 2: F; 3: T

Summary points ❯❯❯❯❯❯❯

In this module on motor skills you learned:

1. Use the same foot to control the accelerator and brake. Learn to accelerate and decelerate smoothly.

2. Weight distribution affects how a vehicle handles. When you accelerate, weight shifts to the rear and when you decelerate, it shifts to the front. Weight shifts to the outside of the car when turning. Traction is reduced on the side or end of the vehicle that's temporarily bearing less weight.

3. Rear-end collisions are caused by following another car too closely. Never take it for granted that the driver behind you will see you stopping.

4. Use the two-second rule to determine the safe distance between you and the vehicle you're following when road conditions are good. Increase the distance as conditions deteriorate.

5. Wheel lock increases your stopping distance. To avoid wheel lock when you have to make an emergency stop, pump the brakes if you don't have an ABS system.

6. Hold the wheel with both hands while steering. Sit upright and comfortably close to the wheel so that your feet reach the pedals naturally and comfortably. Use your safety belt to keep you in the proper driving position.

7. Large and multi-wheeled vehicles and those towing trailers do not handle as easily as small ones. A vehicle that's towing a trailer is more difficult to handle because the trailer has momentum and tries to continue on its own path when going around bends and turns.

8. Generally speaking, the optimum lane position is in the centre of the left lane, moving to the right or left as necessary to avoid hazards. Only move into the right lane to overtake. It is illegal to overtake on the left, except in lines of traffic where the left lane is moving more quickly than the right.

9   Lane weaving is dangerous because it reduces your control and doesn't meet other drivers' expectations. Weaving slows the overall flow of the traffic as drivers have to adjust to accommodate.

10 Skids usually result from driver error. They happen when the vehicle loses traction because the driver failed to drive appropriately and/or due to maintenance problems.

11 If you skid, reduce the pressure on the brakes. Steer in the direction of the skid and try to keep the front of the vehicle in line with the vehicle's trajectory. Avoid abrupt steering or braking when you regain traction so you don't roll the vehicle. It is appropriate to drive on the hard shoulder in an emergency if it is the best way to avoid a collision and/or skid.

9

'Experience is a hard teacher because she gives the test first, the lesson afterwards'

Vernon Law

Safety margin

Introduction

You've already learned a great deal about safety margins in this programme. For example, you know that time gives you a safety margin and that you usually increase your safety margin by slowing down and allowing more distance between you and a hazard or potential hazard.

In this module, we'll revisit the techniques you need to maintain a safety margin and pay special attention the principles that underlie them. In this way, you'll be able to understand why you should apply the techniques – and how you can continuously maintain and modify your safety margin to fit the circumstances that you encounter as you drive.

In this module we will discuss...

- Your safety margin
- Stopping time and stopping distance
- Speed limits
- Following distance
- Tailgating
- Lateral space
- Maintaining your safety margin

Your safety margin

Aidhmeanna
OBJECTIVES 9 ▷ **Look for, and highlight, the answers to these questions**

- What is the main reason you need to have a safety margin while driving?
- Who is responsible for your safety margin?
- Why do you need to constantly adjust your safety margin while driving?
- What can you do to increase your safety margin while driving?

If you ask the average person why you need a safety margin while driving, you're likely to get a common-sense answer like, 'so that I have time to respond and avoid an accident'. It doesn't take genius to figure that out. However, there is an underlying premise that makes a tremendous difference in how you view the importance of maintaining a safety margin. *The main reason a safety margin is necessary while driving is that nobody is perfect. We all need room for error because we all make mistakes from time to time.*

No doubt you know this and, as you've read many times up to now, you can count on making mistakes while driving. Still, even though you'll make mistakes – as will other road users – most of these mistakes will *not* cause a collision as long as you and the other road users have allowed each other an adequate safety margin. Your safety margin provides the time you need to think, adjust and respond.

It's easy to understand this if you think about what's going on when someone *fails* to leave an adequate safety margin.

For example, drivers who tailgate are unconsciously making several significant and incorrect assumptions. Such drivers assume that:

- They can and will anticipate the need to stop as quickly as the driver they're tailgating will stop.
- The driver or drivers ahead won't do anything unexpected or irrational.
- They can *completely and perfectly* anticipate any mistakes the other driver will make.
- They will not make any mistakes themselves.

Clearly, these assumptions are ridiculous. Yet to avoid a collision, a driver who doesn't leave a safety margin is relying on nothing unexpected happening. Fortunately, the unexpected doesn't usually happen – but when something does go wrong, *the result is almost always a collision.* Good drivers have very few collisions not because the unexpected doesn't happen and not because they can anticipate everything that could possibly happen, but because they allow a sufficient safety margin to adjust when a problem does arise.

The main reason a safety margin is necessary while driving is that nobody is perfect. We all need room for error because we all make mistakes from time to time. Always leave an adequate safety margin between you and the vehicle ahead

You are responsible for maintaining your safety margin. You are the only factor you can control while driving – no one else can do it for you. The driver behind you shouldn't follow you too closely but it will happen. You still have the ability to maintain your safety margin by slowing down or pulling over to let the driver go by.

Because circumstances constantly change while you're driving, you need to continually adjust your safety margin to maintain the balance between effective time use and staying out of trouble. On a clear, open road during the day and in good weather, it may be reasonable to cruise at the posted speed limit. But when it starts to rain, you need to slow down to accommodate for longer stopping distances and reduced visibility.

Good drivers will always try to maintain a safety margin while poor drivers are prepared to compromises theirs

You've learned many specific techniques that increase your safety margin, but if you think about it, they all boil down to three broad actions:

- Increase the *time* you have to detect and respond to a hazard by *slowing down* as the situation requires or when in doubt.
- Increase the *time* you have to detect and respond to other drivers by *giving them room* for error and by taking nothing for granted.
- Increase the *time* other drivers have to detect and respond to you by *communicating* your intentions clearly and in good time.

One of the primary differences between being a good driver and being a bad one is the habit of maintaining and refusing to compromise your safety margin.

QUICK QUIZ

1 Other drivers are responsible for your safety margin. T ☐ F ☑

2 You need to constantly adjust your safety margin while driving to maintain the balance between effective time use and avoiding trouble in circumstances that are always changing. T ☑ F ☐

3 To increase your safety margin, slow down as the situation requires, communicate your intentions in plenty of time, give other drivers room for error and do not take what another driver will do for granted. T ☑ F ☐

Answers: 1: F, 2: T, 3: T

Stopping time and distance

- How does your speed generally affect your safety margin?
- What are the three components of total stopping time?
- What factors influence braking time?
- Give an example of how a higher speed can increase your safety margin?

As we discussed in the last module, there is a relationship between speed and your safety margin. Obviously, the faster you're going, the farther you travel in a given period. Also, the faster you're going, the more distance you need to stop because you need to dissipate more momentum. Therefore, speed generally affects your safety margin by lessening it. If you're travelling at speed, you must compensate by increasing the distance you allow to detect and respond to hazards.

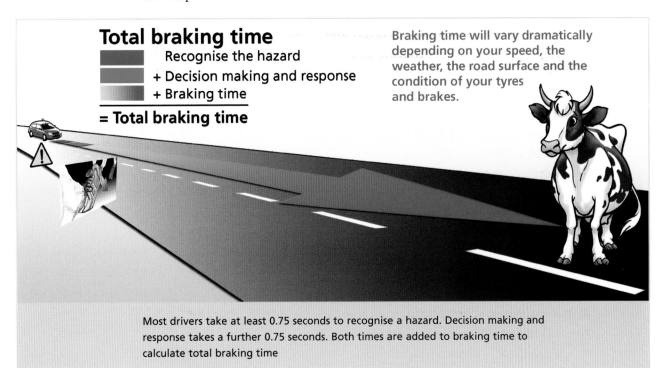

Total braking time
■ Recognise the hazard
■ + Decision making and response
■ + Braking time
= **Total braking time**

Braking time will vary dramatically depending on your speed, the weather, the road surface and the condition of your tyres and brakes.

Most drivers take at least 0.75 seconds to recognise a hazard. Decision making and response takes a further 0.75 seconds. Both times are added to braking time to calculate total braking time

The worst-case scenario is when you have to come to a complete stop in an emergency. Three components determine total stopping time:

1. Most drivers need about 0.75 seconds to recognise a hazard.
2. Decision making and response takes most drivers another 0.75 seconds.
3. Braking time – the time it takes to go from your current speed to zero – depends on how fast you are travelling.

The combination of all three equals total braking time.

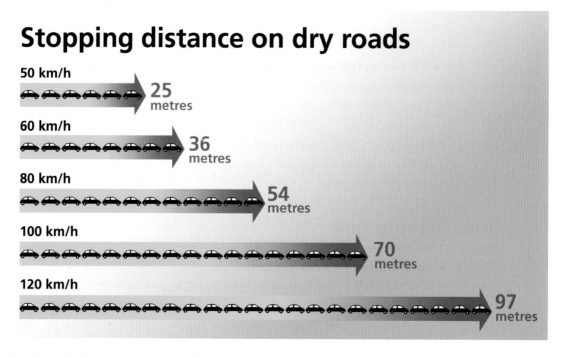

Stopping distance on dry roads

50 km/h — 25 metres

60 km/h — 36 metres

80 km/h — 54 metres

100 km/h — 70 metres

120 km/h — 97 metres

In Module 8, we mentioned that the distance you need to stop in good conditions is greater than you might think. At 100 km/h, the average driver will travel about 42 metres between recognising a hazard and *starting* to brake. Various factors influence braking time and distance. These include:

- Driver alertness.
- Driver skill and experience.
- Road and weather conditions.
- Vehicle condition, including tyre tread.
- Road slope – whether you are headed uphill or downhill.

While speed generally lessens your safety margin, this isn't always the case. Your primary concern is increasing the *time* available to respond to a hazard. And sometimes you might increase your safety margin by decreasing your exposure to a particular hazard.

A good example of this is overtaking on a two-lane road. As soon as you pull out to overtake, you're exposed to the hazard of oncoming cars. The sooner you complete the overtaking manoeuvre and return to your own lane, the better. So, once you have determined that it's safe to overtake, pull out and build sufficient speed to overtake quickly while still remaining within the speed limit. If you can't accelerate enough to overtake quickly, then pull back in behind the vehicle you want to overtake and only try again when you feel confident that it is safe to do so. Remember that a few minutes spent driving at 5 or 10 km/h less than the legal speed limit will only delay you slightly overall. Don't get killed or become a killer just because you don't want to lose a few short minutes.

Remember that a few minutes spent driving at 5 or 10 km/h less than the legal speed limit will only delay you slightly overall. Don't get killed or become a killer just because you don't want to lose a few short minutes.

The principle is that when you've committed yourself to an action, be decisive. Going slowly when overtaking or pulling into traffic may not be as safe as going faster. Adjust your speed to reduce your exposure to risk, whether that means speeding up or slowing down.

QUICK QUIZ

1 Speed affects your safety margin by increasing safety. T☐ F☑

2 The three components of total stopping time include recognising a hazard, initiating a response and calculating the stopping distance. T☐ F☑

3 Driver alertness has a big influence on braking time. T☑ F☐

Answers: 1: F, 2: F, 3: T

Speed limits

Aidhmeanna
OBJECTIVES 9 > **Look for, and highlight, the answers to these questions**

- What is the purpose of a speed limit?
- Why is a speed limit not a target?
- What percentage of collisions in Ireland can be attributed to excessive speed?
- How do you know if you're going too fast?
- Why is it important to stay under the speed limit even when it 'feels' slow?

In our earlier discussions about road design, you learned that roads have a design speed that accounts for sight distances, cross-fall on curves and the type of surface among other factors. These are some of the considerations that help determine the posted speed limit. The purpose of a speed limit is to inform you of the maximum safe speed that has been determined for the road.

Excessive speed *always* increases your risk on the road – and the risk to those around you

Keep in mind, though, that traffic engineers, the National Roads Authority and other groups apply many different criteria to a speed limit. The maximum safe speed is based on common pedestrian activity, traffic density and even the number of collisions that have occurred in an area – not just the road design. For example, a road's design may be suitable for travelling at 80 km/h, but that speed would be too high where the road passes in front of a school. In such a case, the limit will be much lower because of the risk to children, not because of the road design.

Remember that a speed limit is not a target; it is the maximum safe speed based on optimum driving situations. Because you won't always drive in ideal circumstances, you need to account for road conditions, the weather, unusual traffic, vulnerable road users, your alertness, how far you can see and anything else that may pose a hazard or hamper your ability to detect one – and then reduce your speed as appropriate. You must constantly adjust your speed to maintain an adequate safety margin, which often means slowing down to increase the gap between you and something that's ahead of you.

As a novice driver, be vigilant about going too fast – you can find yourself speeding without even realising it.

Be careful of the tendency to drive faster as you gain confidence. Don't forget that as a new driver, you need about five years' experience to reach average driving competence. Don't get overconfident and drive quickly because excessive speed always increases your risk on the road – and the risk to those around you. The faster you're going, the less time you have to recognise and respond to a hazard, and the more momentum you'll have in a collision. If you have too little time and distance to stop, you'll almost certainly crash. Data shows that excessive speed is the primary cause of 82% of collisions in Ireland and is a contributory factor in 40% of fatal crashes.

As a novice driver, be vigilant about going too fast – you can find yourself speeding without even realising it. Here's a rule of thumb: *if you would be unable to stop in time to avoid a possible road hazard, then you're going too fast, even if you're within the posted speed limit.* You need to be able to identify a hazard ahead and respond by stopping without hitting it. In urban areas, you should be able to stop without skidding in a short distance if a pedestrian or cyclist were to dart out in front of you.

Speed kills 9 out of 10 pedestrians are killed when hit at speeds over 60km/hr

If hit by a car travelling at 30km/hr, 9 out of 10 pedestrians will survive. If hit at a speed of 60km/hr, only 1 out of 10 pedestrians will survive

Choose your speed, choose your consequences

It's not always easy to drive at the right speed and there are times when you'll feel like you're driving more slowly than you are. On long straight roads, in poor visibility or when you enter a town or village after an uninterrupted journey on the open road, it can feel as though you are crawling – yet your speed might still pose a threat to your and others' safety. When the speed limit is set at 50 km/h, then that's the maximum safe speed for you, your passengers and the people you are likely to meet on the road. When it feels too slow, remind yourself that it always takes longer to stop safely than most drivers expect and that the consequences of speed-related crashes are dreadful: they are far-reaching, long-lasting and life-altering. When you drive too fast you risk loss of life, loss of mobility, loss of independence, loss of your career, loss of your peace of mind and loss of your licence – all for the sake of reducing your speed by as little as 5 km/h. So slow down and arrive alive.

QUICK QUIZ

1 The purpose of a speed limit is to inform you of the maximum safe speed that has been determined for the road in optimum conditions. T ☑ F ☐

2 A speed limit is not a target because you can usually go a bit faster than the posted speed limit. T ☐ F ☑

3 You're going too fast if you would be unable to stop in time to avoid hitting a potential road hazard. T ☑ F ☐

Answers: 1: T, 2: F, 3: T

Following distance

Aidhmeanna
OBJECTIVES 9 > **Look for, and highlight, the answers to these questions**

- How close is too close when driving?
- When does the two-second rule apply?
- Why should you leave a space between you and the car ahead when stopped in traffic or at lights and junctions?
- How should you judge the size of that space?

The two second rule works well regardless of the speed at which you are travelling. The faster you are moving, the longer the gap will be

In Module 8, you learned that when following another vehicle, the distance between you and that vehicle should be greater than or equal to your safe stopping distance. Anything less is too close.

You also learned that you can use the two-second rule to judge a safe following distance in optimum road conditions. You simply note when the vehicle passes a stationary object and then count two seconds. If you reach the object before the two seconds elapse, you know you're too close.

When conditions are poor, such as wet or icy roads, you should use a longer interval of four or more seconds. It's important to recognise that the two-second rule only applies to determining the gap between you and a vehicle you're following that's travelling at about the same speed as you.

Get into the habit of using the "two second rule" whenever you are following a vehicle. Use any fixed point on the road to measure the distance between you and the vehicle ahead

You need to leave a gap between you and the car ahead even when you're at a complete stop, like at a traffic light. You should be able to see the rear wheels of the car ahead

If you review the stopping distance table earlier in this module, it's easy to see that the two-second rule does not tell you the necessary stopping distance if you're heading towards a stationary object. The two-second rule *only* applies when following a vehicle because it accounts for the fact that the vehicle ahead is also moving and will continue to travel some distance before coming to a complete stop.

The two-second rule doesn't work well in stop-and-go city traffic, either, but the principle behind it still applies: leave ample room to stop between you and the vehicle ahead of you. Remember, if you hit the vehicle ahead of you, you were following too closely and the collision is *your* fault. You are responsible for avoiding obstacles in front of you.

You may not realise that you also need to leave a gap between you and the car ahead even when you're at a complete stop, like at a traffic light. There are several reasons for this. The first is that it gives you enough room to manoeuvre around the car should it stall. Second, should the car behind you fail to stop and then hit you, you're less likely to be pushed into the car ahead. Third, if you're headed uphill and the vehicle ahead is a manual, it may roll back a bit just before moving forward, so you should allow some room so the car doesn't roll back into yours.

The rule of thumb when coming to a complete stop in traffic, you should be able to see the rear wheels of the car ahead.

QUICK QUIZ

1 You're too close to the vehicle in front if you're closer than the total distance you need to stop safely. T ☑ F ☐

2 The two-second rule applies only when judging the gap between you and a vehicle you're following when it's travelling at about the same speed as you and conditions are good. T ☐ F ☑

3 When coming to a stop in traffic, leave a gap large enough to let you see the rear tyres of the vehicle ahead of you. T ☑ F ☐

Answers: 1: T, 2: T, 3: T

Tailgating

Aidhmeanna OBJECTIVES 9 > **Look for, and highlight, the answers to these questions**

- What are the two primary hazards of tailgating?
- What should you do when another vehicle tailgates you?

We discussed tailgating in the last module, but it's worth briefly revisiting while we're looking at safety margins. As you know, tailgating is aggressive, dangerous and illegal. It's also stupid. There is no rational justification for it in any circumstances, even when the vehicle ahead is driving very slowly.

There are two primary hazards of tailgating. The first and most obvious one is that a tailgating car is too close to be able to stop in an emergency without colliding with the car in front. Tailgaters place themselves, the car ahead and other motorists at risk. Pile-up collisions on motorways often start when a tailgater collides with someone who stops suddenly, triggering a chain reaction that can severely injure many people.

The second and less obvious hazard is that tailgating is distracting. It distracts the driver who's being tailgated, and it also distracts other motorists nearby who must adjust their safety margins to keep a tailgate collision from endangering them. The unnecessary distraction pulls everyone's attention away from other possible road hazards. In this way, tailgaters can contribute to collisions that don't directly involve them.

If a vehicle tailgates you, you're being endangered by a selfish, immature driver. To regain control, slow down or pull over to let the driver by at the first safe opportunity. One could argue that by doing so, you're rewarding childish behaviour – and to some degree, that's true. But the alternative is to let the person continue to endanger you and others around you. That choice could turn out far worse.

Tailgating is aggressive, dangerous and illegal. It's also stupid. There is no rational justification for it in any circumstances, even when the vehicle ahead is driving very slowly

1 The two primary dangers of tailgating include distracting other drivers and causing collisions. T❏ F❏

2 When someone tailgates you, you should allow the them to pass at the first safe opportunity. T❏ F❏

3 Driving closely behind another vehicle is OK if it is going more slowly than you would like in the overtaking lane, because the vehicle shouldn't be there in the first place. T❏ F❏

Answers: 1: T, 2: T, 3: F

Lateral space

Aidhmeanna
OBJECTIVES 9 **Look for, and highlight, the answers to these questions**

- What is 'lateral space'?
- Why do you need to maintain a reasonable lateral space while driving?
- What methods can you use to maintain your lateral space during routine driving?
- Where should you position your vehicle when turning right?
- Where should you position your vehicle when turning left?

When discussing safe distances, we normally think about distances in front of and behind the vehicle. This is natural because that's where the primary hazards lie. However, you also need to pay attention to the space on either side of your car. This is called the *lateral space* or safety diamond.

You need to maintain a reasonable lateral space because it provides a safety margin against collisions with hazards on either side of your vehicle. These include vehicles that begin to change lanes without seeing you, pedestrians who step into the road, parked cars opening their doors and vehicles that stick their nose into

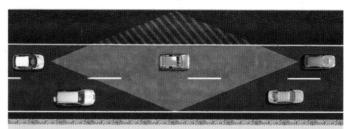

You also need to pay attention to the space on either side of your car. This is called the lateral space or safety diamond

When passing parked cars, try to leave a lateral space equivalent to the width of a car door in case someone doesn't see you coming and opens their door

traffic at junctions. Lateral space also gives you some room to manoeuvre without leaving your lane.

Lateral space is not as easy to control as the space behind and ahead of your vehicle. This is because a road may be very narrow – especially rural roads – or a vehicle in the adjoining lane may be unusually wide. Even so, there are several strategies you can apply to maintain your lateral space:

- As you learned in Module 8, you should generally stay in the lane's centre to give yourself ample lateral space.
- When passing parked cars, try to leave a lateral space equivalent to the width of a car door in case someone doesn't see you coming and opens their door. You may need to move to the right to do this, but be sure you're not making your lateral space too narrow on the right-hand side.
- On multilane carriageways, avoid driving close beside another vehicle for extended periods. Try to keep a space on either side.
- Adjust your speed to maintain optimum lateral space on multilane roads.
- When circumstances reduce your lateral space, slow down just as you do when circumstances reduce your space behind or ahead of you.

Your lateral space is important when you make a turn. When turning right, position your vehicle in the centre of the lane. This allows space for following traffic to pass and prevents you from getting too close to oncoming traffic. It also makes it easier for following traffic to see your right indicator.

When turning left, pull to the left of centre of the lane so you're about a metre from the curb. This allows the maximum possible room for following traffic to pass, while giving you ample space to turn.

Maintaining your safety margin

Aidhmeanna
OBJECTIVES **9** > **Look for, and highlight, the answers to these questions**

- How can you use your headlights to increase your safety margin?
- What three factors should you constantly pay attention to and adjust to control an adequate safety margin?

As you've learned, driving well consists of many mental skills: you have to be a co-operative driver and you have to scan constantly, so you can spot hazards and adjust for them. Part of this is always thinking about maintaining your safety margin.

Safety-margin thinking is a philosophy. It means that you constantly look for and do anything that makes driving safer. A good example is turning on your headlights whenever you drive – not just at night. Headlights make you more visible, which alerts other road users to your presence. At dusk be sure and switch your lights on in plenty of time. Your eyes may fool you into believing that it is brighter than it actually is. If they're already on, however, you've eliminated this problem.

When you drive well, you reduce your exposure to risk in every driving situation. You've already learned a great deal about paying attention to and adjusting the three factors – speed, positioning and communication – that you can control for an adequate safety margin. If you can't maintain adequate safety by adjusting these, then conditions are too bad for driving.

It's a good idea to get into the habit of always driving with your dipped headlights on, even in bright sunlight. This simple practice can make a huge difference to your safety

QUICK QUIZ

1   You can increase your safety margin by using your headlights during the day. T ☑ F ☐

2   Paying attention to and adjusting your speed, position and communications will help you to maintain an adequate safety margin.
T ☑ F ☐

3   It is only important to think about your safety margin in an emergency. T ☐ F ☑

Answers: 1: T, 2: T, 3: F

Having your headlights on at dusk is important. Don't wait until it's dark to switch on your lights

Summary points ▸▸▸▸▸▸▸

In this module on safety margin you learned:

1. Time gives you a safety margin, and you usually increase your safety margin by slowing down and allowing more distance between you and potential hazard.

2. The main reason you need a safety margin is that no one is perfect; we all need room for the mistakes we are bound to make.

3. You are responsible for maintaining your safety margin.

4. Circumstances constantly change while driving, so you must constantly adjust your safety margin.

5. Speed generally decreases your safety margin. However, in a few circumstances, such as overtaking, speed may increase your safety margin.

6. The faster you're going, the longer the stopping distance. Along with braking, the stopping time includes the time it takes to recognise a hazard and the time it takes to decide what to do and to put the plan into action.

7. Alertness, skill, experience, road conditions, vehicle condition and slope are some of the factors that can increase braking time and distance.

8. Speed limits post the designated maximum safe speed. It is not a target and you must adjust within the maximum to allow for hazards and driving conditions.

9. In Ireland, 82% of collisions result from excess speed. Speeding is a contributing factor in 40% of fatal crashes.

10. If you would be unable to stop in time for a potential road hazard, you're going too fast – even if you're within the speed limit.

11   Use the two-second rule to leave a safe gap between you and the vehicle ahead of you when it's going at about the same speed as you in optimum driving conditions. Use a longer gap when conditions are not optimal.

12   When stopped in traffic, leave enough space between you and the car ahead so you can see where the tyres of the vehicle in front touch the road.

13   Tailgating is dangerous because it poses a high collision risk and is distracting to other road users. When someone tailgates you, pull over or slow down at the first safe opportunity to let the tailgater go by.

14   Lateral space is the space on either side of your vehicle. Generally you should stay in the centre of the lane, but adjust your lateral space when passing parked cars or pedestrians or when making turns. When your lateral space gets too small, slow down.

15   Using your headlights during the day has been shown to reduce risk by making you more visible to other road users.

16   To maintain your safety margin, pay attention to and adjust your speed, position and how you communicate.

10

'I will shape my future. Whether I fail or
I succeed will be no man's doing but my
own.... My choice and my responsibility; win
or lose, only I hold the key to my destiny'

Elaine Maxwell

Responsibility

Introduction

As a driver, you affect other people in many ways, both directly and indirectly.
The effects range from how other road users react to your actions to the impact your
vehicle has on the environment. While it is impossible to eliminate *all* the negative
effects driving can have on others, there are ways for you to minimise them.

Throughout this course, you've learned about the many responsibilities you
have as a driver. You've learned that you need to be patient and co-operative, and
that competitive, aggressive driving has no place on the road. You've also learned
that it's important to communicate with other drivers so that they can recognise
your intentions and that you need to pay attention to your own emotional state
and how alert you are. We'll now look at some of those concepts in another light:
in terms of the broader impact your driving has, both on individuals and on
society at large.

In this module we will discuss...

- Sharing the road
- Aggression and driving
- Keeping your cool
- Considerate road use
- Communication
- Self-monitoring
- Safety belts and restraints
- The cost of road traffic incidents
- Energy and the environment

Sharing the road

Aidhmeanna **OBJECTIVES** **10** > **Look for, and highlight, the answers to these questions**

- Who is entitled to use the road?
- What four categories of road users require extra consideration and patience?

Roads are public resources that you and many other people share. No one has a greater right to the road than anyone else. Although engineers build modern roads primarily with motor vehicles in mind, cyclists, pedestrians and others have equal right to use them – apart from restricted roads such as motorways. Some drivers' skills may not be as sharp, developed or as quick as yours, but these drivers are still entitled to use the roads, just as you are. Being slightly inconvenienced by other road users is part of driving and something you should be prepared to deal with patiently. Remember, as a new driver, *you will be inconveniencing other road users*. Does this diminish your right to use the road? No. Do you want other road users to treat you with patience? Yes. A good rule of thumb is to treat others as you would like them to treat you.

Give learner drivers extra space and time, pressurising them to hurry up will only add to their stress

There are four categories of road users who require your extra consideration and patience. These are:

- **Learner drivers.** Experienced drivers need to allow learner drivers to take the extra time they need to accomplish routine manoeuvres. Give them space and don't cause them stress by trying to get them to hurry. You're a learner driver now – remember what it feels like so you'll know how to treat learner drivers when you're no longer one of them.

- **Elderly drivers.** Age affects co-ordination and vision, so elderly drivers tend to drive more slowly to compensate for their longer response times. You may be aware of the stereotype of elderly people as bad drivers. Did you know that the stereotype is wrong? Statistically, older drivers are among the safest road users, accounting for only 7% of serious crashes in Ireland. The reason is that their experience more than offsets their poorer vision or co-ordination. Sadly, elderly drivers are subject to more than their fair share of aggression on the roads. This has to stop, and you can help stop it. This is important because first, older drivers are the safest group of Irish drivers, and second, one day you will be one of them.

Statistically, older drivers are among the safest road users. Sadly, elderly drivers are subject to more than their fair share of aggression on the roads

Collision speeds that produce no injury when two cars are involved can hurt and even kill more vulnerable road users such as cyclists, pedestrians or horse riders

- **Pedestrians, cyclists, children and horse riders.** Non-motorists have as much right to use the road as motorists have. Unfortunately, anyone not in a vehicle doesn't have the protection that a vehicle affords – such as the protective metal shell, crumple zone and air bags – and is therefore extremely vulnerable. Collision speeds that produce little or no operational damage or personal injury when two cars are involved can hurt and even kill these more vulnerable road users. So, be cautious around them, give them a wide berth and be patient.

- **Motorcyclists.** They are especially vulnerable because they travel at the same high speeds as other motor vehicles, yet lack the protection of a vehicle around them. Give motorcyclists extra room and remember that on a dry surface, they can stop more quickly than you. On a wet road, they take longer to stop.

- **Disabled people.** Anyone with an impairment will require extra care and consideration. Be sure to give them extra space and time as required.

Motorcyclists are especially vulnerable because they travel at the same high speeds as other motor vehicles, yet lack the protection of a vehicle around them

QUICK QUIZ

1   The law only gives motor-vehicle drivers the right to use the road.   T ❑   F ❑

2   Elderly road users are the only road users who require your extra consideration and patience.   T ❑   F ❑

3   Giving learner drivers extra room and consideration only gives them a false sense of security.   T ❑   F ❑

Answers: 1: F, 2: F, 3: F

Aggression and driving

Aidhmeanna
OBJECTIVES **10** > Look for, and highlight, the answers
to these questions

- When is it acceptable to drive in an aggressive manner?
- Why does driving have the potential to make people aggressive
  and hostile?
- What types of behaviours or thinking can trigger aggressive
  driving behaviour in yourself and/or other drivers?

By now, you're well aware that aggressive driving is not acceptable at any time. But as you've probably seen, getting behind the wheel can trigger a 'Jekyll and Hyde' transformation in some people. Sometimes, it seems as if the most reasonable, calm and likeable people become unhinged when they get on the road. Since you don't want this to happen to you or to others, it helps to look at why driving has the potential to make people aggressive and hostile.

Getting behind the wheel can trigger a 'Jekyll and Hyde' transformation. The most reasonable, calm and likeable people can become unhinged when they get on the road!

- Driving can be stressful, and people handle stress differently. If stress is not relieved or controlled, it can lead to irritability, anger and aggression.

- Driving a vehicle insulates you from other road users: the vehicle acts as a barrier and it become easy to forget that there's a person in the other car. It is easy to act aggressively toward an inanimate object – a car – and not confront the reality of acting aggressively towards another driver. Inside a car, you may feel that you're anonymous and unrecognisable, and therefore shielded from the consequences of your behaviours. This perception is wrong.

- In some situations, a driver can imagine that he or she wields some power over traffic. You may feel that you can make up time or force traffic to speed up or get out of the way by driving aggressively, but in reality this is not the case.

Although you are now aware of some of the reasons why driving can trigger aggression, there may still be times when you begin to feel angry and tense. Therefore, you must be vigilant and avoid turning into Mr. Hyde – the bad guy – yourself. You can *choose* to think and act as a co-operative, considerate driver. You can choose to relax.

It's equally important to recognise the behaviours and thinking that can lead to aggressive driving. Some of these can make you aggressive, while others can trigger aggression in other motorists.

- Constant moaning and complaining about the behaviours of other drivers doesn't help anyone. You're going to see poor driving all the time, so it's better to accept it. You can be sure you'll do things that others might moan and complain about too.

- Thinking aggressive thoughts, such as fantasising about what you'd *like* to do, isn't appropriate, even if you don't plan on doing what you imagine. Aggressive thoughts tend to affect your concentration and reasoning. They also de-sensitise you, so that you become increasingly likely to do something aggressive.

- Don't verbally abuse other road users, even if they can't hear you.

- Driving competitively takes two forms. The obvious form is the aggressive driving you often see, where a driver is weaving and frantically trying to get ahead of other drivers. This kind of aggressive manoeuvring can trigger aggressive behaviour in other road users. The other form is much more subtle: you may not feel aggressive, but you accidentally do something that another driver *perceives* as competitive. Try to put yourself in the other driver's shoes before executing a manoeuvre, especially when you have little time to communicate it beforehand.

- Tailgating or invading safety margins can provoke aggression in the driver you're crowding.
- When you use your horn, lights or gestures to convey anger or displeasure, you're likely to trigger aggression. (It doesn't matter if the other driver deserves an angry gesture from you.) By the way, if someone honks, flashes or gestures in anger at you, wave in a way that says 'sorry' – *even if you feel you're completely in the right*. It may help to diffuse the other person's anger and help them to relax and drive safely.

Exceeding the speed limit or traffic flow is, by definition, aggressive driving. So is lane hopping and rushing through amber lights

Keeping your cool

Aidhmeanna **OBJECTIVES 10** **Look for, and highlight, the answers to these questions**

- What can you do to prevent yourself from becoming aggressive behind the wheel?
- What should you do when you encounter an aggressive driver?

How you behave while driving is something you *choose*. While you can't control the traffic or the behaviour of other road users, you can choose and control your own reaction to them. You have a responsibility to drive with care and patience no matter how much you're provoked. If you can't commit to this, you should not be driving.

Give yourself plenty of time to reach your destination. If you leave late, accept that you're going to be late. Don't let time pressures influence how you drive.

While you aren't helpless in the face of your feelings and emotions, it's true that it isn't always easy to stay calm while driving. Here are some tips to help you to drive in a co-operative and considerate frame of mind.

- Try to see the driver and not just the car, and to be seen as a driver and not as a vehicle. Communicate well and in a friendly manner with all road users.

- Give yourself plenty of time to reach your destination. If you leave late, accept that you're going to be late. Don't let time pressures influence how you drive.

- Don't take offence if another driver fails to behave as you would like or expect them to behave. If someone is delaying or irritating you, recognise that the behaviour is most likely unintentional.

- Recognise the early symptoms of aggressive driving in yourself. Avoid complaining about the conduct of other drivers. It may seem fun at first, but it can easily lead to aggressive driving.

- Remember that as you move away from being calm and rational, you move away from driving safely. The more anger you feel, the more risk you create because anger impairs your ability to drive well.

If you encounter someone who is driving dangerously, remember that allowing yourself to get upset reduces your ability to drive safely. Concentrate on your own driving. If possible, put some space between you and the other driver to protect yourself and your passengers. If you consider the situation to be a threat to others, you should alert the Gardaí on 999 or 112, or on Traffic Watch, 1890 205 805. Try to make a note of the make, colour and registration number of the vehicle and the direction in which it is heading. Your call could save a life.

- Never allow yourself to respond aggressively to another driver's aggressive behaviour. Two drivers behaving irresponsibly will endanger each other and other road users.

1 Giving yourself plenty of time to reach your destination helps to lessen the tendency to become aggressive behind the wheel.
T ☑ F ☐

2 When you encounter an aggressive driver give back as good as you get. T ☐ F ☑

3 Anger impairs your ability to remain in control and drive well. T ☑ F ☐

Answers: 1: T, 2: F, 3: T

- If you are confronted by an enraged driver, do not engage with the person in any way. Do not even make eye contact. Stay in your car with the doors locked and windows closed and if possible, drive to the nearest Garda Station or to a place where there are people who can help or act as witnesses. If you can't drive away, try to attract attention by sounding your horn or calling for help on your mobile phone.

Considerate road use

Aidhmeanna **OBJECTIVES** **10** > **Look for, and highlight, the answers to these questions**

- What driving practices help you avoid antagonising or irritating other road users?
- Why you should make these driving practices habits?

In the section on aggression and driving, you learned that certain behaviours and ways of thinking can trigger aggressive driving in other drivers and in yourself. Now let's look at the positive side and review some ways of showing consideration for other drivers.

Respect other drivers' space – that is, their safety margin. When you crowd another driver, you're reducing that driver's intended safety margin. It can make them feel threatened, annoyed, defensive, aggressive or distracted. On the other hand, when you respect a driver's space, you increase road safety by reducing stress for both of yourself and them. You also reduce the chances of a collision occurring should either party make a mistake.

Stay left except when overtaking. If you're driving more slowly, allow others to overtake. In general, try not to delay other drivers unnecessarily. Even when you feel another driver is travelling faster than they should be, you gain nothing by being in their way.

Refrain from double parking, parking near corners or blocking traffic just because it's convenient to you – it's often unsafe and inconvenient for those you're blocking

On multilane roads, don't travel in the right-hand lane. Stay to the left unless you're overtaking. Similarly, refrain from double parking, parking near corners or blocking traffic just because it's convenient to you – it's often unsafe and inconvenient for those you're blocking. Put yourself in the other drivers' places before you do something that will impede traffic flow.

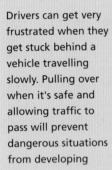
Drivers can get very frustrated when they get stuck behind a vehicle travelling slowly. Pulling over when it's safe and allowing traffic to pass will prevent dangerous situations from developing

Allow other drivers to pass. You are free to choose a safe and comfortable speed below the posted speed limit but don't forget to allow other drivers to pass you should they wish to travel faster. Even normally passive drivers can get very frustrated and aggressive when they get stuck behind a vehicle travelling slowly. Pulling over when it's safe and allowing traffic to pass will prevent potentially dangerous situations from developing due to the frustration of drivers who feel stuck behind you – especially on single-lane or narrow roads with few overtaking opportunities.

Be considerate when you pull out from a junction. No matter how long you've been waiting at a junction, wait until there's ample space to pull out. Remember that you may tend to accept more risk as you become impatient unless you're on guard to avoid it. An alert and considerate driver may slow up to let you out but, failing that, a safe gap will always come along eventually. Pulling out in front of another vehicle causing it to brake hard or slow significantly is not only inconsiderate and antagonising but dangerous. You can't take it for granted that the other driver can or will stop in time, which means you risk causing a collision, not just annoyance.

Don't allow yourself to be pressurised into pulling out dangerously, wait for the appropriate opportunity

Leave plenty of room when returning to a position in front of another vehicle. When overtaking or changing lanes, be careful not to cut in too close in front of other drivers and enter their safety margin. You should be able to see the other vehicle in your rear-view mirror before you move in front. If oncoming traffic will force you to cut in too close to the vehicle you plan to overtake, then there is insufficient room for the manoeuvre.

Maintain your lane. Weaving, lane hopping and other frequent lane changes to try to beat the prevailing traffic flow is rude and unsafe. Lane changing on a busy road requires co-operation and communication – both of which you're not likely to get when you change lanes erratically with little or no warning. It's OK to overtake safely if you'll be able to maintain a higher safe speed after overtaking. But if you repeatedly overtake and end up going the same speed, you're just being inconsiderate. You're creating extra risk and are unlikely to gain any time.

When overtaking or changing lanes, you should be able to see the other vehicle in your rear-view mirror before you move back into the lane

Pay attention at traffic lights. It's a good habit to check right and left before proceeding when a light changes at a junction, even if this means you don't move forward the instant the light changes. Don't delay for too long, though – no one likes waiting because someone's day-dreaming. On the other hand, if someone else stalls or delays at a light, be patient. The delay may be for safety reasons, not necessarily because the driver isn't paying attention.

Dip your lights. At night, dip your lights for oncoming traffic. Full lights can dazzle drivers, making it hard for them to maintain their lane and avoid hazards.

Full beams blind oncoming traffic, so dip your lights in plenty of time

Communicate in a clear and polite way. Communication goes a long way towards making drivers co-operative. Acknowledge drivers who help you in traffic, and wave regrets when you accidentally do something inconsiderate – which you will. Actions like these encourage others to drive in a considerate manner.

Not all drivers will treat you well. You'll see plenty of examples of bad behaviour but, as you've already learned, you're better off *not* assuming you know everything that's on another driver's mind. There are at least three reasons for making considerate driving a habit even though you should expect that others won't always do the same.

1   **Considerate driving makes the road safer for you as well as others.**
    No matter how someone else drives, being considerate in return reduces your risk. It keeps you from antagonising other drivers. To put it another way, being considerate on the road is not only nice – it's in your own best interest.

2   **Considerate driving keeps you from becoming aggressive.** It's hard to take a competitive, aggressive stance while trying to be accommodating and courteous. They're completely different mindsets.

3   **Considerate driving is more enjoyable.** Whether or not you get stressed by heavy traffic usually has more to do with your attitude than with how crowded the road is. You'll find that when you drive generously – such as giving way by helping others to overtake or change lanes – the reward is almost always greater than what you give. Driving selfishly, on the other hand, inevitably makes driving an unpleasant chore. The choice is yours.

Communication

Aidhmeanna OBJECTIVES 10 ▷ **Look for, and highlight, the answers to these questions**

- Why is it important to signal correctly?
- What are the appropriate uses of your indicators?
- What are the appropriate uses of hazard warning lights?
- When should you flash your full headlights or sound your horn?
- What is 'passive' or 'unintended' communication? How does it benefit you as a road user?

Up till now, we've talked a lot about the need to communicate your intentions. You've already learned that signalling correctly is important because it helps others know your intentions and makes for safer driving. Now let's go through specific ways of signalling in more detail.

Your car provides most of your primary signalling methods through various lights and the horn. However, you can also signal by hand to help clarify a situation; for general, person-to-person communication; or in the event of your car's signals failing.

Indicators. Use the indicators to show that you intend to turn, to overtake or to pull over. Don't leave other road users guessing what you may or may not do because they may guess incorrectly. Indicate with ample time for others to adjust, but not so far ahead that people wonder whether you're ever going to do what your indicators suggest. It's important to indicate your intentions even when your intentions seem obvious; you would be surprised how often what you think is obvious is anything but clear to others.

Indicating your intentions clearly allows other road users know what you intend to do, it also shows that you are a considerate driver

If an indicator bulb fails you will be alerted by the rapid flashing of your dash light. Use the hand signals shown in the Rules of the Road and replace the bulb without delay.

Brake lights. Other vehicles know that you're stopping when they see your brake lights come on as you press the brake pedal. This makes it very important to check regularly that your brake lights are working, and to change bulbs promptly when one goes out.

Reverse lights. White reversing lights come on when you put the car in reverse gear. This helps to light the area behind you, but it also warns others that you're backing up. Again, make sure these lights are working, and get in the habit of scanning for reverse lights in parking areas. They can alert you to a vehicle that may be about to reverse – whether you are a pedestrian or a motorist.

Hazard warning lights. Flashing amber lights tell other drivers that you're having a problem; that you've stopped in a place that presents a road hazard; or that you're driving very slowly due to a hazard ahead or hazardous conditions.

Parking lights. Use your parking lights when you're parked somewhere temporarily that does not present a particular hazard. The lights make your vehicle more visible and tell others that you plan to leave shortly. A good example is when parked in a loading/unloading zone at dusk.

Neither hazard nor parking lights give you a licence to park illegally or without consideration for others, even though you'll sometimes see other people do both.

Horn. Use your horn to warn other drivers of an imminent hazard. In most vehicles you sound the horn by pressing the centre of the steering wheel or buttons along the edges, but the location varies. Make sure you know where the horn is. Be aware that it is illegal to use the horn in built-up areas between 11:30 pm and 7 am, except in an emergency.

Using the horn allows you to alert other road users to imminent danger. It is illegal to use the horn in built up areas between 23:30hrs and 07:00hrs, except in an emergency

Full headlights. Normally you only use full headlights on unlit roads when there is no oncoming traffic. However, you can flash your 'high beams', as they're known, to alert other drivers of your presence, to warn oncoming

Polite hand gestures are useful for thanking other drivers and for acknowledging when you've inconvenienced someone

traffic of a hazard, or to remind someone who forgets to dip their headlights – but don't leave them on to 'get even' if the other driver doesn't take the hint. Don't leave them on full when following or approaching other vehicles, because this will dazzle the other drivers and impair their vision.

Waving and hand gestures. Polite hand gestures are useful for thanking other drivers and for acknowledging when you've inconvenienced someone. They provide a personal touch that helps people be more considerate.

Be cautious about what you signal. You shouldn't wave anyone to cross a road because you may not be able to see all the potential hazards.

Be cautious about what you signal, however. For example, you shouldn't wave anyone to cross a road because you may not be able to see all the potential hazards.

Considerate, clear communication between you and other road users makes driving safer and less stressful. Keep these points in mind:

- Use your mirrors and scan to ensure that the manoeuvre you have in mind is safe. Your signals indicate intent. They do *not* give you right of way.
- Signal your intentions early and clearly prior to a manoeuvre.
- Confirm that your indicators are off after a turn or lane change. Forgetting and leaving them on can cause miscommunication and lead to collisions.
- Make sure your intention is clear. For example, if you're turning and there's another turn just ahead of the one you want to make, be cautious not to signal too early or in a way that leads others to think you're taking the first instead of the second turn.

- Not everyone uses signals correctly – often circumstances make even the most skilled driver's communications unclear. Therefore, don't rely entirely on an indicator or other signal. Instead, be prepared to react based on the worst case. For example, if someone indicates a turn and the manoeuvre would be hazardous to you, adjust accordingly. On the other hand, if the indicator is on, never assume that the driver will turn until it is unmistakeably clear that they *will*.

- Make a habit of waving thanks when someone does you a favour or when you accidentally inconvenience someone. It goes a long way toward making the roads more friendly, safe and efficient.

- Blaring your horn or flashing your lights to alert drivers of their mistakes is illegal. It's also provocative and serves no useful purpose.

It would be great if everyone signalled correctly and consistently, but that's not what happens in reality. Drivers can fail to indicate because of bad driving habits – but even excellent drivers forget once in a while. To help offset this, you need to learn to recognise *passive* or *unintended* communication. Thats when a driver's behaviour alerts you to their intention without the driver purposely *signalling* the intention. For example, if you're approaching a junction and the car ahead begins to slow, the driver may be planning to turn even though the indicator isn't flashing. On multilane carriageways, you may notice a driver move to the side of the lane or checking the mirrors, alerting you to a possible lane change without indicating.

You can anticipate many intentions by paying attention to passive communication. But a driver's ability to do this does not excuse those drivers who fail to signal their intentions properly. Being able to recognise passive communication is a skill that helps drivers accommodate each other's imperfections and mistakes; it's not a replacement for good driving habits.

QUICK QUIZ

1 It is important to signal correctly because it helps others to know your intentions, which makes for safer driving. T ☑ F ☐

2 Use your indicators when you want someone to overtake you. T ☑ F ☐

3 Only use your horn or flash your full headlights to warn other drivers of a hazard. T ☑ F ☐

Answers: 1: T, 2: F, 3: T

Self-monitoring

Aidhmeanna
OBJECTIVES **10**

Look for, and highlight, the answers to these questions

- What is the best way to ensure that you continue to improve as a driver?
- What aspects of your driving should you consider when assessing your driving ability and the effect your road use has on others?

One habit that distinguishes bad drivers from good drivers is that bad drivers often focus more on the mistakes others make rather than on how they could improve their own driving. Good drivers focus more on assessing their own actions and the effects their behaviours have on others. This goes back to the fact that you can only control one thing while driving – yourself. Therefore, the best way to ensure that you continue to improve as a driver is to evaluate what you do on the road throughout your driving career.

Self-monitoring means that you constantly assess your attitude, your driving skills, your safety margins, the decisions you make and anything else that affects how you drive. When you're accustomed to self-monitoring, you'll find yourself thinking things like, 'Oops, I made that turn without looking far enough down the road. If another car was coming, I would have had a collision. Better not do that again!' Or suppose you notice that you invade another driver's safety margin after you make a lane change. You say to yourself, 'OK, I got away with the lane change, but what if the other driver hadn't been paying attention? That was risky and inconsiderate.' You wave an apology, thank your lucky stars and resolve not to repeat the mistake.

QUICK QUIZ

1 To ensure that you continue to improve as a driver, you should constantly evaluate what you do on the road. T ☑ F ☐

2 Focusing on the mistakes other drivers make will help you to learn from them. T ☐ F ☑

3 Self-monitoring means occasionally evaluating your attitude. T ☐ F ☑

Answers: 1: T, 2: F, 3: F

Safety belts and restraints

Aidhmeanna OBJECTIVES 10 ▷ Look for, and highlight, the answers to these questions

- What are the benefits of safety belts in a vehicle?
- Who is responsible for the wearing of safety belts in a vehicle?
- What is the proper way to use and adjust safety belts?
- How do you restrain children who are too small to use an adult safety belt?
- What is the proper way to use and position rear-facing child safety seats?
- What is the function of a head restraint in a vehicle?
- What is the correct position for a head restraint?

You're already aware that safety belts save lives during collisions and that they can help you drive safely by keeping you in the best position for driving. We'll now take a closer look at how safety belts and other types of restraints should be used.

Safety belts have been mandatory in all Irish-registered cars since 1992, and since before then in many other countries. In the event of a collision, people wearing safety belts are less likely to be injured or killed. Is this a guarantee? Of course not – but statistically speaking, safety belts are the safest bet. Safety belts help to transfer the momentum of the occupants to the vehicle in a collision. Those who wear safety belts are more likely to be conscious and able to help themselves and others after a crash.

Safety belts save lives during collisions and they can help you drive safely by keeping you in the best position for driving

You should never drive without your safety belt. More than half of all collisions occur within a few kilometres of home, so there's no justification for leaving the safety belt off for a short trip.

You should never drive without your safety belt. More than half of all collisions occur within a few kilometres of home, so there's no justification for leaving the safety belt off for a short trip.

The law requires you to wear a seat belt, it will protect you and others in the event of a crash

Safety belts and the law

Irish law requires everyone in a regular vehicle to wear safety belts, including children and pregnant women. The law states that you are responsible for wearing your safety belt, and for ensuring that all passengers under 17 wear theirs. Passengers over 17 are legally responsible for themselves and can be fined for not wearing a safety belt. Even so, don't allow anyone to travel with you if they refuse to wear a safety belt because, as the driver, *you* are ultimately responsible for passenger safety. If a passenger objects, politely remind them that going without a safety belt endangers *everyone* in the vehicle. Certain categories of vehicles and professions may be subject to special exemptions regarding the use of safety belts, such as classic cars and members of the Gardaí – but this is the exception rather than the rule.

Of all the children who were killed in collisions in Ireland from 1996 to 2000, over three-quarters died because they weren't wearing safety belts or seated in special child restraints

Safety-belt placement

Safety belts are only effective when worn properly. The lap portion should go across your hips, and the shoulder belt should sit between your neck and shoulder and across your chest. Adjust the height, if possible, so that it doesn't lie right next to your neck. Wear the belt snugly so there's no slack, though it shouldn't be uncomfortably tight. On long journeys you may have to readjust the belt's position from time to time for comfort and maximum protection.

Child safety belts and restraints

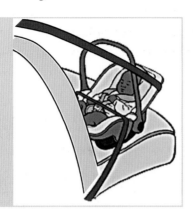

Infants weighing up to 9 kg can be placed in rear-facing baby seats that you attach to the car seat with the normal safety belt or with special hooks or straps

Research shows that of all the children who were killed in collisions from 1996 to 2000, over three-quarters died because they weren't wearing safety belts or seated in special child restraints. It is not safe or effective to carry a child in an adult's lap because in the event of a crash, momentum will either push the adult forward, crushing the child, or momentum will tear the child from the adult's arms. Remember from Module 2 that when you double your speed, you quadruple your momentum. In a sudden impact at 70 km/h, it takes more than *100 kg* of force to hold an unrestrained five-kilogram child on your lap. Few people are strong enough, so the child would be thrown onto the windscreen and out of the vehicle.

Because of their size, children need special safety restraints. Infants weighing up to 9 kg can be placed in rear-facing baby seats that you attach to the car seat with the normal safety belt or with special hooks or straps. It is best to place all child restraint seats in the back seat. Never put a child restraint seat in the front seat of a car fitted with airbags, unless the passenger-side airbag can be deactivated. This is because airbags can cause severe injury to infants and children.

Larger infants and toddlers who are up to four years old or who weigh less than 18 kg can be carried in forward-facing child safety seats

Larger infants and toddlers who are up to four years old or who weigh less than 18 kg can be carried in forward-facing child safety seats. When installing a safety seat, consult the manufacturer's guidelines or get professional help.

Children under 12 should also sit in the back. They may use adult safety belts if they fit properly. If necessary, use a booster seat so that the child is sitting at the proper height for an adult safety belt. If the child is too small to use the adult safety belts, then he or she should sit in a child safety seat.

Children under 12 should also sit in the back. They may use adult safety belts if they fit properly. If necessary, use a booster seat so that the child is sitting at the proper height for an adult safety belt

With any child car seats, make sure the seat carries the ISO certification mark and get advice about fitting the seat properly in your car. Be careful if you are buying a second-hand car seat because the technology is improving all the time; a seat only a few years old may be far less effective than a new model in the event of a collision.

The head restraint will help to reduce neck injuries and whiplash in the event of a crash, be sure and set the height to suit you

Head restraints

Head restraints are designed to reduce neck and spinal injury in the event of a crash. When positioned correctly, they keep your head from snapping backward in a collision, preventing severe neck and spinal injury. The main mistake drivers make with head restraints is failing to adjust them properly. You and your passengers should set the height so that the centre of the restraint is level with your eyes and ears, and as close to the back of your head as is comfortable.

QUICK QUIZ

1 As the driver, you are responsible for wearing your safety belt, and for ensuring that all passengers under 17 wear theirs. T ☑ F ☐

2 Wear your safety belt so the lap portion is high above the hips and the shoulder portion rests against your neck. T ☐ F ☑

3 Head restraints are primarily for resting your head on long journeys. T ☐ F ☑

Answers: 1: T, 2: F, 3: F

The cost of road traffic incidents

Aidhmeanna
OBJECTIVES **10** > Look for, and highlight, the answers to these questions

- How does a death or serious injury affect the community?
- What effects do road incidents have on individuals, on society and on the economy?

You've already learned that currently 87% of Irish road collisions result from driver error. At first glance, you might think that traffic incidents have a limited effect on others – that they only affect the people directly involved in the crash. The reality is that bad driving is a burden on Irish society at large. Road incidents have broad social, personal and economic effects that can reach well beyond those directly involved. It's worth considering this because as a driver, you have the potential to trigger an unfortunate chain of events that can upset many lives.

Let's look at an example. Karen is a secondary-school physical-education teacher. She's planning a trip to France in two weeks with her class, and she's getting married in three months' time. She's the primary caregiver for her aging mother. Driving home at 2:00 a.m., a driver exceeding the speed limit collides with her. Fortunately, she was wearing her safety belt and was able to take some evasive action; she survives but loses her leg. Besides Karen, who does this collision affect?

- The Gardaí and medical personnel who have to respond to the collision.
- Others who need help at the same time but who now have to wait because the emergency personnel are helping Karen.
- The hospital personnel who must attend to Karen.
- Those waiting on trolleys in the accident and emergency ward who would be receiving care if the hospital personnel weren't helping Karen.
- Karen's class of 30 students who will have to postpone their trip to France.
- Karen's workmates at school who must find a way to cover her classes, temporarily or even permanently.

Bad driving is a burden on Irish society at large. Road crashes have broad social, personal and economic effects that can reach well beyond those directly involved

- Karen's students in each class period who will, in the short term, not have a PE teacher.
- Karen's mother, who will lose her primary caregiver.
- Karen's brother, who has to either take over as their mother's caregiver, or find a professional aide.
- Karen's fiancé, who suddenly finds himself having to help Karen recover her quality of life and change their plans for their wedding and their future.
- Everyone involved in the wedding plans.
- *You,* to the degree that Karen's emergency care, recovery, artificial limb and therapy will be largely funded by taxes. That is no small sum.

The list could go on. Karen's injury will have an enormous effect not just on her own and her family's lives, but on the lives of people she had never met before the collision – and on people she will never meet.

Things might be a bit better if those injured in a crash could count on a full and quick recovery. Unfortunately, however, people involved in collisions often suffer physical and psychological damage for years if not permanently. Crash survivors may need years of follow-up surgery, therapy and medication just to cope with the aftermath. They have to deal with financial effects that range from medical costs to losing a career because they're no longer physically capable of working. Even so-called 'minor' injuries can have devastating psychological effects, such as injuries that cause disfigurement.

Even those who aren't hurt may suffer long-term consequences. In Karen's case, the driver who caused the crash wasn't hurt, but will spend the rest of their life regretting a bad decision that changed another person's life forever. They face legal charges, court actions, a possible jail sentence and may spend years recovering financially. There is even a significant cost to you, the taxpayer: road-traffic incidents cost about 1.1 billion per year.

In psychological and legal terms, there is a huge difference between being involved in a bad collision that injures others if you were driving reasonably and responsibly, and being involved in a collision as a result of showing off or driving in a reckless manner.

Life is precious and fragile. Road collisions take away more young lives than any other single cause. No amount of time or money can ever ease the grief that these lost lives cause. Until you're a parent, you cannot begin to imagine how devastating it is to lose a child; loving parents would rather give their lives than to see their children lose theirs. Likewise, it's almost impossible to imagine what it would be like to grow up without one or both of your parents. Driving is a serious endeavour that may involve far greater risks than anything else you do. Remember, you have a choice. Choosing to be co-operative and conservative, and to drive well within your safety margin, isn't simply about avoiding collisions. It's also a conscious decision that you make not to destroy or damage the lives of others through your actions.

The following table lists some scenarios. Give some of the possible social, personal and economic effects these events might have. You should be able to give an example of each effect for every scenario in the list.

Situation	Social	Personal	Economic
Car crashes into a bridge resulting in closure for repairs			
Car and truck collide blocking a motorway			
Person killed following a crash			
Driver is prosecuted following an incident			
Crash victim suffers spinal injury and is wheelchair-bound			
Truck driver loses licence after a crash			
Young person cannot afford insurance renewal after a crash			
A multi-vehicle incident closes the centre of the town for three hours			
Driver receives penalty points and a fine and must go to court following an incident			

Energy and the environment

Aidhmeanna OBJECTIVES 10 Look for, and highlight, the answers to these questions

- How do cars affect the environment?
- What are the benefits and negative effects of different types of fuels?
- How can you reduce the emissions you produce and the amount of fuel you consume?
- What is the law regarding the disposal of vehicles and accessories?

Although cars give us great mobility, they are damaging the environment that we all depend upon for life

Cars give us great mobility and freedom, and they're important to the economy. Without the modern automobile, society as we know it would not exist. However, the car is damaging the environment that we all depend upon for life. A few environmental effects of cars include:

- Air pollution from toxic exhaust gases.
- Global warming caused by carbon dioxide released from burning fossil fuels (*i.e.*, petrol and diesel).
- Groundwater contamination by oil, coolant and engine fluids, and by the dozens of chemicals used in manufacturing.
- Roads reshape the natural terrain, alter water runoff and disturb wildlife.

- Building cars devours resources: it takes a tremendous amount of material and energy to make a car.
- Noise and light pollution reduce our ability to relax, affect animal behaviour and have been linked to allergies, migraines and sleeping disorders.
- Disposing of vehicles once their useful life is over uses up substantial resources.

The more cars on roads around the world, the greater all these effects will be. The solution isn't to stop driving, because the social consequences of that would be unimaginable. Rather, technology must improve to reduce environmental effects and repair the damage that's already been done. This is already happening, and you can now make choices that reduce the impact your driving has on the environment.

Emissions

Your choice of fuel affects the quantities and types of emissions your car releases. All internal combustion engines create carbon monoxide, nitrous oxide, hydrocarbons, sulphur dioxide, particulates and other toxic gases. Leaded petrol has been replaced by unleaded or lead replacement petrol (LRP), an important advance because lead in the environment affects brain function and causes cancer and acid rain. Unleaded petrol is not only kinder to the environment, but is also necessary in engines that have catalytic converters. These devices change carbon monoxide into less toxic carbon dioxide. However, carbon dioxide is still a problem because it is a greenhouse gas that contributes to global warming.

New technologies are also helping to reduce emissions. Eco-cars that run on vegetable oils, solar power, rechargeable batteries and hydrogen fuel cells are coming onto the market. These help by reducing or better containing the pollutants. Vehicles that run on vegetable oil still release carbon dioxide through combustion, but because the carbon dioxide originates from a plant source, the net contribution to global warming is less than it would be if the car ran on fossil fuels.

Even if you're driving a conventional petrol vehicle, you can still reduce the amount of fuel you consume and therefore the amount of pollution your

Vehicles that run on vegetable oil still release carbon dioxide through combustion, but because the carbon dioxide originates from a plant source, the net contribution to global warming is less

vehicle creates. You can reduce your fuel consumption by reducing how much you drive and by modifying your driving to use fuel in a more efficient way. The following steps will help you reduce the amount of fuel you use, which is not only better for the environment, but also saves you money.

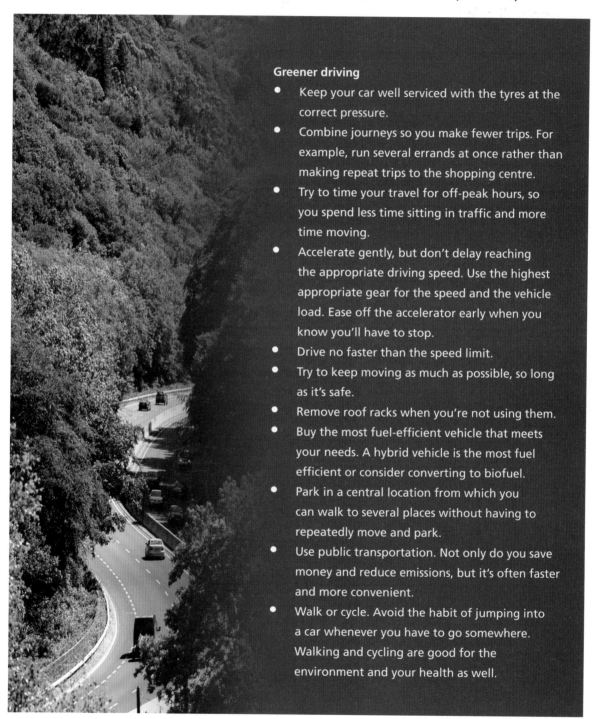

Greener driving

- Keep your car well serviced with the tyres at the correct pressure.
- Combine journeys so you make fewer trips. For example, run several errands at once rather than making repeat trips to the shopping centre.
- Try to time your travel for off-peak hours, so you spend less time sitting in traffic and more time moving.
- Accelerate gently, but don't delay reaching the appropriate driving speed. Use the highest appropriate gear for the speed and the vehicle load. Ease off the accelerator early when you know you'll have to stop.
- Drive no faster than the speed limit.
- Try to keep moving as much as possible, so long as it's safe.
- Remove roof racks when you're not using them.
- Buy the most fuel-efficient vehicle that meets your needs. A hybrid vehicle is the most fuel efficient or consider converting to biofuel.
- Park in a central location from which you can walk to several places without having to repeatedly move and park.
- Use public transportation. Not only do you save money and reduce emissions, but it's often faster and more convenient.
- Walk or cycle. Avoid the habit of jumping into a car whenever you have to go somewhere. Walking and cycling are good for the environment and your health as well.

As of 2007, the last owner of a car is responsible for end-of-life vehicle (ELV) disposal

Disposing of a vehicle

Even a vehicle that has reached the end of its useful life continues to affect the environment. By law, you must have it scrapped in an authorised disposal centre. The disposal centre dismantles and recycles parts of the vehicle and disposes of potentially toxic components such as fluids, oil, batteries and tyres. As of 2007, the last owner of a car is responsible for end-of-life vehicle (ELV) disposal. Laws also require that you dispose of batteries, oil, fluids and other toxic components in the proper manner during the vehicle's normal service life.

By law, you must have your old car scrapped in an authorised disposal centre when it has reached the end of its working life

Summary points ▸▸▸▸▸▸▸

In this module on responsibility you learned:

1   Everyone is entitled to use the road. You should have more patience and consideration for learner drivers, elderly people, pedestrians, cyclists, disabled people, horseback riders and motorcyclists.

2   It is never acceptable to drive in an aggressive manner. Driving has the potential to make people aggressive because it can be stressful.
It's easy to forget that there are people just like you in the other cars.

3   Moaning and complaining and thinking aggressive thoughts can trigger aggressive driving. Competitive driving is, by definition, aggressive.

4   Keep your cool behind the wheel by seeing the other driver, not the car.

5   Give yourself plenty of time to reach your destination and don't take offence when someone does something unexpected or improper.

6   Never respond aggressively to another driver's aggressive behaviour.

7   You can avoid antagonising or irritating other drivers by respecting safety margins, staying left except when overtaking, being considerate when pulling out and by communicating clearly. These simple habits make the road safer; keep you from becoming aggressive; and also make driving more enjoyable.

8   Signal correctly so that others will know your intentions. Use indicators, hazard lights, full headlights and the horn in the appropriate way.

9   Pay attention to passive communication by other drivers.

10 Throughout your driving career, you can keep improving as a driver by constantly monitoring anything that affects your driving behaviours.

11   Safety belts reduce the risk of injury and death in a collision and are required by law.

12   Children under 12 should be in an appropriate child safety seat.

13   Position your head restraint properly to reduce the risk of neck or spinal injury.

14   Road incidents have significant personal, social and economic costs. Drive responsibly to avoid them. A single collision can affect hundreds of people, and it can go on affecting people for the rest of their lives.

15   Motorised vehicles damage the environment. Your choice of fuel and driving habits can minimise these effects.

16   Follow the proper procedures to dispose of your vehicle when it reaches the end of its useful life.

11

'What you risk reveals what you value'

Jeanette Winterson

Risk management

Introduction

Everything we do involves some risk. We constantly weigh the possible risks of actions against their benefits. Simply crossing the road involves risk: you must decide when and where to cross to minimise the risk of getting knocked down. Using a pedestrian crossing substantially lessens the risk. Weighing the risks versus benefits and choosing the least risky option is called 'risk management'.

Driving constantly involves taking calculated risks and, while nobody expects to have an accident, they do occur. Risk management not only helps you to avoid problems but it also improves your chance of survival should the worst happen. It can be as simple as always wearing your safety belt or keeping your vehicle in good working order.

To effectively manage risk you must recognise it and adjust your driving accordingly. In this module we look at situations that increase risk such as changes in the weather, road types and conditions and at ways to improve your safety by managing the risks.

In this module we will discuss...

- Different road types and challenges
- Weather conditions
- Night driving
- Loading and towing
- Driving in unfamiliar areas and in other countries
- Emergency procedures

Different road types, different challenges

Aidhmeanna OBJECTIVES 11 Look for, and highlight, the answers to these questions

- In terms of risks, what are the advantages and disadvantages of the various road categories – motorways, dual carriageways, rural roads, urban roads?
- How do you manage the risks on the different types of roads?

Different types of roads present different driving circumstances. Let's look at the differences between motorways, dual carriageways, rural roads and urban roads with an eye toward their relative advantages and disadvantages, and what you should do to manage the risks unique to each.

Motorways are denoted by the prefix 'M' on road maps and they provide an efficient and controlled environment with at least four lanes of traffic separated by a central median. The vehicles on either side of the median travel in the same direction. Motorways are by far the safest roads to travel as they do not have traffic crossing on the same level. Entries and exits are well marked and allow for seamless merging and diverging.

Motorways are generally kept in good repair, have wide lanes and have good signage, road marking and reflective aids.

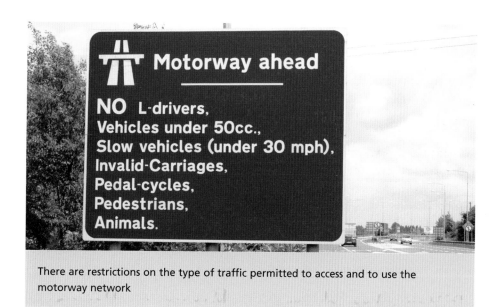

There are restrictions on the type of traffic permitted to access and to use the motorway network

As traffic can travel very fast on motorways it is very important to stay alert. Be aware of the position of other vehicles in relation to your own and scan well ahead for hazards. Watch for brake lights in the distance; you may have to stop because of congestion ahead and decelerating safely from 120km/h will take approximately the distance of 24 average car lengths. So leave ample space between you and the vehicle in front.

It is easy to underestimate your speed on a motorway, so watch your speedometer to be sure you are driving within your capacity to stop and within the speed limit. Travelling on this type of road is often less interesting than on a rural or smaller road, so it is important not to get hypnotised by the monotony of motorway driving and to use the techniques outlined in Module 3, to help you stay alert.

The speed limit for cars on a motorway is 120 km/h for trucks, single-deck and mini-buses it is 80 km/h; and for double-deck buses and larger mini-buses it is 65 km/h.

Dual carriageways are denoted with the prefix 'N' on road maps. They have two or more lanes in each direction and allow traffic to enter directly from the side roads. They may or may not have a dividing median. National and Secondary routes are often dual carriageways. Dual carriageways have less restrictions than motorways and are accessible to most road users.

The speed limit on dual carriageways is generally 100km/h unless otherwise posted and is therefore higher than the limit on all other types of roads apart from motorways. Driving on a dual carriageway requires extra vigilance because you have to deal with crossing traffic, vehicles entering from junctions and vulnerable road users such as cyclists and pedestrians.

Rural, regional and local roads are prefixed with the letter 'R' on road maps. They tend to be two-lane roads – one lane in each direction – and are less likely to be well maintained than the major routes. Local roads tend to have many twists, turns, intersections, homes and surprises awaiting you around the corner. Rural roads are interesting to drive on but they are deceptive; they are rarely as empty or as safe as they seem. They are less forgiving than major roads, have little room for taking evasive action and conceal many potential hazards.

Watch out for hazards such as slow-moving agricultural vehicles, pedestrians on your side of the road, cyclists, horses and riders, narrowing of the road where it may be impossible for two vehicles to pass safely, blind bends, sudden sharp turns, concealed entrances, uneven road surfaces and animals.

To manage your risk, stay alert and be prepared to stop at short notice. Slow down on the approach to blind bends and leave space between your car and the road margin; the absence of footpaths does not mean there are no pedestrians and anyone walking on rural roads will, quite literally, be sharing the road with you. Once again the speed limit on these roads varies but it is rarely safe to drive at more than 80km/h. Speed limits of 60km/h and 50km/h may be posted.

Urban and suburban roads are often congested. Bikes or pedestrians weaving between cars can catch you unawares if you are not scanning properly. The footpaths are crowded with pedestrians and vulnerable road users. Traffic flow is controlled by numerous junctions, signals and road markings so you will need to drive carefully but decisively if you are to negotiate busy streets and junctions safely and effectively. Remember that other road users may not take you into account or even be aware of your presence when they decide to cross the road, change lanes, pull out of a parking space or reverse into one. They may not be patient with drivers who are not alert or decisive when trying to join a busy stream of traffic.

You need to pay particular attention to your driving environment to stay safe in towns. Be observant, filter out distractions, scan for and anticipate hazards and distribute your attention.

Take particular care on the roads around schools, which can become chaotic around opening and closing times, and never park at or close to a school entrance. The speed limit in our towns and cities is usually 50km/h and on busy streets it is unwise to drive above 30 or 40km/h.

QUICK QUIZ

1 Disadvantages of motorway driving include wide lanes and shoulders and no cross traffic.
   T ☑ F ☐

2 A disadvantage of dual carriageways is that they have junctions and intersections where traffic can cross paths on the same level, exposing drivers to more risk. T ☑ F ☐

3 Generally speaking, rural and urban roads require that you drive at slower speeds, stay alert and be prepared for the unexpected.
   T ☑ F ☐

Answers: 1: F; 2: T; 3: T

Weather conditions: wind and rain

- What kinds of weather conditions can make driving more hazardous?
- What steps can you take to manage the risks posed by all adverse weather conditions?
- What kinds of hazards can strong winds cause?
- What should you do to retain control when strong winds affect driving?
- What are the four primary hazards caused by rainy conditions?
- What should you do to manage the four primary hazards caused by rain?
- What are the dangers of a light rain after a dry spell?
- What is aquaplaning and how can you avoid it?
- What should you do if you begin to aquaplane?
- What should you do if you must cross a flooded area on the road?

Wind, rain, snow, ice, mist, fog and even sunshine present different driving challenges, but they all require you to do two things to help you stay safe:

- Slow down. This gives you more time to detect hazards and a greater response time. It also makes your vehicle easier to handle. The worse the weather conditions, the slower you should go.
- Increase your safety margin. Increase your following distance and allow more room when attempting to join traffic or when overtaking.

Wind

You might not think wind is a road hazard but it can affect you directly and indirectly, depending on its strength, what type of vehicle you're driving, and the other vehicles around you. The stronger the wind, the lighter the vehicle and the more areas of the vehicle that are exposed to the wind, the more the wind will affect you.

Strong winds have a greater effect on motorcycles, bicycles, lorries and trailers than they have on cars. Strong gusts can easily blow them sideways or off their course. In windy conditions, be alert for vehicles getting pushed in front of you, and leave extra lateral space when overtaking or when someone is passing you. Wind that is blocked momentarily by an obstacle such as a lorry can hit you suddenly when you get past the obstacle. This is of particular concern when overtaking, so allow plenty of lateral space as you go by.

Strong winds have a greater effect on motorcycles, bicycles, lorries and trailers than they have on cars. Strong gusts can blow them sideways or off their course

If you feel a loss of control due to wind, slow down immediately. As you recall, air passing rapidly under your car creates lift that reduces traction. Slowing down reduces lift, increases traction and improves your ability to hold the road and to regain control.

Rain

Driving in the rain presents many more hazards than driving on dry roads. The four main hazards are reduced visibility, reduced road holding, compromised steering and increased stopping time and distance.

Reduced visibility

Rainy weather can interfere with your ability to see other road users and with their ability to see you. Rain shortens the distance you can see due to the water droplets in your line of sight. Mist rising off a warm road or spray from the wheels of other vehicles, especially from large trucks, can obscure your view even more. The cool rain falling on your windows can cause them to mist up

You can take steps to improve your visibility on rainy days but it is physically impossible for it to be as good as it is on a clear day

on the inside, compounding the problem. Rain clouds obscure the sunlight and make the road darker – especially close to dawn and dusk. Other drivers will have the same problems, which means that in rainy weather, everyone on the road cannot see as well as they would in dry conditions. You can take steps to improve your visibility, but it is impossible for it to be as good as it is on a clear day. Use your wipers and window washing fluid to keep the outside of the windscreen clear.

Turn on your dipped headlights to make yourself more visible. Keeping the inside of your windscreen clean will reduce interior condensation. Use the heater to clear the windows and mirrors. Stay well back from other vehicles so you don't have to contend with their spray on your windscreen as well as the rain. Use extra caution when overtaking in the rain – but note that overtaking may only be appropriate on dual carriageways or motorways. Switch your wipers to the fastest setting before you start to pass, because the vehicle in front may have been acting as a barrier against the rain while you were behind it. This way, you'll be ready to deal with the added spray that will wash across your windscreen as you go by. Stay alert and keep scanning. Turn down or off any distractions so that you maximise your ability to hear.

Keeping the inside of you windows clean will help reduce fogging, always drive with your lights on in the wet

Reduced road holding

Water on the road acts as a lubricant that reduces your tyres' traction, making you more likely to lose control or skid in wet conditions. Reduced traction means there is less grip to counteract the centrifugal force that tries to make your vehicle go straight when you are going around a bend. When the road is wet, you can easily lose control at speeds that would be fine on a dry road. Slow down. Remember, the slower you go, the more control you have because you maximise traction and minimise the forces trying to overcome traction. Take care of your tyres, inflate them properly and be sure you have adequate tread. Remember that tread design forces water away from your tyres to help maintain traction. You should be extremely careful when there is a light rain after a long dry spell. The small amount of water combines with accumulated oil, debris and dirt on the road surface, resulting in a particularly slick mixture.

Aquaplaning can occur when you're travelling at a speed of 50 km/h or more. At a high speed on a road that's very wet, your tyre tread cannot

Water on the road acts as a lubricant that reduces your tyres' traction, making you more likely to lose control or skid in wet conditions

eject water quickly enough. When you aquaplane, you literally drive up onto the water. Because there's a thin layer of water between your tyres and the road, you have no traction. The steering will become unresponsive and braking will simply cause you to skid. If this happens, immediately take your foot off the accelerator. Braking isn't likely to help while you're still aquaplaning, but once you slow down enough, you'll regain traction.

You can prevent aquaplaning altogether by slowing down and avoiding accumulated water patches on the road. If you must drive through standing water, slow down even more.

Increased stopping time/distance

Regardless of speed, it takes far more time and distance to stop when the road is wet. So slow down and allow at least twice as much stopping distance as you would in dry weather. The two-second rule becomes the four-second rule. Look well ahead and try to anticipate having to slow, stop or take evasive action, when necessary. Begin decelerating and braking lightly sooner than you normally would.

ROAD FLOODED

Driving through a flooded area

Where possible, avoid driving through any significant flooding. It is generally much safer to turn around and use an alternative route or to wait for the water to drain. If you must drive across a flooded road, these guidelines will help:

- Stay out of deep puddles near the curb. When you drive through a deep puddle, the puddles create drag on the wheels on that side, causing the car to swerve toward the puddle. The faster you're going, the more pronounced the swerve. If you must go through a puddle, slow down even further.
- Stay where the water is shallowest. On a level road, this is normally in the centre where the high point of the camber is. On a sloped road, it is naturally on the uphill side.
- Try to drive on the same track as the vehicle ahead of you. The vehicle's tyres displace water so, if you follow in their tracks, you'll be driving on a surface that is temporarily a little drier than the rest of the road.

Drive slowly and steadily through a flooded area to prevent engine damage and avoid splashing pedestrians

- Do not cross a flooded area if you can't determine how deep it is. If you're unfamiliar with the road, it's better to wait and watch another vehicle go through. If there's little traffic, you may be able to pull off the road safely and inspect the flooded area on foot.

- Do not attempt to cross a flooded area with high water flow, even if it looks shallow. You could end up trapped in a flooded vehicle, or worse, washed away and drowning in conditions like these. The most dangerous floods occur where a river, creek or drainage canal has overflowed its banks due to heavy rain.

- Do not drive through water deeper than just below the centre point of your wheels unless you're in a vehicle that's specially equipped for such conditions.

- Stop as you approach the flood, scan the area, and then proceed slowly if you deem it safe to do so. Stay in low gear to keep the engine speed up – this also helps keep water out of the exhaust.

- After leaving the water, drive slowly and gently test your brakes to be sure they're dry and working properly.

QUICK QUIZ

1 Most weather conditions can make driving more hazardous. T ☑ F ☐

2 Generally speaking, you don't need to worry about a light rain, especially if it's the first rainfall in a long while. T ☐ F ☑

2 If you begin to aquaplane, take your foot off the accelerator, but do not brake. T ☑ F ☐

Answers: 1: T, 2: F, 3: T

Weather conditions: ice, snow and fog

Aidhmeanna
OBJECTIVES 11 > **Look for, and highlight, the answers to these questions**

- What are the primary hazards associated with driving in icy conditions?
- What are the primary hazards associated with driving in snow?
- What are the primary hazards associated with driving in fog?
- When is it appropriate and inappropriate to use your fog lights?

Ice

When temperatures drop in winter you need to watch for icy road surfaces. Before you start to drive warm up the engine according to the manufacturer's guidelines, ensure that all windows and lights are clear of ice, and check that your tyres are correctly inflated and have at least the minimum amount of tread required by law. The main hazard associated with icy conditions is loss of traction. Your stopping distance on ice may be as much as 10 times longer than it is on a dry road, making you more likely to lose control and skid on ice. Slowing down and *substantially* increasing your following distance and safety margins will help in icy conditions. Watch closely for signs of ice in near freezing or sub-zero temperatures.

Take note of signs of frost ice on windows, cars, puddles and grass verges. If you have trouble walking to your car due to ice, you can assume it will be a problem on the road. Be especially careful when crossing bridges and overpasses because these areas freeze more quickly than the normal road. This is because cold air passes over and under them, taking away heat more rapidly. When conditions warm up and the ice melts, watch out for parts of the road that are in shade which may retain ice long after the rest of the road has thawed. Be particularly careful if a light rain falls in sub-freezing temperatures because this can form *black ice*. Black ice is a very thin but slick ice patch that is difficult to see – hence the name. It is extremely dangerous. Change speed gradually and with caution in icy conditions, gear down to slow down, and avoid heavy braking. Sharp manoeuvres

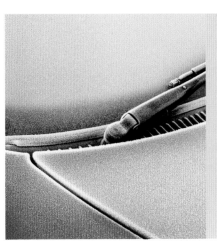

Watch closely for signs of ice in near freezing or sub-zero conditions.
Take note of frost ice on windows, cars, puddles and grass verges

of any kind tend to cause skidding and loss of control. If you find yourself skidding, take your foot off the accelerator and turn gently in the direction of the skid.

Winter-grade windscreen wash used during the winter will prevent ice from forming on your windscreen and protect the reservoir from cracking. Be sure that you have adequate antifreeze in the engine's cooling system. If you don't have much experience of driving in icy conditions, build experience in the safest situations possible. If you can, get an experienced driver to take you to a clear, open area, like an empty car park, to practice driving on ice.

To stay safe in snowy conditions your first defence is to slow down. Use your gears to control your speed and brake gently

Snow

Think of driving in snow as driving in a combination of rain and ice. The main hazards are reduced visibility and reduced traction. Although it's preferable to avoid driving in snowy conditions, in many regions that would mean not driving all winter. If possible, try to avoid driving while it's snowing heavily. Wait until the snow stops and there's been enough time for the roads to be ploughed and/or gritted. To stay safe in snowy conditions your first defence is to slow down. Assume there is ice under the snow and give yourself the same safety margin you would allow on ice. Before you set out dress in warm clothing and bring along the following in your car: a mobile phone, rug,

Clear snow from all windows and lights before setting out

shovel, scraper, brush and some emergency food and drink if you'll be in a rural area. In this way, you'll be prepared for a breakdown or severe traffic delays due to the weather conditions.

Clear snow from all windows and lights before setting out. Carefully drive in the ruts left by other vehicles to help your traction. If you get caught in a snow storm, slow down gradually and avoid overtaking, lane changes or sudden movements. Drive carefully with dipped headlights on, increase your stopping distance and look as far ahead as possible. Turn off the radio and all distractions because driving in snow requires your full attention. If conditions are very bad, you should get off the road and park in a safe place. If you're within a couple of kilometres of home, the best choice may be to leave the car safely parked and walk. If you get stuck in a snow storm somewhere hazardous and cannot leave the vehicle, turn on your hazard lights and use your engine sparingly to stay warm. Open the window slightly for ventilation.

Fog

Loss of visibility is the main hazard in fog. It's hard to see and to be seen. If the fog is very bad, the prudent measure is to wait until it lifts. If the fog sets in while you're driving, however, you need to deal with it, at least until you can pull over somewhere safe. Here are some ways to help you stay safe while driving in fog:

- Slow down. Stay well back from other vehicles. If you can see their lights clearly, you're probably too close. Be aware that the vehicle ahead can displace fog a little, creating the illusion that visibility is better than it really is.

Don't use high beams because they tend to reflect off the water droplets that make up the fog, reducing your visibility

- Keep your headlights on. Don't use high beams because they tend to reflect off the water droplets that make up the fog, reducing your visibility.
- Don't speed up in the clear patches between fog banks. There may be something hidden just inside the next fogged area.
- Use the road lines and reflective markings to maintain your lateral safety margin.
- Drive at a speed that allows you to stop safely within the distance you can see clearly.
- Slow down gradually and give ample warning to following traffic that may be too close or that may not be able to see your brake lights.
- If you have fog lights, use them. They won't obscure other drivers' view if the fog has reduced visibility to 100 metres or less. It is inappropriate and hazardous to use fog lights when there is no fog or in any conditions that interfere with another driver's ability to see, so be sure to turn them off when the fog clears. You may find it helpful to alternate between the high beams and fog lights as the fog density changes.
- If conditions deteriorate and you feel that you are not in control, find a safe place to stop well off the road and wait for conditions to improve.

Weather conditions: sunshine

Aidhmeanna
OBJECTIVES 11 ▷ Look for, and highlight, the answers to these questions

- How can sunshine cause a driving hazard?
- How should you respond to problems associated with sunshine?

Although rain, snow and fog are the obvious weather-related driving hazards, sometimes sunshine causes significant problems, too. The greatest hazard is when the sky is clear and the sun is low in the sky: the sunlight impairs your view either when you turn towards the sun or when you see the sun's reflection in your rear-view mirror. This is not only a dry-weather concern. When the sun shines on a wet road or snow it can cause blinding glare. Lowering the sunshade or putting on sunglasses will help. It's a good idea to keep sunglasses in the car at all times so that they will always be available when you need them. Remember, if sunlight is obscuring your view, it's doing the same to other drivers. It will be harder for those behind you to see your indicators or brake lights – or when the sun is low and behind you it will be hard for oncoming traffic to see you in the glare. Be extra vigilant for pedestrians in these conditions, since they're usually unaware that the dazzling sunlight conceals them. More often, they think they're plainly visible because the sun is shining brightly. As always slow down as you would in other adverse conditions, because this gives you a greater safety margin.

Low sun light impairs you view either when you face it or when you see the sun's reflection in your rear-view mirror

QUICK QUIZ

1. Sunlight can cause a hazard by obscuring your view when the sun is low in the sky. T ☑ F ☐

2. To cope with reduced visibility due to sunshine put your hand up in front of your eyes to shade them. T ☐ F ☑

3. Other drivers will also have an impaired view due to low sunlight or sun reflecting off wet roads. You may be difficult to see if the sun is behind you. T ☑ F ☐

Answers: 1: T, 2: F, 3: T

Night driving

Driving at night can be deceptive. Because it's dark, you have less colour and contrast to help you perceive depth and make speed judgements. It's harder to estimate how fast a vehicle is approaching or how fast you're closing a gap. Your eyes must constantly re-adjust as you pass from areas with streetlights to areas that are in darkness. Night driving often coincides with times when you'd normally be sleeping, which can make it difficult to stay alert. In the evening you are more likely to encounter other road users who are tired or who may have been drinking, so extra care is needed.

It is more difficult to identify hazards at night particularly in poorly lit areas, watch your left side for pedestrians and cyclists

Irish roads are rarely empty, and some of the most serious crashes happen on regional roads at night. Part of the problem is that drivers mistakenly believe that they're alone on the road and, if driving conditions are good, they also believe that they can afford to take risks. Unfortunately, the harsh truth is that it's more difficult to see hazards at night, which means you'll have less time to respond and more difficulty avoiding hazards when they arise. When people drive recklessly at night, collisions are inevitable. The National Roads Authority's statistics for 2004 show that 1,360 people were killed or injured on Irish roads that year between the hours of 11:00 pm and 5:00 am.

Clearly, driving at night requires caution and a conservative approach. Here are a few things that you can do to reduce your exposure to risk when driving at night-time:

- Slow down and increase your safety margin.
- Be sure all your lights are switched on and working. Remember to carry spare bulbs and to replace failed bulbs immediately. It's against the law and it's dangerous to drive if any of your vehicle's lights aren't working.
- In areas well lit by streetlights, beware of cars driving without lights on. This sometimes happens because the area is so well lit that drivers forget that they need to switch on their lights. If you encounter such a driver, quickly flash your headlights as a reminder.
- Watch closely for pedestrians, especially in areas around housing with patchy streetlight.

Slow down on bends and turns. Your headlights point straight ahead, so you have reduced ability to see to the sides and around the bend

- Scan the dark areas as well as the illuminated ones. Hazards aren't always in the well-lit places – it's more likely that they will be hidden in the darker patches.

- You must be able to stop in the distance you can see clearly – that is, as far ahead as your headlights illuminate. If you drive faster than this, you may not see a hazard until it is too late to stop and avoid hitting it. Note that visibility can be deceptive in traffic. For example, you can see lights coming towards you from a long way off, creating the illusion that you can see much farther than you really can. Hazards can be waiting in the unlit area between you and the distant car.

- Slow down on bends and turns. Your headlights point straight ahead, so you have reduced ability to see to the sides and around the bend. After you complete the turn and your headlights illuminate the road ahead, you can resume a higher safe speed if the way is clear.

Dealing with headlights

Headlights can be both a curse and a blessing. You can't drive at night without them, but other cars' headlights can easily obscure your view, and you can obscure their view with yours. You should use your high beams on unlit roads when there are no other vehicles around. Dip them when you see another road user approaching and when you approach another vehicle from behind.

Dip your lights when in view of other traffic ahead of you travelling in either direction

Don't use high beams on well-lit roads or in urban and suburban areas that have streetlights. Be sure to keep your lights properly adjusted. You may need to adjust your lights when carrying heavy loads because the load tends to lower the back of your car, tilting the lights upward. Dip your headlights when passing oncoming cars. If an oncoming car forgets to dip theirs, flash yours briefly as a reminder. However, don't leave them on to 'get even' if the other driver doesn't take the hint. Two blinded drivers just increases the risk of a collision. Leave enough room when following a vehicle so that your headlights don't create glare inside it. Keep your windscreen clean inside and out. Dirt on your windscreen diffuses and intensifies headlight glare. Don't look at oncoming headlights. Look slightly to the left to avoid being temporarily blinded, especially when an oncoming driver forgets to dip their headlights. Adjust your mirrors as necessary to reduce glare from headlights behind you.

Overtaking at night

Overtaking at night demands extra care and plenty of room. Be sure the way forward is clear and that it will remain so until you complete the manoeuvre. This isn't always easy to judge. Be patient and wait for the right time. *Don't get killed because you don't want to be inconvenienced.* Switch on your high beams only after you've pulled past the vehicle that you're overtaking. When another car overtakes you, leave your lights on high beam until the overtaking driver draws level with you. This provides the overtaking driver with a better view of the road. Dip your lights as the car passes and pulls back into lane in front of you.

Reflective road markings

To make night driving easier, Irish roads have colour-coded 'cat's eye' reflectors that are embedded in the road surface, reflective delineator posts and reflective road markings. The first general rule for using these is that the closer reflectors are to each other, the greater the potential hazards. For example, cat's eyes in the centre of the road are normally 24 metres apart. When you are near an intersection or slip road, they are 12 metres apart; at a bend or dangerous area, they're placed at smaller intervals of six metres.

Cats eyes are colour coded to assist you when driving at night, sign posts are reflective for easy recognition

- White cat's eyes indicate the centre of the road, the divisions between lanes on main roads and motorways, and the edge of cross hatchings that mark a prohibited space.
- White delineators mark the grass verge where there are no intersections.
- Yellow cat's eyes appear on the left-hand side where you would see broken yellow lines by day, and on the centre medians of motorways to represent the white unbroken line you see in the daytime.
- Green cat's eyes indicate that you're approaching side roads, slip roads and lay-bys. Green reflective delineators mark the grass verge beside the road, and are placed in the centre median where a junction is on your right.
- Red delineators are posted on the far left-hand side of the centre median of a right-hand junction.
- Bright amber flashing lights warn you that there are roadwork hazards ahead.
- Construction cones have white reflective bands, and may be topped with rotating amber reflectors that appear to flash, alerting you to roadworks ahead.

QUICK QUIZ

1 Many fatal crashes occur at night in Ireland because some drivers believe they have the road to themselves and can therefore afford to take risks.
T ☑ F ☐

2 To avoid being blinded by oncoming traffic, look slightly to the left, not at the headlights.
T ☑ F ☐

3 If an oncoming driver forgets to dip their headlights, leave your headlights on full until the other driver dips their lights.   T ☐   F ☑

Answers: 1: T, 2: T, 3: F

Loading and towing

Aidhmeanna **OBJECTIVES** **11** ⟩ Look for, and highlight, the answers to these questions

- Why should you load luggage securely inside your vehicle?
- How could an unrestrained pet be dangerous in your vehicle?
- Why is correct loading on top of or outside the vehicle so important?
- What are the risks associated with towing trailers and how do you manage them?

Luggage

Anything in or on top of your car needs to be well secured. In the event of a sudden stop, anything that isn't fastened down continues to travel forward with the force of its own momentum. Imagine being hit by a mobile phone that is travelling at 100 km/h!

Load your luggage so that it doesn't block your field of view and be sure it's secure so that it doesn't shift when you take a corner – otherwise it may tumble and block your view, or hit you or a passenger.

Unrestrained pets can cause collisions by leaping into your field of view or by creating other distractions

Pets

The guidelines for securing luggage also apply to pets. An unrestrained pet will be injured or killed in a high-speed collision, and it could injure you or a passenger as it hurtles through the car. Pets can also cause collisions by leaping into your field of view or by creating other distractions. If you're carrying a pet, you need to be sure it's properly restrained behind a barrier or in a pet carrier.

Heavy loads

Remember that the more weight you have in your car, the more momentum the car has. This means you need longer stopping distances, making it important to increase the space you allow for braking when you are carrying a heavy load. You will also need more power to accelerate and it will take longer to reach a given speed, which means you need more space to enter traffic and more room when overtaking. It's also important to distribute the weight as evenly as possible so that you can maintain traction. Uneven distribution puts more weight on some tyres than others, which can substantially affect road handling.

Longer stopping distances are required when your vehicle has increased momentum due to the additional weight of passengers or load

Roof racks and boxes

Roof racks and boxes are a handy way to add luggage capacity, and they're often ideal for carrying things that don't fit in the car. Put luggage on the roof with care, however, because too much weight up high shifts the centre of gravity and can make your car unstable. This makes it easier to roll the vehicle over when making a turn or sharp bend.

Limit the weight you add to the top of the vehicle as it will shift the centre of gravity and reduce stability

To avoid problems with roof racks, remember that they're best used for lighter items. Load the car with heavier goods so that the centre of gravity stays low. Be sure the items on the roof rack are firmly attached. You should have multiple attachments so that if any one of them fails, the load will still be secure. You are responsible for anything that falls off the roof, including any damage it causes.

If something does fall, pull over in a safe place and retrieve it only if it is safe to do so. If you can't retrieve it safely – on a motorway, for example – don't create an additional hazard by running out onto the road. Instead, report it to the Gardaí so they can remove it for you.

Keep in mind that roof racks add to your car's profile, substantially increasing drag. This reduces your efficiency, which means you'll get fewer kilometres per litre of petrol; it can also make you more vulnerable to buffeting by strong winds.

Towing

In addition to giving you more momentum, towing a trailer has other risks because you need longer stopping distances and longer acceleration distances. Also, in a bend, the trailer tries to keep going straight. When you take the

Towing a trailer requires special care. The load needs to be properly secured and lit plus you need to allow for the extra momentum and overall length

bend the trailer tries to push the rear of your vehicle in the trailer's original trajectory. This is why it's important to slow down substantially before making turns or sharp bends with a trailer. You also need to allow a much wider turning radius.

Perhaps the greatest challenge when learning to tow a trailer is learning how to drive in reverse. When you're in reverse, the trailer leads and tends to travel in the opposite direction to that of the car. The easiest way to reverse with a trailer is to turn so you're looking backwards over the trailer. Put your hand on the top of the steering wheel, then reverse slowly. If you want the trailer to go right, move your hand to the left. For left, move your hand right. Always go slowly. If the trailer is large use your wing mirrors or have one or two people outside the car spotting for you. Keep the windows down and the radio off so you can hear them.

It's a good idea to go to an open clear area, like an empty parking lot, to practice reversing with a trailer. If necessary unhitch the trailer and turn it around manually.

QUICK QUIZ

1 There is no need to secure luggage as long as it is on the back seat or in the boot of the car.
   T ☐   F ☑

2 An unrestrained pet can be dangerous because it can injure you in a sudden stop, and it can cause a collision by being a distraction.   T ☑   F ☐

3 When towing trailers you need to leave more space and time for accelerating, turning and stopping.
   T ☑   F ☐

Answers: 1: F, 2: T, 3: T

Driving in unfamiliar areas and in other countries

Aidhmeanna
OBJECTIVES 11   **Look for, and highlight, the answers to these questions**

● How should you prepare for driving in an unfamiliar area?
● What do you need to do to prepare for driving abroad?

Unfamiliar areas

As you'll quickly discover, you tend to drive better in familiar areas – provided you don't let yourself become complacent. You know where many potential trouble spots are, such as blind turns or lanes that end abruptly, so you can compensate and adjust before you see them. Since you know your way around, you focus on the road, not on navigation.

Driving on unfamiliar routes and in unfamiliar areas is more difficult because you have to detect all hazards by coming upon them. In addition, you may be trying to read street signs and road markings to find your way, forcing you to divide your attention between driving and navigating. There are several things you can do to prepare for driving in an unfamiliar area:

- If possible, take a passenger who knows the road and the area.
  This person can forewarn you of trouble spots and upcoming turns in plenty of time.
- Trying to read a map while driving is a huge distraction. Instead, read the map while safely parked and then write down the directions in simple steps for easy reference while driving. If you have a difficulty during your journey, pull over to consult the map again.
- Some websites generate driving directions for you. Before you set out, you can use them to print maps and the route to follow; they also give the distance of each leg of the journey and the estimated driving times. These are of great help, but take a comprehensive map with you, just in case a wrong turn takes you off course.
- Modern GPS driving devices can be an excellent navigation aid. The most sophisticated ones are much like passengers who know the area and verbally alert you to upcoming turns. These systems don't alert you to hazards, however. Don't let a GPS device distract you from watching the road.

Modern GPS driving devices can be an excellent navigation aid but don't let a GPS device distract you from watching the road

International driving

If you're travelling outside of Ireland and are planning to drive, you need to find out how local driving laws, regulations, customs and practices differ from our own. You may need to get a local driving permit, and you should invest in an area map in advance. There may be differences in how you drive in another country; for example, often you will be required to drive on the right-hand side of the road. It takes some time to adjust to this, and if you are using your Irish vehicle abroad, in these circumstances you will need to adjust the headlights to conform to the local regulations.

When driving abroad you are required to be aware of the driving laws and regulations of that country

Road signs frequently differ. You'll have to become familiar with signs of many different shapes and colours. Also, different countries apply different rules to pedestrian crossings. In some places, pedestrians always have right of way over cars. In others, cars have right of way; in some countries, who has right of way depends on the circumstances. It is important to know this whether you're a driver or a pedestrian. Some countries, such as the United States, allow vehicles to turn right after stopping at a red traffic signal. Ignorance of local driving regulations is never an excuse for poor driving. In all countries, if you're operating a motor vehicle, you're expected to know the laws, rules, regulations and road markings. Don't make assumptions and don't get behind the wheel until you're properly equipped to drive.

QUICK QUIZ

1   You can prepare for driving in an unfamiliar area by planning your journey with a map in advance. T ☑ F ☐

2   Most countries are lenient on foreign drivers because they recognise that they're not familiar with local driving regulations.
    T ☐   F ☑

3   If you forget where you are going it is ok to check the map as you drive. T ☐ F ☑

Answers: 1: T, 2: F, 3: F

As well as adjusting to driving on the right, you'll have to become familiar with signs of many different shapes and colours

If the worst happens: emergency procedures

- When should you stop or not stop for a collision?
- How do you stop and park a car during an emergency situation?
- How do you alert the emergency services?
- How do you stop traffic in a safe way?
- Why should you avoid moving a person who has been injured in a collision?
- When might it be necessary to move an injured person?
- Why should you complete a course in basic emergency first aid?
- What are the steps for basic immediate assistance?
- What items should you include in a first aid kit?

You cannot be a driver without direct or indirect involvement with collisions. It is inevitable. If you drive in a co-operative manner, allow an ample safety margin, remain alert and drive according to your experience level, it is possible to go your entire lifetime without being involved in a major collision. However, minor 'fender benders' are almost certain, though they may not always be your fault. It is likely that at some stage, you will also come upon major collisions that involve casualties. Therefore, you should know what to do in an emergency situation.

Stopping for road incidents

You may find it a relief to learn that you are *not* expected to stop for every road incident you come upon. In fact, it is often best if you don't. However, there are times when the law *requires* you to stop.

Stop for a road incident if:

- You were involved in the incident – this is the law.
- You witnessed an incident occurring. Alternatively, you should at least call the Gardaí and report that you witnessed the collision. They may wish to get a report from you.
- There are casualties, if you're qualified and able to provide first aid and if there are no emergency personnel already on the scene.

At some stage of your driving career you will encounter a serious crash either as a passer-by or as a witness but hopefully not as a victim

Slow down but do not stop for a road incident if:

- You are not involved in the incident directly or as a witness.
- You cannot provide aid, if aid isn't needed or if emergency personnel are already there.

If you don't need to stop, don't add to the problem. Keep moving and *keep your eyes on the road*, not on the incident. Be especially cautious because unfortunately, many drivers divert their attention and 'rubber neck' – they take their eyes off the road to get a better view of the crash scene. This can result in more collisions near the initial crash – all caused by motorists running into each other in the slowed traffic because they're not watching the road.

When you come upon a serious collision, watch for emergency vehicles coming from either direction and give way to them, even if there are already emergency vehicles on the scene. Remember that in a serious collision, emergency personnel may need to summon more help.

If you don't need to stop, don't add to the problem. Keep moving and *keep your eyes on the road*, not on the incident

If you are involved in a crash or incident, or if it's appropriate for you to help people involved in a collision, you must pull over in a way that will not make the scene more dangerous. If you're the first one there, you need to warn and divert approaching traffic before helping the people involved in the crash. Before trying to make a situation better, you need to make sure that it doesn't get worse.

Whether you pull over or are stuck on the road, use your hazard lights and/or flash your headlights to alert other drivers. If you're not injured and you get out of your vehicle, do so with great care, especially if your car is on the road. Wear reflective clothing, or at least light-coloured clothing if you have it, especially at night. Watch for debris, broken glass or spilled fuel on the road. *Take care of yourself first.* Remember that you can't help anyone else if you get hurt and you'll take valuable medical assistance from others if you suffer an injury while trying to help at the scene of a crash. Taking care of yourself first isn't selfish; it gives those who need help the best possible chance of survival.

Summoning and providing aid

Make a quick assessment of the scene and phone emergency services by dialling 999 or 112. You can do this from your vehicle if you don't feel it is safe to leave, or if you are injured and capable of making the call without risking further injury. Try to tell the operator the location of the collision and the number of injured people, and give a sense of how serious the crash is. Do not disconnect the call – allow the emergency services operator to do so. That way, you won't accidentally hang up before the operator gets all the necessary information from you. Sometimes, the emergency services operator stays connected until the emergency personnel arrive.

If you don't have a mobile phone and there isn't one readily available on the scene, you can try to stop traffic to wave down another motorist. Stand clear of traffic and wave something brightly coloured or, if it's night-time, a torch to get attention. Then hold out your hand indicating 'stop' to a specific driver and wave the driver to pull over to a safe spot. If the driver doesn't respond, let that car go by and try the next one. When someone stops, ask that person if they can call the emergency services. If the driver doesn't have a phone, ask if they can find a public telephone and call the emergency services for you. Then you'll know that help is on the way – though you may want to try waving down another driver to see if they have a mobile phone. Use the same procedure to stop traffic when necessary, but get the driver you wave down to remain in the lane, blocking the cars behind. *Never step in front of traffic to try to stop it* – remember that many motorists get distracted by road collisions and you may get run over.

Due to the high risk of spinal injury, normally you *do not* move a person injured in a collision or try to remove them from a vehicle.

Phone emergency services by dialling 999 or 112

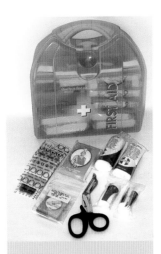

Keep a first aid kit in you car, they are not expensive and can be purchased in most pharmacies

Do not move an injured person's head. Instead, if possible, hold or have someone hold the person's head in the position you find it until help arrives. Similarly, if you are injured and feel neck or back pain, or if you feel numbness or as if something is out of place, do not move. Do not turn your head. You can speak or call for help, but stay in the same position until help arrives.

One exception to the rule of not moving an injured person at a crash scene would be to save them from greater danger. If the vehicle is on fire or at risk of sinking underwater, for example – both very rare events, despite what you see on television – you need to get the driver out of the car. If the driver isn't breathing and has no pulse, you may need to change his or her position to administer CPR (cardiopulmonary resuscitation). With training, you can learn to move a victim in a way that minimises the risk of further injury to the neck and spine.

Some countries require first aid and CPR training for all drivers but in Ireland it is still optional. It doesn't take much time to get this training, yet it can make a tremendous difference if you're involved in an emergency – traffic-related or not. It's worth remembering that the majority of people who use their training in emergencies do so for people they know and love. If you're not already qualified, you should enrol in a course; some can be completed in just one day. We cover first aid in more detail in Module 12.

First aid kits

First aid kits are inexpensive and readily available and you should keep one in your car. You'll probably use it more to care for cuts and scrapes that have nothing to do with driving but first aid kits are invaluable in the event of a collision. Make sure your kit includes at least two pairs of disposable gloves, a rescue-breathing mouth barrier, roller bandages and hand wipes. You can add a torch, reflective vest, pen and notebook, and some chemical lights. You should also carry a rug or blanket in your vehicle, a safety triangle, some water and a mobile phone.

Summary points

In this module on risk management you learned:

1 Motorways, dual carriageways, rural roads and urban roads have different advantages and disadvantages. Be familiar with the differences and adjust your safety margin to manage the various risks these roadways pose.

2 Weather can make driving more hazardous by reducing traction and by affecting your ability to see. You can reduce the risks in all weather conditions by slowing down and increasing your safety margin.

3 Strong winds are most likely to directly affect light vehicles like bicycles and motorcycles, and high-profile vehicles like lorries. They can blow vehicles into your path and sudden gusts can cause you to swerve, especially after passing an obstacle that was shielding you from the wind.

4 Rain reduces visibility and at least doubles your stopping distance. Slow down, dip your headlights and use the four-second rule. Keep your tyres properly inflated and have adequate tread. Be especially cautious when driving after a light rain that follows a long dry spell.

5 Stay out of deep puddles because they can cause you to swerve. If you must go through one, slow down. Avoid aquaplaning by reducing speed.

6 Do not cross a flooded area if you can't tell how deep it is. Nor should you cross if the area has a high water flow – even if it looks shallow. Don't drive through water that's deeper than the centre point of your wheels. Stop before you reach the flood, check the area and then drive through the shallowest part if it's safe. Check your brakes carefully after you emerge.

7 Compared with dry roads, icy conditions can increase your stopping distance tenfold. You need to allow a far greater safety margin than usual. Be cautious of parts of the road that are in shade even after the thaw and watch out for black ice if a light rain falls in sub-freezing temperatures.

8   Snow reduces both visibility and traction. Try to avoid driving when it's snowing. Before setting out in snow, pack warm clothing and supplies. Assume that there is ice under the snow.

9   When driving in snow, drive in the ruts that other vehicles have left to help your traction. If you get caught in a storm, slow down gradually, use your dipped headlights and allow a greater stopping distance. If possible, pull over somewhere safe to wait it out or walk the rest of the way.

10   Slow down substantially in fog. Use dipped headlights and fog lights if you have them. Don't use fog lights when there's no fog, or when the visibility in fog is greater than 100 metres.

11   Sunshine can obscure your view with glare when the sun is low in the sky. Use your sunshade and sunglasses. Keep good sunglasses in your car.

12   Night driving can be deceptive. Many fatal car crashes happen at night-time because it's more difficult to determine distances and to spot hazards in the darkness. Slow down; you should be able to stop within the distance you can see ahead.

13   Don't use your high beams when there are other vehicles nearby or when driving in lit urban or suburban areas. When passing oncoming traffic at night, look a little to the left to avoid looking directly at the approaching cars' headlights.

14   Be familiar with the different types of reflective road markings. They help you navigate and drive safely at night.

15   Secure luggage and pets inside your vehicle. Use caution with roof racks to ensure that the load doesn't fall off and that you don't raise your car's centre of gravity too much. Put the heavier luggage inside the car and lighter baggage on the roof. The more luggage you have, the longer your acceleration and stopping distances.

16   Trailers increase your acceleration and stopping distances. They also increase the risk of a skid and require a larger turning space. Slow down substantially when towing a trailer, especially at bends and turns. Practice reversing a trailer in a safe location such as an empty car park.

17   Prepare for driving in unfamiliar areas by writing down directions ahead of time. Remember that you can make mistakes more easily when you divide your attention between looking for hazards on unfamiliar roads and trying to navigate. Don't try to read a map while driving – pull over to read it.

18   If driving in another country, familiarise yourself with local driving laws, regulations and customs before you start to drive. Ignorance is no excuse for poor driving.

19   Only stop for a collision if you're involved in it or if you can provide aid to the injured when the emergency services have not yet reached the scene. Pull over carefully, use your hazard lights and take care of yourself first. Get help by calling 999 or 112.

20   Do not move an injured person because of the risk of neck/spine injury, unless you must move them to avoid a greater danger or to administer CPR.

21   Enrol in a first aid course today if you're not already qualified.

12

'Kaizen – The need for continuous improvement in your abilities and actions to truly benefit yourself and others'

Japanese philosophy

The road ahead

Introduction

Congratulations! You have almost completed the knowledge development section of the Steer Clear™ Driver Education system. You've learned a lot about how to use the road which will stand to you in the years to come – but the underlying message will always be that learning never ends. There will always be new situations to deal with, new technology to take on board and plenty of room for improvement.

So let's conclude this part of the Steer Clear programme by looking at ways in which you can continue to learn and improve your driving; at some pointers that will help when you buy your first vehicle; and at some of the legal, financial and moral obligations that go with driving and vehicle ownership. We'll also see how to prepare for the driver theory test and how to apply and prepare for the full driving test and licence.

In this module we will discuss...

- Learning for life
- First aid
- Buying a vehicle

- Financial and legal obligations and regulations
- The driving tests

Learning for life

Aidhmeanna **OBJECTIVES** **12** **Look for, and highlight, the answers to these questions**

- How should your driving skills and knowledge change over time?
- What will you learn in parts 2 and 3 of the Steer Clear programme?
- What personal, financial or career incentives would encourage you to take further driver training?

Think back five years. Do you know more now than you did then? Have you learned from experience and do you have better ways of approaching problems or of thinking about things now than you did five years ago? Of course you do – and in another five years, you'll look back and say the same. It stands to reason that because of your life experience, you will be wiser at 47 than at 17. Learning only stops when you refuse to learn.

Now think about the technology changes that you have seen in the last five years: mobile phones, personal music systems and digital cameras are among the devices that have advanced rapidly as designers and engineers come up with new ways of solving problems. Living in an age of constant change means that you need to continue to adapt to use the new technology as it evolves. What you know today may be obsolete in the future. This also applies to driving. Continuing to learn as a driver will not only improve your ability and skills, but it will also also enable you to stay up to date and get the most benefit from advances in vehicle technology.

Your knowledge and skills should change over time. Every time you experience and handle a new driving situation, you should improve as a driver. When you run into that situation again, you'll be better prepared to anticipate any hazards, and better able to respond to them – as long as you continually assess your driving and accept that learning never stops. Also, as new laws come into effect, you may need to modify your driving habits to accommodate them. Remember that

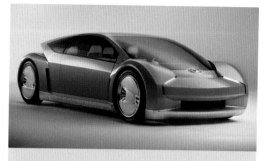

Tomorrows cars will be more environmentally friendly, giving greater fuel efficiency, fewer emissions and running on renewable energy sources

getting your full driving licence doesn't mean that you're a fully capable driver. It just means that you've demonstrated that you're not likely to pose an unreasonable hazard to yourself or to other road users. Don't forget that it takes about five years to reach average driving competence.

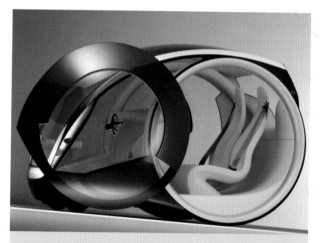

Peugeot's Moovie is an electric concept car with wheels that rotate at different speeds, a bit like a wheelchair

We are at an exciting junction in the history of vehicle technology. Previous generations drove cars with conventional internal combustion engines. Your parents' generation learned to drive conventional cars, but many of them are already or will soon be driving hybrids and cars that use alternative fuels. The drivers of your generation will be the first to learn to drive in these new vehicles. The basic skills you need on the road aren't likely to change significantly in the next 10 years, but what you need to know about how your car operates and how to care for it will.

Further training

One way to speed your learning and skill as a driver is to continue your training. Your next immediate step should be to enrol in Steer Clear™ Part 2, which develops your practical driving skills under the guidance of a qualified instructor. Then you can progress to

Your next step should be to enroll in Steer Clear part 2 which develops your practical driving skills under the guidance of a qualified instructor

Part 3, to get valuable structured driving practice with a mentor. These steps will better prepare you for the driving test and for becoming a fully licenced driver.

Later you may want to take further training to qualify for a motorcycle or commercial vehicle licence, for example, which may help your career. Additional licences permit you to carry goods or passengers for payment.

QUICK QUIZ

1 Your knowledge and skills as a driver should change over time because learning is a continuous process; your driving skills and knowledge should continue to improve; and you will need to adapt for new laws and automotive-technology changes over time. T ☑ F ☐

2 In Parts 2 and 3 of the Steer Clear™ driver training system, you could learn as much as you would from five years' driving experience. T ☐ F ☑

3 Further driving training is required if you wish to carry fare-paying passengers or to drive a freight lorry. T ☑ F ☐

Answers: 1: T, 2: F, 3: T

First aid

Aidhmeanna **OBJECTIVES** **12** > **Look for, and highlight, the answers to these questions**

- Where can you obtain first aid training?
- In layman's terms, what is the 'Good Samaritan' law?
- What do the ABCD's of first aid stand for?
- What are the steps and techniques for basic life support?

You learned in Module 11 that you need to protect yourself before helping others, and that it's very important to avoid moving someone who has been injured in a collision – unless you need to get the victim away from further danger. Now we'll look at ways of getting first aid training and at an important legal principle regarding administering first aid. We'll also look at some specifics of first aid practice.

First aid training

By definition, first aid is the first care someone gets before professional medical help arrives. It is not necessarily professional care, but it is provided by a knowledgeable and qualified care giver. Although Irish drivers are not required to have first aid training, drivers in most of the other EU countries are. Because you're highly likely to come upon a crash at some point, having first aid skills can make a tremendous difference in your ability to assist someone who is injured. It can mean the difference between life and death, or between full recovery and a disability for life. Furthermore, you may be required to have first aid training if you plan to drive abroad. So it makes sense to do a first aid course – and remember that it doesn't take much time.

Having first aid skills will allow you to help an injured person and could mean the difference between life and death

There are many ways of getting first-aid training:

- Organisations such as Emergency First Response or the Red Cross.
- School, college, club or your workplace.
- Local community-based schemes.
- Teach-yourself courses*.
- Online*.

*Independent study and online courses that meet legal or professional requirements usually require at least one session with an instructor. This is because it takes a trained teacher to evaluate your practical skills such as moving a patient or administering CPR.

Good Samaritan

'Good Samaritan' precedents provide a reasonable degree of legal protection for those who provide first aid. They enable you to help an injured person without fear of being sued. For these precedents to protect you:

- Provide care only within the scope of your training.
- Ask the person if you can provide care, and do not force it on someone who refuses.

There are many excellent first aid programmes available in Ireland including those run by the Red Cross, Order of Malta and Emergency First Response

- You can assume that an unconscious person consents to care. This is called 'implied consent' and recognises that no rational person in that condition would turn away aid.
- Act as a reasonable person would.
- Once you begin providing care, do not stop until professional help arrives, or unless circumstances require you to stop to protect yourself.

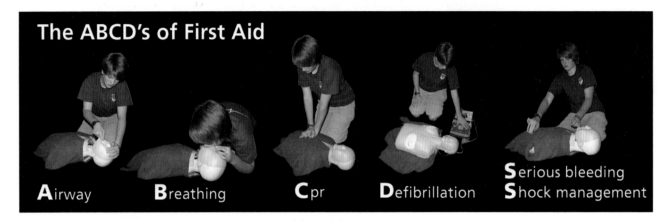

The ABCD's of First Aid

Airway   **B**reathing   **C**pr   **D**efibrillation   **S**erious bleeding **S**hock management

The ABCD's of first aid

Let's look at the complete ABCD's you'll learn in your first aid course. ABCD's stands for:

- **A**   Assess scene, Alert medical care and clear Airway
- **B**   Breathing
- **C**   Circulation and CPR
- **D**   Defibrillation
- **S**   Serious bleeding, Spinal injury and Shock

If you come across a collision, or any situation where someone is injured, you should follow these basic life-support steps:

1. Assess the scene. Ensure that there is no danger to yourself or to others. Stop traffic if necessary. Protect yourself first.
2. Alert emergency services, giving your name, the precise location, the nature of the emergency, and what assistance is needed.
3. Check for patient responsiveness. Speak to the person in a loud voice and tap the shoulder firmly to determine if the person is conscious; conscious but in an altered mental state; or unconscious.
4. Get the airway clear to allow breathing. Ensure that an unconscious person's throat and mouth are open to the lungs by tilting the head back, or by lifting the chin if you suspect a head injury.

5 Check for breathing. Listen at the person's mouth for 10 seconds for breathing or to feel the warmth of their breath on your ear. Watch to see if the chest rises and falls.

6 If the person is breathing, keep the airway open until help arrives and recheck breathing at close intervals. If the patient isn't breathing, give rescue breaths. Pinch the nose, tilt the head and lift the chin – or just lift the chin if you suspect a spinal injury – and give two slow breaths.

7 Check for circulation. If no signs of circulation are present, provide CPR (Cardiopulmonary Resuscitation). Expose the chest, place the heel of one hand on the breast bone between the nipples and place the heel of the other hand on top of the first. Kneel to one side of the patient with your shoulders directly over your hand position, and compress the chest 3 to 5 cm thirty times in quick succession. Follow this with two rescue breaths. Repeat the sequence of thirty chest compressions and two breaths four times, and then check for breathing and circulation again.

8 If there are no signs of breathing/circulation, continue with CPR until help arrives or you are too exhausted to continue.

9 If the patient has no circulation and an AED (Automated External Defibrillator) is available, then it should be used as soon as possible. An AED must only be used by someone suitably qualified.

10 If the breathing/circulation returns, place the person in the recovery position. Turn the patient on to the left side with the upper leg and arm bent and in a position that keeps the patient facing forward with a clear airway. Monitor for breathing until help arrives.

11 Remember: do not attempt to move a patient at all if you suspect spinal injury. The only exception is if the patient is in danger of death due to fire, drowning or another hazard – or if you must move them to provide effective rescue breaths and CPR.

12 Reassure a conscious patient, and keep them warm to prevent shock.

Remember that in the case of a serious road collision, the probability of a spine or other serious injury is high, but these injuries aren't easy to detect. Moving a victim can cause further injury and result in paralysis. As much as possible, avoid moving an injured person, and ask the person to remain still and to refrain from head movements. Ideally, hold or have someone hold the person's head gently to keep it still until help arrives.

1 Getting first aid training is a waste of time because accidents never happen to you. T☐ F☑

2 Good Samaritan precedents protect you if you give aid within the scope of your training. T☑ F☐

2 The B in ABCD's stands for bandaging. T☐ F☑

Answers: 1: F, 2: T, 3: F

Buying a vehicle

OBJECTIVES 12 ⟩ **Look for, and highlight, the answers to these questions**

- What are the most important considerations when choosing a vehicle?
- What financial considerations do you have when choosing a vehicle?
- What are the legal requirements for purchasing or selling a vehicle?
- What hidden charges might you come across when purchasing a car?
- What are the pros and cons of buying a new car versus buying a used car?
- How can you get an independent assessment of a used vehicle?

When the time comes to buy your first car, you will probably imagine yourself driving something new and exciting, but end up in your auntie's old banger. Not to worry – you'll always think of your first car fondly, provided you choose it wisely and that the purchase is within your means.

There are several things you need to consider when choosing a car: the finances – not just the cost of the car, but payments, maintenance, fuel, insurance, taxes and other fees; the conditions in which you'll be driving; and the purpose for which you intend to use it. If you're into adventure sports like scuba diving or kayaking, you'll need to be prepared to carry more luggage than if your pastimes centre around the movies or walking. Will you be making mainly short, urban commutes or long journeys in rural areas? Do you plan to tow a trailer or take passengers? Do you see yourself getting married and having children in the near future or is that something to allow for when you get your next car?

New cars have the advantages of the latest safety features and, in general, low maintenance costs. The downside is that your investment is higher, and you lose more through depreciation

Whatever car you buy, the most important considerations are roadworthiness, safety and suitability for your needs. You shouldn't even consider a car that's not roadworthy or safe for obvious reasons. A car that won't meet your needs may be safe to drive, but it will constantly frustrate you or, worse, you may be tempted to push it beyond its capabilities and use it in unsafe ways, such as overloading it with passengers or luggage.

Funding your car

The biggest mistake you can make as a first-time car buyer is thinking that it will only cost you the advertised purchase price. It's easy to overlook the cost of running, taxing, insuring and maintaining it, which often amount to more than the cost of buying the vehicle. Failure to consider all the expenses can make your life difficult, leave you with a car that you can't afford to drive or, even worse, a financial institution may reclaim your car, destroying your credit rating with lending institutions. This will make buying your next car or house or make other investments even more difficult. Consider *all* these expenses together and look at your financial picture over time against your income:

- Initial costs – initial payment, taxes, registration fees and so on.
- Monthly payments.

- Insurance – cost varies significantly depending on the size and condition of the vehicle.
- Fuel costs.
- Maintenance including tyres, oil changes, cooling system upkeep and the NCT.

It's very important to consider all these costs, because sometimes a vehicle that costs more at the outset is better value in the long run. Fuel efficiency, lower maintenance costs and insurance savings from safety features can make the 'more expensive' choice less expensive in a relatively short time.

Getting and keeping a car on the road can be far more costly than you think. Apart from purchase payments, there are maintenance, fuel, insurance, taxes and other fees

Like many people, you may need to borrow money to buy a car. Generally, you have two options: a hire-purchase agreement or a car loan. The Financial Regulator has developed an independent consumer guide to personal loans and credit. You can look at this guide on their web site if you're considering getting a loan or taking out credit.

Whatever credit system you use, be sure to read the paperwork carefully and shop around for the best deal. There are two pitfalls to avoid when borrowing. The obvious one is to ensure that you don't borrow more than you can afford to repay. Defaulting on a loan hurts your credit rating and will make future borrowing more difficult and more costly, because lower credit ratings result in higher interest rates. If you realise that you won't be able to make your repayments, sell the car or refinance *before* you miss an installment.

The less obvious pitfall is borrowing more than you should for a long period instead of borrowing less for a shorter period. This can end up costing you far more and reducing the funds you have available for your next car or for other purposes. For example, suppose you figure that you can afford €150 per month. You qualify for a loan at 10% interest to be paid back over three years. This would allow you to borrow about €4,650, and pay €750 in interest over the life of the loan. But suppose you want a 'better' car, so you finance €7,060 for five years. The monthly payment is the same, but you will have to pay €1,940 in interest, and your monthly payments will continue for two years longer. In addition, the higher-priced car may have higher road tax and other fees associated with it. This is fine if you are able to afford the payments, higher interest and fees without any difficulty. Just be aware and know what you're doing in advance.

You should borrow the minimum amount of money over the shortest period of time, the longer the term the greater the amount of interest paid

Hire-purchase agreements. This is an arrangement whereby you pay monthly installments to hire the vehicle for an agreed period. At the end of the period, you don't own the car, but may pay a lump sum if you wish to purchase it. In some cases, the hire-purchase agreement does result in you owning the car at the end of the period, but you don't become the owner until the period ends and you've made all the payments. Be sure you know which type of agreement you're signing.

Hire-purchase agreements can be appealing because you can get more car for less money up front. However, you don't end up owning anything, or if you do, it generally costs you more than if you'd bought the vehicle to begin with. Hire-purchase agreements are an attractive option for people who change their vehicles every year or two rather than keep the same car for three or more years.

Loan Application. If you get a loan, you own the car from the start. You have to put up more money initially compared to a hire-purchase agreement, and you repay the financial institution a monthly installment that covers the loan and interest. Depending on your credit rating, your loan may be personal – trusted against your proven reliability in handling credit – or secured against your car. This means that if you don't make the payments, the institution can take the car. Most loans run for two to five years.

Direct purchase. Whether with or without a loan, buying the car directly is generally recommended for more economical purchases. It is ideal if you plan to save money by keeping your vehicle for three or more years. Over the long term, this is the least costly way to invest in cars.

However you decide to finance your car, be aware that advertisements don't always tell you everything. Incentives like 'free' car tax or a personal stereo may not be the best offer. Offers for very low payments may have excessive interest rates for long periods or added loan fees up front. If you don't understand a contract, don't sign it. Get independent advice from someone with knowledge of financial matters. You can get free and confidential advice at your local Citizens Advice Centre or from the Comhairle web site.

Legal requirements

When buying or selling a vehicle in Ireland, you must meet some legal requirements. First, you need to check whether or not the vehicle is taxed and that there is no outstanding tax due. As the new owner, you will have to pay the outstanding tax. Anyone selling a car must have a vehicle registration certificate in their name. If this is not available for the car you're looking at, the sale may be invalid – so don't buy the car. When you sell a car, you must complete the transfer of ownership form RF200, or the change of ownership section on the vehicle registration certificate and send it to your local motor tax office.

To buy a car, you will require adequate insurance for the vehicle and the appropriate driving licence.

Anyone selling a car must have a vehicle registration certificate in their name. If this is not available for the car you're looking at, the sale may be invalid

Buying a new car

New cars have the advantages of the latest safety features and, in general, low maintenance costs. It is also easier to compare new vehicles because different dealers will have the same type of car in their showrooms. The downside is that your investment is higher, and you lose more through depreciation – the car loses value as soon as it becomes 'used'.

If you're buying a new car, the price quoted may be subject to a delivery fee and other surcharges. Prices are usually negotiable and will vary so shop around and find out what costs apply. Don't hesitate to check with various dealers for competitive offers.

Buying a second-hand car

Second-hand cars have the advantages of a lower initial investment and less depreciation in the car's value. However, depending on the car's age and history, maintenance and replacing worn parts may be more costly in the short term. A very worn second-hand car may cost very little but end up costing more, in just a few months, than a newer second-hand car with a higher initial cost.

A second hand car has a lower purchase price but may have higher service and maintenance costs, be sure to have the vehicle fully checked by a qualified mechanic before purchasing

When buying a second-hand car, it's a good idea to get an independent assessment of the car's condition. This is essential when buying from an individual rather than a dealer. You can buy directly from an individual, but you'll have little or no recourse should you have a problem with the car after the deal is done. Car dealers must sell cars of a certain quality, which means that if a problem arises within a defined period, they must repair or replace the car for you. There are a number of companies who specialise in car assessment and who can provide mechanics to check the car. You can find assessors in the Golden Pages, through insurance companies and through motoring associations like the RAC and the AA. You can also look on websites such as the Car Buyer's Guide.

You should always be careful about who you deal with and where you buy a second-hand car. If you are ever in doubt about the authenticity of the deal, look elsewhere. If a deal seems 'too good to be true', it usually is. When buying a second-hand car you should check the following – or better yet, have an expert do the checks:

- **Full service history.**
- **Tyres.** What is the condition of the tyres – will they need to be replaced?
- **Tracking.** If the tyres show more wear on one side than on the other, it may indicate that the wheels need to be re-aligned. Get the vehicle checked out professionally because this may be minor and routine, or it may indicate a major, expensive problem.
- **Body.** Is the paintwork in good condition or are there areas that have slightly different colouration or texture? This may indicate hidden damage from a crash.

Excellent company car. Especially if you work from home

- **Windows and doors.** Check for rust and seal damage around the doors and windows. Do the windows and doors open and close properly? Are there any cracks on the windows?
- **Engine.** How does it sound? Are there any knocking or grating sounds? Any smell of burning? Look at the engine and see if any of the visible belts are in good condition. See if the exhaust rattles or is noisy as you drive it. When the engine is cool, look inside the radiator for rust and to see what condition the coolant is in.
- **Steering and brakes.** Drive the car and check on its overall handling – how it steers, brakes and changes gear. Have an expert inspect the brakes.
- **Instrument panel.** Check all the dials on the dashboard to ensure that they function properly. How many miles/kilometres are on the odometer?
- **Lights and fuses.** Check that these function properly by testing the lights, wipers, heaters, radio and brakes.
- **Interior condition.** Look at the condition of the seats and the pedals; they can indicate how much the car has been driven and how it has generally been treated.

Don't expect everything to be in brand new condition – it is a second-hand car, after all. There may be some things that will require your attention in the short term, such as new tyres or brake pads. It may still be a worthwhile purchase – just be aware of the cost of such repairs along with the total purchase price when making your decision to buy.

Importing a car

If you import a car from another country you will have to pay Vehicle Registration Tax (VRT). Once you have paid the tax, you will get the Vehicle Registration Certificate and registration number for the car. The VRT is a percentage of the expected retail price of the vehicle or 'Open Market Selling Price' (OMSP). You can make enquiries about VRT costs online.

QUICK QUIZ

1 The most important considerations when choosing a vehicle are roadworthiness, safety and suitability for your needs. T ☑ F ☐

2 Hidden charges you may come across when purchasing a vehicle can include excessive interest rates or added loan fees up front. T ☑ F ☐

3 You can get a good assessment of a used vehicle by asking the seller to be completely honest. T ☐ F ☑

Answers: 1: T, 2: T, 3: F

Financial and legal obligations

The fiscal responsibilities of owning a vehicle mean being prepared to cover the cost of operating the vehicle. You must allow for insurance, taxes, maintenance, servicing, repairs and running costs like petrol, oil and even parking fees. If you can't afford them, then you're better off delaying your purchase until you can. You need to plan your budget for these costs before you make your purchase so that you will be able to afford the costs as they occur; that way you will be able to keep your car safe and on the road.

Maintenance

Maintenance is necessary to keep your car operating in a safe and efficient manner. Although maintenance costs money, it actually costs less to maintain your car than to neglect it. A small amount of checking and maintenance ensures reliability and catches minor problems before they become serious. If you don't tend to a minor problem, it can quickly develop into a more serious one that's both dangerous on the road and expensive to repair. You must carry out regular basic maintenance checks and you should have your car serviced professionally no less than once a year.

Your regular checks should include: oil, water, battery fluid, brake fluid, coolant, lights, tyre pressures and tread, wipers, and windscreen wash and power-steering fluid levels. In the practical skills part of this course, you'll learn how to do these checks, how to top up the fluids, and how to change failed light bulbs and wiper blades. If you find problems such as unusual smells, noises or anything that affects the driving or braking of the car, get a mechanic to investigate.

The NCT checks brakes exhaust emissions, wheels and tyres, lights, steering and suspension, chassis and underbody, electrical systems, glass and mirrors, transmission, interior, and fuel system

The national car test

You learned about preparing for the National Car Test (NCT) earlier in this course. The NCT makes a positive contribution to road safety, the economy and the environment by eliminating poorly maintained and dangerous cars. It is a very useful gauge of your car's roadworthiness, and it also serves as a helpful and independent guide when buying or selling cars. Compulsory car testing for vehicles over four years old was introduced in 2000 as part of an EU directive that makes car testing compulsory in all member states.

If you don't display a valid NCT disc, you can be fined up to €1,500. The NCT is carried out on behalf of the government by the National Car Testing Service Ltd (NCTS). It is completely independent of the maintenance and motor trade and does not benefit if your car passes or fails. All cars older than four years must be tested and then re-tested every two years after that.

The NCT ensures your vehicle is road worthy, helping to keep you safe and giving you peace of mind

The NCT procedure is computer-controlled and largely automated to be as objective and accurate as possible. The NCT checks brakes, exhaust emissions, wheels and tyres, lights, steering and suspension, chassis and underbody, electrical systems, glass and mirrors, transmission, interior, and fuel system. To prepare your car for the test ensure that:

- It has adequate oil and water.
- The boot is empty and the seats are clear of personal belongings.
- It is reasonably clean – especially the underbody.
- The wheel hubcaps are removed and the tyres are inflated to the correct pressure.
- The safety belts and clips are fully visible.
- Your vehicle registration plates comply with current regulations.
- In the case of a diesel vehicle, the timing belt has been replaced within the timeframe specified by the vehicle manufacturer.
- The lights are working and adjusted properly prior to the test.

Road tax and insurance

You're required to pay car tax and insurance, and you must display certificates for both along with the NCT certificate in your car window any time your car is on a public road or in a public place

If you own a car, you're required to pay car tax and insurance and you must display certificates for both in your car window any time your car is on a public road or in a public place. You will receive penalty points, a fine and may have your car impounded if you fail to do so.

The taxes you pay fund the construction and upkeep of the road system. The motor-tax rate varies with vehicle size, and you can pay it quarterly, half-yearly or yearly. You can now pay your motor tax online and the disc will be sent to you in the post.

Your car insurance costs can vary significantly because they're based on the insurance company's estimation of the risk in insuring you. Typically, young male drives with big sport cars pay higher rates because they figure highly in the collision statistics. If you have previous claims or driving convictions the rates go up. It pays to shop around or to get an insurance broker to help you find the best rates. However, the best way to keep your insurance costs down is to drive a modest car and to drive it well. Over time, a good driving record will save you thousands of euro.

To get your full driving licence you must complete the driving test. This allows you to drive unaccompanied and on all roads, and to tow a trailer that weighs up to 3,500 kg

Driving licences

At present, new drivers start out with a provisional licence before getting the full driving licence. This will change in the near future when a *learner's permit* will be required to start learning to drive. A provisional licence is temporary and allows you to learn to drive and practice. Under a provisional licence, you must have a fully licenced driver in the car with you. (This rule does not apply to learners on their second provisional licence.) To get your provisional licence, you must first complete the theory test. As a provisional driver you must display L-plates on your car and you may not drive on motorways, carry people for payment or tow a trailer. New legislation aims to restrict provisional drivers from driving under the influence of alchol.

To get your full driving licence you must complete the driving test. This allows you to drive unaccompanied and on all roads, and to tow a trailer that weighs up to 3,500 kg. The law requires that you carry your driving licence with you whenever you drive.

QUICK QUIZ

1 It is important to do regular maintenance checks on your vehicle to keep it running in a safe and efficient manner, and so that minor problems don't become major ones.
T ☑ F ☐

2 The NCT benefits drivers by making it illegal for a car more than four years old to be on the road. T ☐ F ☑

3 When operating your car on a public road or in a public place, you must display tax and insurance certificates in the window.
T ☑ F ☐

Answers: 1: T, 2: F, 3: T

The driving tests

Aidhmeanna
OBJECTIVES **12** > **Look for, and highlight, the answers to these questions**

- How should you prepare for the Driver Theory Test?
- What steps do you take to get your provisional driving licence?
- How should you prepare for your driving test for a full driving licence?
- What steps do you take to get your full driving licence?
- What are the requirements for obtaining an international driving permit?
- What documentation do you need to drive in another country over an extended stay?
- How and why would you take a driving education refresher course?

The Driver Theory Test

The Driver Theory Test assesses your knowledge of the rules of the road, proper procedures, road signs and signals, and your ability to perceive hazards. By completing this course you will have a very good understanding of the rules of the road but, to prepare for the exam, you should also study the Driver Theory Test questions and answer book.

Driver Theory Test
Tástáil Teoirice Tiomána

The DTT uses a computerised test system to test your knowledge of the rules of the road and road user information

Begin by filling out the theory test application form which is available online or you can book your test over the telephone by dialling 1890 606 106. Test centres are located nationwide and use a simple computerised test system, where you answer 40 questions by pressing a touch screen. The minimum passing score is 35 correct answers. You can change your answers as you take the test and after reviewing your answers at the end before submitting your test for scoring. You can do a practice session before you take the real test and there's a voice option that will read questions aloud if you have difficulty reading. You also have the option to take the test in English or Irish. The computer scores your test automatically and gives you the results and a certificate straight away when you pass.

Getting your provisional driving licence

Once you pass your theory test, you can apply for your provisional licence by completing form D201. You can request the form on the government's Oasis website, then send it by post or bring it to your local motor tax office.

www.dtts.ie

Your application needs to include:

- Your completed D201 form.
- Your Driver Theory Test certificate.
- Two identical passport-type photographs with your signature on the back of each.
- A birth certificate or passport.
- A completed eyesight report – the official form is available from the Oasis web site.
- A medical report if you suffer from any of the disabilities, dependencies or diseases listed on the D201 form that would be likely to impair your ability to drive safely (the medical forms are also available online).
- Your last driving licence if you are renewing a provisional licence.
- The application fee.

Getting your full driving licence

When you're ready for your full driving test, you can apply online or pick up a form at a motor tax office and apply by post. Waiting lists vary from county to county, so you should allow yourself up to 10 months waiting time for the test. Use this opportunity to gain plenty of driving practice to improve and to build your confidence.

Before the day of your driving test, take a few steps to prepare yourself. First, be sure that your car is in good condition. You can fail the test if your car is not roadworthy. Check the following:

- Current motor tax and insurance discs and an NCT certificate, if applicable, must be displayed on the vehicle you are using.
- L-plates should be displayed at the front and rear of the vehicle.
- The vehicle should be roadworthy.
- Everything should be in working order, *e.g.*, windscreen wipers, indicators and mirrors.

Be mentally prepared for the test by reviewing what you've learned in this course. You should have been driving recently and feel that you've had plenty of practice and are ready. Get a good night's sleep the night before and arrive in plenty of time.

The test takes about 30 to 40 minutes and consists of a driving section and a knowledge test. Expect the examiner to assess how well you move off, drive in traffic, stop, reverse around a corner, park, make an about turn

The driving test takes about 30 to 40 minutes and consists of a driving section and a knowledge test. Be mentally prepared for the test by reviewing what you've learned in this course

and start on a hill. The examiner will also evaluate your road positioning; overtaking and passing; anticipation and observation; use of mirrors and signals; progress; speed; compliance with traffic lights; adherence to road signs and road markings; and how you use the vehicle's controls. At some point during your test, the examiner will ask you to demonstrate the standard hand signals. You can also expect to make a number of left and right turns, encounter a roundabout and stop at traffic lights. You will be asked to identify items under the bonnet where you would carry out routine checks, such as fluid levels.

When you return to the test centre, your examiner will bring you back into the examination room to give you the result. If you pass, you will be given a Certificate of Competency, which is valid for two years, during which time you may apply for your full driving licence. If you don't apply during these two years, you will have to take the driving test again.

If you fail your test, the examiner will give you a detailed list of your mistakes. You should study and rectify these before you repeat the driving test. However, if you brush up on your driving knowledge, drive as you've learned, obey the rules of the road, be conservative and use common sense, you should be successful on the first try.

Once you have passed your driving test, you can apply for your full driving licence by downloading a form from the web, or by getting one from a motor tax office and sending it in along with:

- Two identical passport-type photographs, signed by you on the reverse.
- Your current or most recently issued provisional or full driving licence.
- A medical report if you are over 70 years or if you suffer from any of the disabilities, diseases, or conditions listed on the D401. A registered medical practitioner should carry out your medical examination and then complete the form. You must sign the declaration on the medical report form in the presence of the registered medical practitioner.

the road ahead · module twelve **345**

- A Certificate of Competency if you have recently passed a driving test.
- The appropriate fee.

Your full driving licence does not entitle you to drive all vehicles. It entitles you to drive vehicles with up to eight passengers and a maximum weight of 3,500 kg. The table sets out the additional licencing requirements for motorcycles, large passenger vehicles and goods vehicles.

Category	Licence type	Requirements	Minimum age
A1	Motorcycles under 125 cc or 11 kW	Motorcycle licence	16 years
A	Restricted: motorcycles up to 25 kW (approx 300 cc)		18 years
A	Any size motorcycle (after two years on a full licence)		18 years
B	Vehicles with seats for up to eight passengers and weighing up to 3,500 kg	Driver's licence	17 years
M	Moped with maximum speed of 45 km/h and engine size up to 50 cc		16 years
W	Works vehicle such as tractor or JCB		16 years
C1	Goods vehicles weighing 3,500 kg to 7,500 kg	Full C1 licence	18 years
C	Goods vehicles weighing over 3,500 kg	Full C licence	18 years
D1	Buses or passenger vehicles with accommodation for more than eight but less than 16 people	Full D licence	21 years
D	Buses or passenger vehicles with accommodation for more than eight people	Full D licence	21 years
EB	Cat B vehicle with trailer	Full EB licence	
EC1	Cat C1 vehicle with trailer	Full EC1 licence	
EC	Cat C vehicle with trailer	Full EC licence	
ED1	Cat D1 vehicle with trailer	Full ED1 licence	
ED	Cat D vehicle with trailer	Full ED licence	

The ability to drive safely gives you the means to travel independently, explore the country you live in or embark on the journey of a life time

The AA (Automobile Association) is responsible for issuing International Driving Permits and can tell you if you need a permit for a particular country

International driving

In Module 11, you learned that different countries have differing driving laws, regulations and customs. If you plan to drive abroad you're responsible for knowing and following the rules. You may also need to get an International Driving Permit for a specific country before you go there or in some cases, you can obtain it after you arrive. Either way, check before you travel.

The AA (Automobile Association) is responsible for issuing International Driving Permits and can tell you if you need a permit for a particular country. International Driving Permits are issued for one year to holders of full driving licences. You can download the application from the AA. When you submit the application, you must include your full driving licence, a passport photo and the fee.

Different countries have different laws regarding driving tests and requirements for international visitors. Most countries will allow you to drive using your Irish driving licence or an International Permit for six months, but after that you may have to take a local driving test. Check with the driving authority, the AA or equivalent motoring body in the country you'll be visiting and be sure to inquire about time limits if you're planning to relocate there for a permanent or extended stay.

www.aaireland.ie

Refreshing your driving knowledge and skills

When it comes to any knowledge or skill, there's a principle that says 'use it or lose it'. The skills you use regularly remain fresh and grow stronger, but those you don't use as much become stale and are temporarily forgotten unless you take steps to bring them back to mind. This certainly applies to driving.

You may think that if you drive nearly every day, you don't have to worry about keeping your knowledge fresh. That isn't true, because there are some skills that you won't use much at all. This isn't necessarily bad, though – for example, you shouldn't be handling a skid or regaining lost control on a regular basis. A good driver can go years without a serious loss of control. For those skills you won't often need, you can refresh your memory by rereading this manual once in a while. You shouldn't get into skids for practice, but as you review how to handle emergencies, visualise yourself doing what you're supposed to do. This is called *mental rehearsal* and studies show that this enhances your performance with almost any motor skill. For a more formal review, take a driver education refresher course. This gives you more hands-on practice and is especially helpful if, for some reason, you have not been driving for an extended period. As a graduate of Steer Clear™, you'll be able to do a refresher course that takes just half a day. This refresher course will brush up your knowledge and driving skills, bring you up to date with any changes in the rules and regulations, and help you to retain premium reductions on your insurance renewals.

Remember to assess your own driving performance on a continuous basis and to improve your skills. You are not perfect and never will be; there will always be room to drive better. You should be a better driver a year from now, even better than that four years on and you should be quite accomplished 20 years from now.

A clean driving record without penalty points or collisions and conservative, co-operative driving go together for good reason. Remember this and you will contribute to making Ireland's roads safer and more enjoyable for everyone.

QUICK QUIZ

1 Once your pass your theory test, you receive your provisional licence automatically.
T ☐ F ☑

2 After you complete the full driving test, you have three years to apply for your full driving licence, after which you must retake the test if you have not applied. T ☐ F ☑

3 You can take a driving education refresher course to refresh little-used driving skills and to learn of changes in driving laws and regulations. T ☑ F ☐

Answers: 1: F, 2: F, 3: T

Summary points ⟫⟫⟫⟫⟫

In this module on the road ahead you learned:

1. Your driving knowledge and skills should improve over time because learning is a continuous process. It is also necessary to keep up with changes in the law and technology.

2. Continuing your training in driving can help you qualify to carry goods or passengers for payment.

3. You can get first aid training from organisations such as Emergency First Response and the Red Cross, through local community schemes and at other locations. Good Samaritan precedents help to protect you from legal action if you provide aid as a reasonable person would, within the scope of your training and with the injured person's consent.

4. The ABCD's of first aid guide you through the steps and techniques for basic life support. Learn these by completing a first aid course.

5. The most important considerations when buying a vehicle are roadworthiness, safety and suitability for your purposes. You need to consider the cost of the car, the monthly payments, insurance, taxes, maintenance and operating costs. You can finance a car through hire-purchase agreements or by getting a loan from a bank or other institution.

6. When you buy a new car, it will have the latest safety features and will cost less to maintain. However, the car costs more and its value will depreciate more quickly. Buying a second-hand vehicle is cheaper at the outset but you may have more maintenance and repair costs due to wear. When choosing a used car, have a professional assessor check the vehicle.

7. If you cannot afford all the costs of owning a car, wait until you can before you get one. Perform regular maintenance checks to keep your car running safely and to prevent minor problems from becoming major ones. Have your vehicle professionally serviced at least once per year.

8   The National Car Test helps remove dangerous and environmentally unsound vehicles from the road. A car must pass the NCT when it turns four years old and every two years after that.

9   You must display certificates showing that you have paid your motor tax and have insurance coverage whenever you operate your car on a public road or in a public place.

10   A provisional licence requires that you are accompanied by a fully-licenced driver. You may not drive on motorways or tow a trailer. A driver with a full licence does not need to be accompanied and may drive on motorways and tow a trailer.

11   Prepare for your Driver Theory Test by reviewing the test question and answer book. You must apply to sit the test at an appropriate test centre.

12   When you apply for your test for a full driving licence you can expect to wait up to 10 months until your test date. When the day arrives, be sure your car is roadworthy and that you're displaying the necessary certificates – motor tax and insurance and NCT if necessary. Get a good night's sleep the night before.

13   After successfully completing your driving test, you have two years to apply for your full driving licence. The required documents, photos and fees must accompany both provisional and full driving licence applications.

14   International Driving Permit requirements vary from country to country. The AA or its equivalent in each country can help you find out the requirements for the country you plan to visit.

15   Take a driving education refresher course periodically to keep your knowledge and skills up to date.

Acknowledgements

Acknowledgements

The Irish Drivers Education Association are indebted to all those who have contributed to the research, development and production of the Steer Clear Driver Education Manual. Since the beginning of the project, nearly five years ago, we have received encouragement and support from countless individuals and organisations within Ireland and abroad. We would like to thank you all.

Development, consultation and review

David Baddeley (Volvo Irl.), Helen Bates, Inspector Michael Brosnan (Garda National Traffic Bureau), Michael Byrne (DCC), Ron Christie (RACV Melbourne), Des Cummins (DIR), Maire Daly, Jean Duffy, Justin Delaney (Modified Motors), Gerry Duffy, John Dusch (MVA. Maryland), Conor Faughnan (AA), Robert Flanagan, Tom O'Connor (Motor Distributors Ltd.), Philip Quinlan (Spinal Injuries Association), Prof. Ray Fuller (TCD), John Kinsella (DSAT), Mary Kinsella, Letterpress Inc., Sorcha Mc Donagh, Simon Mc Loughlin, Trish Mc Loughlin, Colin Montgomery, Donal Murphy, NCT Centre Deansgrange, Tricia O'Connor, Nicole O'Neil, Julie O'Shea (ELC), Angelika Renger, Alan Richardson and the staff of the NSC, Dan Rohan (DEHLG), Marina Schaefer, Eddie Shaw, Specs Xpress Bray, Denise Sweeney, Peter Taylor, Stephanie Taylor, John Walsh (ISM), Forbes Zigors (NRA)

Editing team

Maire Daly, Julie O'Shea, Karl Shreeves, Sorcha McDonagh, Mary Kinsella, Mark Loughran

Director of operations

Brian Murphy

Design and production

William Siddall, Mark Loughran (Identikit Design Consultants), Tani Pratchayaopak, Anneke Calis, (Tanika Design)

Illustrations and photography

William Siddall, Getty Images, Volvo, NRA, RoSPA (UK), Haynes Publishing, Big Bad Wolf Animation Team

Author and editor-in-chief

Monica Schaefer

Road Signs

Regulatory Signs

These signs indicate the existance of a road regulation and show the course that you, the driver, must follow. They can also show the action you are permitted to take, or action you are forbidden to take.

50 km/h Speed Limit 50 km/h	**60** km/h Speed Limit 60 km/h	**80** km/h Speed Limit 80 km/h	**100** km/h Speed Limit 100 km/h	**120** km/h Speed Limit 120 km/h	STOP Stop Sign	YIELD Yield Right of Way

GÉILL SLÍ
Géill Slí

No Entry

No Left Turn

No Right Turn

No U Turn

Parking Permitted

Parking Prohibited

Turn Left

Straight Ahead Only

Keep Left

Keep Right

Pass Either Side

Turn Left Ahead

Turn Right Ahead

STOP
School Wardens Sign

3t
Weight Restriction

4t
Axel Weight Restriction

14'3" 4.4m
Height Restriction

P 3t *Ceantar* ZONE
Parking Weight Restriction

Pedestrian Zone

Clearway Stopping or Parking Prohibited

Cycle and Pedestrian Track

Approaching a Bus Lane

Bus Lane

Contra Flow Bus Lane

Maigh Chromtha MACROM

Ná Scoitear

Sli Rothar CYCLEWAY
Pedal Cyclists only

Raon Rothar CYCLE TRACK
Pedal Cyclists Access only for vehicles

No Entry except for Trams

Tram Lane

50 km/h
Speed Limit entering Town or Village

DO NOT PASS
No Overtaking

Road Signs

Warning Signs

These signs give advance warning of a hazard. They are diamond shaped with black symbols / letters on a yellow background.

Junction ahead with road or roads of equal importance

Junction ahead with road or roads of less importance (the latter being indicated by arms of lesser width)

Staggered junction ahead with roads of less importance.

Staggered junction ahead with roads of equal importance.

Merging and / or diverging traffic ahead

Dangerous bend ahead with junction or junctions

  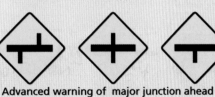

Dual carriageway with junction

Warning of major junction with dual carriageway

Advanced warning of major junction ahead

Roundabout ahead

Mini roundabout

Dangerous corner ahead

Dangerous corner ahead

Dangerous bend ahead

Series of dangerous bends ahead

Series of dangerous corners ahead

Road Signs

Warning Signs *continued*

These signs give advance warning of a hazard. They are diamond shaped with black symbols / letters on a yellow background.

Two-way traffic ahead

Road narrows dangerously

Road narrows ahead

Road narrows on left side

Road narrows on right side

Dual-carriageway ends

Road divides ahead

Steep ascent

Steep descent

Sharp depression

Sharp rise ahead

Series of bumps or hollows

Tunnel ahead

Unprotected Quay ahead

Slippery stretch of road ahead

Low flying aircraft

Tramway Crossing ahead

Level Crossing ahead Unprotected

Level Crossing ahead protected by gates

Level Crossing ahead with lights and barriers

Crosswinds

Aire Leanaí CAUTION CHILDREN

School Children crossing ahead

School ahead

Pedestrian crossing ahead

Possibility of riders on horseback

Risk of wild deer

Low Bridge ahead

Motorway Signs

Motorway ahead

NO L-drivers,
Vehicles under 50cc.,
Slow vehicles (under 30 mph),
Invalid-Carriages,
Pedal-cycles,
Pedestrians,
Animals.

Motorway ahead

Entry to Motorway

Approaching end of Motorway

End of Motorway

Countdown markers for Motorway sliproad at 100m intervals

Road Signs

Warning signs for Roadworks

These are the same shape as ordinary warning signs but are orange coloured instead of yellow

| Roadworks ahead | Road narrows on left side | Traffic crossover ahead | Traffic Lights ahead | Manual traffic control ahead | Two way traffic | Road narrows ahead |

| Left Lane closed ahead | Inside Lane closed ahead | Middle Lane closed ahead | Outside Lane closed ahead | Lane closed Deviate to right | Mid lane closed Deviate to right | No Through Road |

MAJOR ROAD WORKS AHEAD

Major Road Works ahead

Móroibreacha Bóthair Romhat

Móroibreacha Bóthair Romhat

Bóthar Dúnta **ROAD CLOSED**

Road Closed

DETOUR 400m

Detour Ahead

DIVERTED TRAFFIC →

Direction of Diverted Traffic

Information signs

These signs show direction, distance and route number etc. They also show facilities and places of interest.

N6

Áth Cliath **DUBLIN** *An Longfort* **LONGFORD** N4 →

Advance Direction Sign

Gaillimh	km
GALWAY	94
Sligeach	
SLIGO	29
(*Dún na nGall*	
DONEGAL	49)

Route Confirmation Sign

↑ R430 *Main. Laoise* **ABBEYLEIX**

Advance Direction Sign

Baile Bachaille km **BALLYBOUGHAL 5** R129 →

Direction Sign

Car Park with access facilities

Alternative route for high vehicles

Naomh Caoimhín **ST KEVINS** 3 km

km *Tearmann Éan* 2 **BIRD SANCTUARY**

← *Dolmain* **DOLMEN**

Tourist Information signs showing route and distance

← *Áth Cliath* M7 **DUBLIN**
Luimneach → **LIMERICK** M7

Motorway Advance Direction Sign

H 100m

Hospital Distance Sign

Index